Numeracy Skills for Business

Numeracy Skills for Business

Jon Curwin and Roger Slater

with Mike Hart

Department of Business Policy and Marketing
University of Central England
Birmingham
UK

CHAPMAN & HALL
University and Professional Division
London · Glasgow · Weinheim · New York · Tokyo · Melbourne · Madras

Published by Chapman & Hall, 2–6 Boundary Row, London SE1 8HN, UK

Chapman & Hall, 2–6 Boundary Row, London SE1 8HN, UK

Blackie Academic & Professional, Wester Cleddens Roads, Bishopbriggs, Glasgow G64 2NZ, UK

Chapman & Hall GmbH, Pappelallee 3, 69469 Weinheim, Germany

Chapman & Hall USA, One Penn Plaza, 41st Floor, New York NY 10119, USA

Chapman & Hall Japan, ITP Japan, Kyowa Building, 3F, 2-2-1 Hirakawa-cho, Chiyoda-ku, Tokyo 102, Japan

Chapman & Hall Australia, Thomas Nelson Australia, 102 Dodds Street, South Melbourne, Victoria 3205, Australia

Chapman & Hall India, R. Seshadri, 32 Second Main Road, CIT East, Madras 600 035, India

First edition 1994

© 1994 Jon Curwin and Roger Slater

Typeset in Palatino by EXPO Holdings, Malaysia
Printed and bound in Hong Kong

ISBN 0 412 59000 X

∞ Printed on permanent acid-free text paper, manufactured in accordance with ANSI/NISO Z39.48-1992 and ANSI/NISO Z39.48-1984 (Permanence of Paper).

CONTENTS

SECTION 3
COLLECTING DATA   71

SECTION 4
FORECASTING   129

SECTION 5
MODELS   165

SECTION 6
UNCERTAINTY   201

SECTION 7
REFLECTIONS
227

Index

Preface

The understanding and application of numeracy are important parts of dealing with business situations, and yet are often shunned by students. This may be because some students feel that they are 'no good at sums' or that they may fail to see the relevance of techniques that they have been taught. We have long felt that the value of the methods will be much more readily appreciated by putting the various techniques into a business context. This context will make the numerical skills meaningful by being directly relevant to the reader's current or potential work situation, and integrating numeracy with his or her other units of study. *Numeracy Skills for Business* does this by working from specific business problems and bringing in the techniques as and when necessary. We hope that you can identify with the various people in the scenarios and see how their use of numerical skills allows them to gain a greater insight into the problem that they are trying to solve.

By including a copy of MICROSTATS we intend to take the 'hard work' out of long (and tedious) calculations, but we still include hand-worked examples in the text to aid understanding of the methods being used. Similarly, the larger data sets are on the disk in both MICROSTATS and Lotus 1-2-3™ formats.

We have also included a refresher in basic numeracy skills as an appendix, to help those who feel that they need some assistance with the basics.

We would also like to take this opportunity to thank our reviewers who have carefully read early editions of the manuscript and made many helpful suggestions to enhance the readability of the text.

Jon Curwin
Roger Slater

The aim of this book

The aim of this book, as the title suggests, is to allow the reader to work effectively with the numbers likely to be met in his or her place of work. Most substantial organizational problems will have a numerical element even if they are mostly concerned with the management of people. An investigation into the motivation of a workforce, for example, is likely to require some description of hours worked and overtime paid. One major skill is to know when a particular numerical method, or indeed any method, is appropriate. This book is about some methods – those that involve numbers. One dictionary definition of method is 'manner of proceeding'. This book is intended to help you proceed with numerical problems in a confident manner. The book is divided into sections and the sections into parts. Each part is introduced using a **scenario** or storyline to provide a problem to work with. The use of formulae is kept to a minimum and they are only referred to as a necessary part of problem solving. A formula sheet is given as Appendix G for your reference.

The outcome of any method also needs to be applicable. A model answer is presented for each of the 20 scenarios. It is possible to do additional calculations for some of these scenarios and challenge the assumptions being made – we would encourage you to do this. Problem solving in the workplace is likely to include some fairly standard calculations, but it can also involve taking a different perspective and questioning the status quo. A few statistics could be used to describe the current stock levels of a company, for example, but an alternative purchasing procedure may be seen as the way of improving the management of stock. Try to be creative in your use of this book. You could decide to look at a few of the scenarios first just to get a feel for the book. You could work completely through one of the early sections to build up your confidence. You could compare what you already know against the content of the book for consistency and completeness. The book does include a refresher in numeracy skills and this is given in Appendix A.

One outcome of any analysis is likely to be more numbers. You may well find that it is your job to explain these results to others who are even less familiar with the methods described in this book. A skill of major importance is being able to communicate the results of your work in a variety of ways. We would encourage you to think about this skill whether you are working with this book or any other. Ask the question 'How can I make my work and my ideas be better understood by other people?' The book does focus on the presentation of numerical information and many of the scenarios do include interpretive reporting. The emphasis is on understanding why certain techniques can be used and interpreting

answers calculated by hand and those available from computer printout.
    Each section of this book will include:

- a set of problem scenarios covering general business, the hotel industry and local authorities;
- a discussion of the ways the problem can be explored and answers developed;
- an outline of the statistical methodology;
- a worked answer;
- often an illustrative computer printout;
- an interpretation of the results.

Your work is supported by two complementary computer packages that come with this book, MICROSTATS and EZESTATS, and by frequent reference to computer output. MICROSTATS is designed as a general purpose, easy-to-use statistics package capable of working with relatively large sets of data. It is described in Appendix B. The symbol ⊡ is used in the text to indicate that MICROSTATS provides one possible means of problem solution. You can, of course, use the book without reference to any of the computer packages. EZESTATS is an independent computer-based tutorial system designed to help you practise and understand statistical calculations. You may find that 30 minutes' work on EZESTAT is all you have to do, or you may find that returning to the tutorial on several occasion is more helpful. EZESTATS is there to help you – why not try it! More details of EZESTATS are given in Appendix D. Most of the spreadsheets referred to in this book have been constructed on Lotus 1-2-3™. To be able to model numerical problems is an important skill which you should try to develop using Lotus 1-2-3™ or any other spreadsheet package. A Lotus guide is given as Appendix C for those who require a brief overview of the facilities offered by the package.

Section 1
What is numeracy?

Numeracy is much more than the ability to add two numbers together and get the right answer! Numeracy is knowing when to use numbers and being confident that these numbers have meaning. It is a competence of:

- knowing when to use numbers and when to ignore them;

- knowing that the numbers being used are meaningful and likely to be correct;

- being able to select appropriate methods to make numbers more meaningful;

- being able to use results produced by others;

- being able to interpret results and communicate this interpretation to others.

Most business-related courses will expect students to enhance their numeracy skills. BTEC courses explicitly require students to meet numeracy requirements as one of the 'common skill' areas.

The use of scenarios

Scenarios are an important part of this book. A topic or a method is not introduced by a theory or a formula but rather a problem context. We want you to think about the type of problems that you might face that involve numbers and see the course material being used to solve these types of problem. It is scenarios that provide the problem context. To illustrate the role of the scenario we have included the first scenario in this introductory section.

SCENARIO 1: Midshires General Hospital

The Midshires General Hospital has recently achieved trust status. The Senior Management Group are keen to monitor the performance of all departments. Your manager has asked you to produce a report on waiting times. You have been advised to refer to *The Patient's Charter* and whatever data can be found.

You have found that according to *The Patient's Charter*, hospitals should use their best endeavours to ensure that all patients attending out-patient clinics do not have to wait excessively long periods of time before they are seen by a consultant. Specifically, all patients should be seen within half an hour of their appointment time. You have decided to look at one clinic in particular and analyse the results of a recent survey carried out for other purposes. Summary results are given in Table 1.1.

Table 1.1

Waiting time (minutes)	Number of patients
Before time	40
0 but under 10	16
10 but under 20	32
20 but under 30	8
30 but under 40	20
40 but under 50	8
50 but under 60	4
60 or above	4

However, discussions with the clinic staff revealed a number of concerns with this table. The result were recorded on a day that did not typify the work of the clinic. Patients who arrived late (for whatever reason) were included in this table. Some patients were obliged to visit another department in the hospital before they could actually be seen by the consultant (blood tests for example) which added to their waiting time. For these and other reasons, the clinic staff were rather sceptical about the value of the exercise.

If delayed patients were excluded from the table, then Table 1.2 for the non-delayed patients could be used. This apparently simple exercise did present the problem of what was meant by 'delayed'. Was 5 seconds to be regarded as late or 5 minutes? When clinic staff were questioned, it was only when patient arrival was 10 minutes later than the relevant appointment slot that the patient was regarded as late and this had been used in the construction of the new table. If any lateness was regarded as 'late' then the table would be different. The outcome of analysis does depend on the definitions used. Another issue that had to be resolved was how to record the time of those patients that arrived early and were seen early. The question was whether these patients should be given a zero waiting time or a negative waiting time. The inclusion of negative values could make a considerable difference to the value of such statistics as the average. This issue you still had to resolve.

Table 1.2

Waiting time (minutes)	Number of patients
Before time	16
0 but under 10	8
10 but under 20	24
20 but under 30	4
30 but under 40	4

You have also been given the following information from a computer printout:

Number of consultations	132
Number of split consultations	8
Mean waiting time	11.8 minutes
Median waiting time	15.0 minutes
Maximum (ID 123456)	70 minutes
Minimum	–60 minutes
Mean consultation time (all)	23.1 minutes
Mean consultation time (new)	57.4 minutes (sample 20)
Mean consultation time (continuing)	17.0 minutes (sample 112)

You have a meeting with your manager tomorrow to clarify the requirements of your assignment and have decided to do some provisional analysis.

There are clearly a number of issues for you to consider in this scenario. You have two tables describing waiting times. Table 1.1 refers to all 132 patients included in the recent survey (40+16+32+8+20+8+4+4). By adding the patients included in the first four rows we can find that 96 were seen in under 30 minutes (40+16+32+8) or 72.7%. In Table 1.2, only the 56 patients that arrived on time are included (16+8+24+4+4), and of these, 52 were seen in under 30 minutes (16+8+24+4) or 92.9%. The percentages 72.7 and 95.9% are both meaningful and valid but we need to be careful as a user, to understand fully the basis of such calculation. It is important to understand all the assumptions that are being employed. It can be seen from the information provided by the computer printout that the minimum waiting time is given as –60 minutes. It is clear that negative values are being used for those patients who are seen early. This may be quite acceptable but we do need to know that it is being done and we do need to know what effect it will have on the figures we calculate. Section 2 of this book is particularly concerned with describing situations and the use of descriptive diagrams and descriptive statistics.

The scenario mentions that you do have a meeting with your manager tomorrow. You will need to clarify a number of issues with your manager. You have been asked to 'produce a report on waiting time' without any indication of what that might include, the resources that you have available and the time-scale. You will at least need to agree the general purpose or objectives for this report. You will also need to clarify the advice to refer to 'whatever data can be found'. The data must be suitable for the purpose and should at least be judged against criteria like completeness, consistency and correctness. In many ways your report is only going to be as good as the data you use. You could express your concerns about the results of the recent survey. A survey should be representative of the people of interest, but we are told that the data was collected on a single day which did not typify the work of the clinic. Section 3 of this book is concerned with the collection of data and the methodology necessary to ensure that the data is meaningful.

Sections 4, 5 and 6 of this book are more advanced and introduce the techniques you can apply to problems to ensure a better understanding of the problem and support the generation of possible solutions to the problem. We would suggest that business skills include the ability to generate many possible options, the ability to evaluate options and finally propose methods of implementation. Section 4 presents forecasting methods, which are clearly important if you wish to anticipate future demand. If the Senior Management Group intend to 'monitor performance', they are likely to be interested in any trends over time. Section 5 presents a number of models that could be adapted to meet the management needs of Midshires General Hospital. If you look back at the figures from the computer printout, you will see that the mean consultation time for new patients was 57.4 minutes and that for continuing patients was 17.0 minutes. You could consider (develop a model of) what would happen if patients were not allocated equal consultation times. On the basis of the information given, you could argue that new patients should be allocated an hour and continuing patients only 20 minutes. Section 6 develops the ideas of probability. In dealing with any queue of people there is likely to be uncertainty, and probability provides the language and tools to work with that uncertainty. Management may want to know what the chances are that a patient has to wait for more than 30 minutes and has to wait for more than 1 hour, for example.

On the completion of this book there will be lots of things that you will be able to do with numbers. In our view, an overriding consideration is 'does it make sense?' Should negative values be included in mean waiting time calculation if we know that this is likely to distort the figure? If we again look back at the figures from the computer printout we can see the maximum waiting time as 70 minutes for a patient identified with the (ID) number 123456. Should we not ask the question whether this number was correct or were there special reasons for the delay such as a fire alarm. Working with numbers is to manage an enquiry (like any other enquiry) which needs careful design, investigation, analysis and interpretation. We hope that this book can help you develop the skill with numbers referred to as numeracy.

Section 2
Describing situations

Objectives

After studying this section you should be able to:

- identify the role of numbers in describing situations;

- draw basic diagrams such as bar charts, pictograms, histograms and ogives;

- recognize when the use of diagrams is and is not appropriate;

- use a spreadsheet to create diagrams;

- identify where calculated descriptive measures are useful;

- distinguish between different types of summary statistic;

- calculate means, medians and modes, where appropriate;

- identify the meaning of dispersion;

- interpret the meaning of numerical answers to measures of dispersion;

- use MICROSTATS or a spreadsheet to find numerical measures to describe situations.

Introduction

Wordy descriptions of business situations are important in conveying an idea of how different people within an organization perceive what is happening, the market faced by the company, the reaction of tenants to new housing legislation or why guests come to stay at a particular hotel. However, such descriptions only give a part of the picture, and usually at some length. Numbers have the ability to convey some of the same perceptions, and more details of the situation, by summarizing large amounts of data into a few diagrams or **summary statistics**.

This section is concerned with looking at where it would be appropriate to use such numerical ideas (and where it would not) and the ways in which you might interpret these figures if they have been provided by someone else.

SCENARIO 2: Amber PLC – coffee consumption survey

You have just been appointed as a marketing assistant to a large hot drinks manufacturing company, and your first assignment is to prepare a short report which describes the market faced by the company for its coffee.

You have been fortunate enough to find a copy of a MINTEL™ report from 1990 on the coffee market in the United Kingdom (which was left in the office by your predecessor). Within this there are two tables which are particularly interesting in terms of describing who buys coffee. Table 2.1 relates to the age distribution of the UK population, and Table 2.2 to the age distribution of housewives who purchase coffee.

Table 2.1 Demographic analysis of population by age, 1984–94 (millions)

Age	1984	1989	1994
0–4	3.6	3.8	4.1
5–14	7.4	7.0	7.5
15–29	13.3	13.4	12.2
30–44	11.2	11.8	12.2
45–54	12.6	12.3	13.0
Over 64s	8.4	8.9	9.1
Total	56.5	57.2	58.1

Source: MINTEL Market Intelligence, March 1990.

Table 2.2 Demographic analysis of selected types of coffee for home use, 1989

Age	Instant granules	Instant powders	Decaffeinated	Filter ground
15–24	57	28	11	4
25–34	61	18	20	15
35–44	59	22	21	19
45–54	55	20	23	19
55–64	52	25	24	14
65+	51	25	14	5
All	55	22	19	13

Source: MINTEL Market Intelligence, March 1990.
Note that the percentages are the percentage of *that age group* who buy that type of coffee.

Finally, there was some information on the value, in money terms, of the instant coffee market 1988 and 1989, and this is shown in Table 2.3 in millions of pounds.

Table 2.3   Value of instant coffee market, 1988 and 1989

Type	1988 (£m.)	1989 (£m.)
Mainstream	360	370
Premium	80	96
Decaffeinated	74	90
Mild	29	24
Cheap	23	24
Filled	6	4

Source: MINTEL Market Intelligence, March 1990.

What do we need to measure?

We need to measure facts about this market which are relevant to the manufacturer of coffee. This could be in terms of:

- Who buys?
- What do they buy?
- Why do they buy?
- How often do they buy? etc.

Which parts can we describe?

To describe one aspect of this market-place (Who buys?) we need to construct a profile of the overall population. Coffee drinking may well be related to age and thus we need to describe effectively the age characteristics of coffee drinkers; we could also look at the overall age profile of the UK population, to act as a comparison.

One way of describing the market would be to construct diagrams which illustrate the situation. There is a wide range of such diagrams, but we will look at the most frequently used ones. The aim here is to create a visual impact rather than to convey detail; to allow people to get 'a feel for the situation' rather than specify exact statistics.

STATISTICAL BACKGROUND: diagrams

Bar charts

A bar is used to show the number of items with a particular characteristic, say the number of people who work at a certain site, or vote in a particular way.

To set up a chart, draw a vertical line and mark out a suitable scale for the data you wish to represent. Draw a horizontal line from the zero point, and label the items or characteristics you wish to represent. Now draw a vertical bar for each item or characteristic where the height of the bar is proportional to the amount, or size, of the characteristic.

Pictograms

A pictogram is similar to a bar chart except that instead of using bars to represent the quantity, we use pictures that are related to the subject matter. This should be better at attracting the attention of readers.

One version just replaces the bars of a bar chart by the pictures (see the coffee cup example in Figure 2.4), but it is possible to use the actual size of the picture to represent a change in quantity. Once we move over to using size, then we could use height, area or volume as the measure.

Histograms

Here we want to represent the frequency by the area on the graph, not just by the height. We therefore need to take into account the width of each group as well as the number of people or things in it.

Pie charts

A pie chart consists of a circle divided proportionately into segments, each of which represents a part of the whole. It is a suitable method of illustration where there are up to about six categories, but over this, it can become rather confusing! Some computer packages allow you to create pie charts with 'exploded slices' (that is, with one or more slices separated out from the main circle). You can also create three-dimensional pie charts on some of these packages.

Ogives

An ogive is a graph of the cumulative frequency from a table, i.e. the number so far. It is useful when we are looking for the percentage who are a certain age or less, or who have a certain level (say income) or more.

Calculating an answer by hand

Bar charts

Looking at the market for coffee, we can see from the scenario that there are four different types of coffee sold in the UK. A suitable way of representing the relative volume of sales of each type would be to use a bar chart.

The percentage of consumers of each type of coffee are repeated in Table 2.4 (note that they add up to more than 100% because some people will buy and drink more than one type of coffee). To construct the bar chart we draw the two axes and mark on the scales (Figure 2.1).

Table 2.4   Percentage of consumers of each type of coffee

	Instant granules	*Instant powders*	*Decaffeinated*	*Filter ground*
Overall	55%	22%	19%	13%

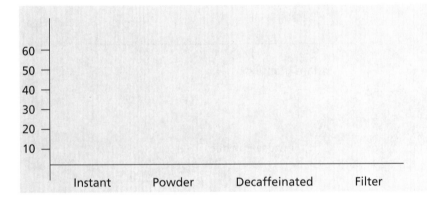

Figure 2.1

Now draw on a vertical block for each of the types of coffee (Figure 2.2).

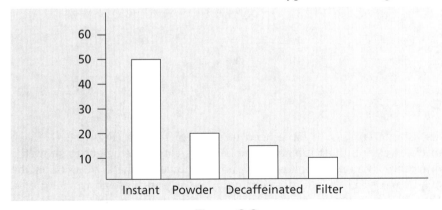

Figure 2.2

A similar result can be obtained by using a spreadsheet such as LOTUS 1-2-3™ (Spreadsheet 2.1).

SPREADSHEET 2.1   PRINTOUT OF LOTUS 1-2-3™ SPREADSHEET

	A	B	C	D	E	F	G	H
1	Coffee type	Per cent						
2	Instant granules	55						
3	Instant powders	22						
4	Decaffeinated	19						
5	Filter ground	13						
6								
7								

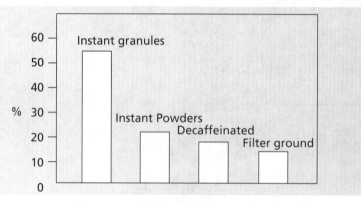

Figure 2.3

Pictograms

An alternative would have been to use a pictogram (Figure 2.4). If we move away from just replacing the bars, we could use height to show the differences (Figures 2.5). It is worth noting, however, that if you double the height and scale the width accordingly, the area increases by a factor of 4. Visual presentations can also have a distorting effect on data presentation (Figure 2.6).

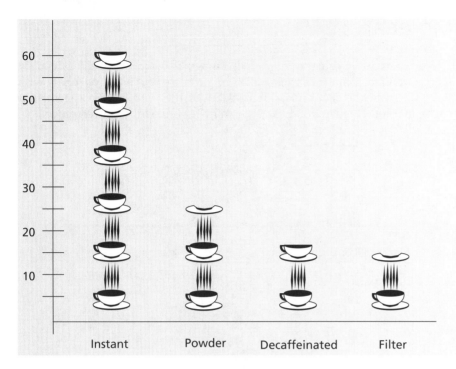

Figure 2.4

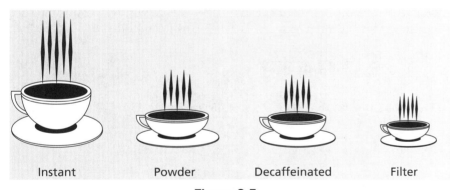

Figure 2.5

Figure 2.6

Pie charts

These are useful in illustrating the percentage of the market held by certain types of coffee because of their visual impact. We will use a pie chart with the data from the scenario which relates to the segments of the instant coffee market. The data for 1988 is given in Table 2.5 for your reference.

Table 2.5	
Type	*1988 (£m.)*
Mainstream	360
Premium	80
Decaffeinated	74
Mild	29
Cheap	23
Filled	6

To draw a pie chart we can work directly with the numbers given, or work with the percentage profile. To find the percentage profile we first add up the total value of sales of instant coffee in 1988 (this comes to £572m.), and then we can work out the percentages. For the mainstream coffee, this will be

$$\frac{360}{572} \times 100 = 62.937\%$$

Doing the same for the other types of instant coffee will give us Table 2.6.

Table 2.6		
Type	*1988 (£m.)*	*%*
Mainstream	360	62.937
Premium	80	13.986
Decaffeinated	74	12.937
Mild	29	5.070
Cheap	23	4.021
Filled	6	1.049
Total	572	100.000

Since a circle has 360 degrees, we need to work out each percentage as a proportion of 360° in order to draw the pie chart. For the mainstream coffee, this would be

$$\frac{62.937}{100} \times 360° = 226.5732$$

There is really no point in going to lots of decimal places, because we cannot draw a diagram that accurately anyway, so we will call this 227°, and we can do the same for the other types of instant coffee (Table 2.7). Now, at last, we can draw the pie chart! (Remember that you will need a protractor if you are going to draw it by hand.) Once completed, your pie chart should look like Figure 2.7.

Table 2.7			
Type	1988 (£m.)	%	% of 360°
Mainstream	360	62.937	227
Premium	80	13.986	50
Decaffeinated	74	12.937	47
Mild	29	5.070	18
Cheap	23	4.021	14
Filled	6	1.049	4
Total	572	100.000	360

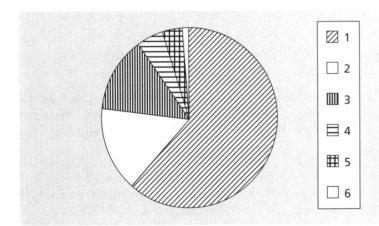

Figure 2.7 Pie chart of instant coffee types.

Using suitable computer packages, we could 'explode' a particular slice which interested us, say the premium type (Figure 2.8). Alternatively, we could make the pie chart three-dimensional, and have an exploded slice (Figure 2.9).

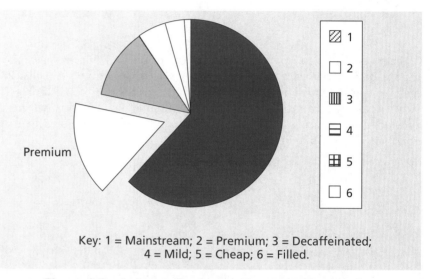

Key: 1 = Mainstream; 2 = Premium; 3 = Decaffeinated; 4 = Mild; 5 = Cheap; 6 = Filled.

Figure 2.8   Instant coffee types with premium 'expoded'.

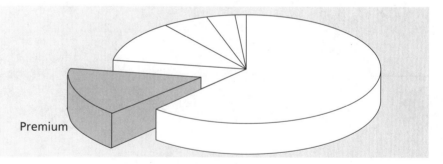

Figure 2.9   Three-dimensional pie chart.

Histograms

Histograms are used to represent frequency distributions such as the number of people in an age group who drink coffee, or the total number in the population of a certain age. We can now draw two histograms from Scenario 2.

Looking at the age distribution of instant coffee purchasers, from the scenario we have the data shown in Table 2.8. Notice that all of the groups are of the same width except the last one, which does not have an upper limit. We could 'cheat' and just make this 10 years wide (like all the rest) but you must know people who are older than 74! Let us take a reasonable assumption, and make the upper age limit as 84 years. We can now work

Table 2.8 Age distribution of instant coffee purchasers

Age	Instant granules
15–24	57
25–34	61
35–44	59
45–54	55
55–64	52
65+	51

out the appropriate height for each block in the histogram (Table 2.9). The actual width is the number of years in each age grouping whilst the relative height is the frequency divided by the actual width. We can now draw the diagram (Figure 2.10).

Table 2.9

Age	Instant granules	Actual width	Relative height
15–24	57	10	5.7
25–34	61	10	6.1
35–44	59	10	5.9
45–54	55	10	5.5
55–64	52	10	5.4
65–84	51	20	2.55

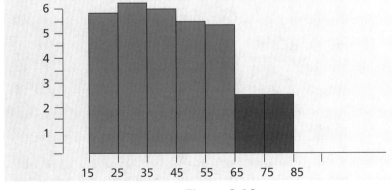

Figure 2.10

TASK

> **TABLE 2.10 GIVES THE EXPECTED AGE DISTRIBUTION FOR THE UK FOR 1989; USE THE METHOD ABOVE TO GET A HISTOGRAM FOR THIS DATA.**

Table 2.10

Age	1989 (m.)
0–4	3.8
5–14	7.0
15–29	13.4
30–44	11.8
45–54	12.3
65–84	8.9

Ogives

To construct an ogive we need to determine the cumulative frequency. Using the data on the age of the UK population, the number 'under 5' is 4.1 million, and the number 'under 15' are these 4.1 million plus the 7.5 million who are 'over 5 but under 15'. The full table is shown as Table 2.11.

Table 2.11

Age	1994 (m.)	Cumulative frequency (m.)
0–4	4.1	4.1
5–14	7.5	11.6
15–29	12.2	23.8
30–44	12.2	36.0
45–54	13.0	49.0
65–84	9.1	58.1

We can now plot the cumulative frequency against the upper limits of the age groupings (remember that the upper limit of 0–4 years is 5 years since 4 implies age at last birthday!) (Figure 2.11). This diagram allows us to

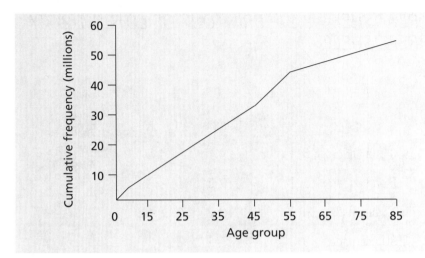

Figure 2.11

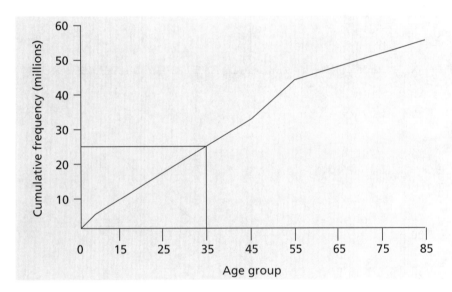

Figure 2.12

determine statistics of order; for example, we can now estimate the number of people under 35 by drawing a line up from 35 on the horizontal axis until it meets the ogive, and then drawing a horizontal line across to the vertical axis (Figure 2.12). You can see that then estimate is that approximately 26 million people will be under 35 in 1994. The printout in Spreadsheet 2.2 gives an example of how such an ogive could be produced using a spreadsheet.

An alternative to using diagrams or pictures would be to calculate some numbers which summarize the situation.

SPREADSHEET 2.2   PRINTOUT OF LOTUS 1-2-3™ SPREADSHEET

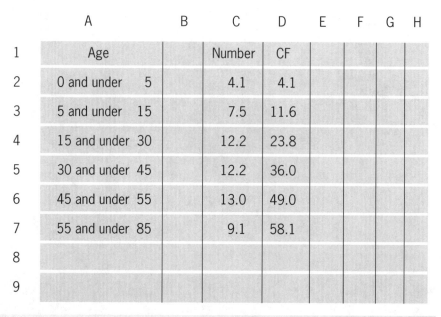

	A	B	C	D	E	F	G	H
1	Age		Number	CF				
2	0 and under 5		4.1	4.1				
3	5 and under 15		7.5	11.6				
4	15 and under 30		12.2	23.8				
5	30 and under 45		12.2	36.0				
6	45 and under 55		13.0	49.0				
7	55 and under 85		9.1	58.1				
8								
9								

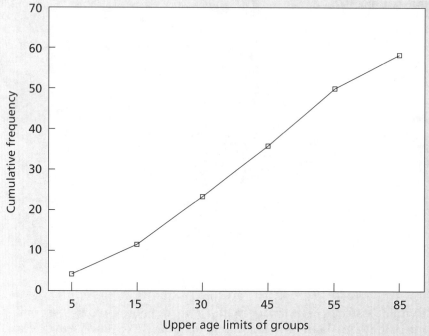

Figure 2.13   Ogive of ages.

STATISTICAL BACKGROUND: averages

Mean

This is the common average which everyone can already calculate – for example, you know that the average of 4 and 6 is equal to 5!

If you needed a formula to work it out it would be

$$\overline{X} = \frac{\Sigma X}{n} \text{ (pronounced } X \text{ bar)}$$

This means add up all of the numbers (that is what the Σ sign means) and then divide by the number of numbers (Σ is pronounced 'sigma').

If we started with a frequency table, then the formula would be

$$\overline{X} = \frac{\Sigma fX}{\Sigma f}$$

This means that we must first of all multiply the frequency of the group by the mid-point of the group, and then add up all of these results to get a total. We then divide this total by the sum of all of the frequencies (i.e. the number of numbers).

Median

This is defined to be the value of the middle item of data when that data is arranged into numerical order. For very simple data, in small amounts, we can just put them into order and then count up until you come to the middle one. For example, if we have

2 4 6 4 3 5 3 5 4

putting them into order gives

2 3 3 4 4 4 5 5 6

so the middle one is the fifth item (since there are nine items), and in this case the median is equal to 4.

For larger amounts of data, especially when they are presented as a frequency distribution, it is easiest to read the median from an ogive.

Mode

This is the most frequently occurring value from the data. It is particularly useful when dealing with categorical data, but its use is very limited when dealing with quantitative data.

For simple data we can just count how many times each value occurs, and then pick the most frequent one, for example:

$$2 \quad 3 \quad 4 \quad 2 \quad 3 \quad 4 \quad 5 \quad 3 \quad 6 \quad 2 \quad 3 \quad 5 \quad 3$$

Here you can quickly see that the number 3 occurs more frequently than any of the others (five times).

The problem with the mode is that it can easily change; for example, if we got more data which consisted of two more 2s and a 4, then both 2 and 3 would be modes, since they both occur five times.

A distribution of data does not necessarily have a mode!

Calculating the answer by hand

Before we go back to the scenario, it is worth looking at a few simple examples of calculating these averages.

If we have collected data on the number of people served in a bar between 8.00 p.m. and 9.00 p.m. for 10 nights, we may get results such as:

$$15, \quad 30, \quad 35, \quad 34, \quad 30, \quad 45, \quad 40, \quad 38, \quad 50, \quad 44$$

To work out the mean, we need to add all of the numbers together to get a total, and this will be 361. Now since there are 10 numbers, the mean will be 361 divided by 10, to give a mean of 36.1 people.

To work out the median, we first of all need to put the numbers into numerical order:

$$15, \quad 30, \quad 30, \quad 34, \quad 35, \quad 38, \quad 40, \quad 44, \quad 45, \quad 50$$

and then count up to find the middle one. However, there is an even number of numbers, so we do not have a middle one; we need to take a simple average of the middle two. This will give us a median of (35 + 38) / 2 = 36.5 people.

The mode is the number which occurs most frequently, and here there are two occasions when 30 people are served, so the mode is 30 people.

 MICROSTATS   If you put the 10 numbers into the first column of MICROSTATS and type in DESCRIBE C1 you will get these answers. Try it!

Where we have rather more data, it would probably be arranged into a frequency distribution, so if the data given above had formed part of a much larger survey, we might have overall results as shown in Table 2.12. For each line of the table, the frequency column tells us how many times each number appeared, so, for example, 40 people were served during the hour on 24 occasions. To find the mean, we need to multiply each number by its frequency, and then add up the results to get the total number of people served. This would give us Table 2.13. The mean will be

$$\frac{\Sigma fX}{\Sigma f} = \overline{X} \quad \frac{12\ 959}{350} = 37.0257$$

or approximately 37 people.

Table 2.12

Number of people served	Frequency
15	1
29	8
30	25
32	31
34	35
35	32
36	37
37	34
38	32
39	29
40	24
42	20
44	15
45	14
48	10
50	2
53	1

Table 2.13

Number of people served (X)	Frequency (f)	fX
15	1	15
29	8	232
30	25	750
32	31	992
34	35	1 190
35	32	1 120
36	37	1 332
37	34	1 258
38	32	1 216
39	29	1 131
40	24	960
42	20	840
44	15	660
45	14	630
48	10	480
50	2	100
53	1	53
Total	350	12 959

To work out the median, we need to count up until we get to the middle. (Note that the numbers are already arranged into order.) Half-way will be the 175th and 176th items as shown in Table 2.14. The **cumulative frequency** is the 'number so far' and is found by adding up the frequencies to that line of Table 2.14. For example, there are 9 occasions when 29 or less people are served; adding the frequency for '30 people served' we get 9 + 25 = 34, so there are 34 occasions when 30 or less people are served. From Table 2.14, we can see that both the 175th and 176th items are occasions when 37 people were served, so the median is equal to 37 people.

The mode is the most frequent number, so looking down the frequency column, we find that the highest frequency is 37, and that this relates to '36 people served'. Therefore the mode is 36 people.

MICROSTATS   If you wanted to analyse this data on MICROSTATS, then you would have to type in all 350 numbers. You could, of course, do the sums on a spreadsheet.

Table 2.14

Number of people served	Frequency	Cumulative frequency
15	1	1
29	8	9
30	25	34
32	31	65
34	35	100
35	32	132
36	37	169
37	34	203
38	32	
39	29	
40	24	
42	20	
44	15	
45	14	
48	10	
50	2	
53	1	

Return to Scenario 2

The mean

The age range of those people using instant granules (in 1989) was given in Table 2.8. However, we have to remember that the percentages shown in the second column are the 'percentage of the age group' that drink instant

Table 2.8   Age distribution of instant coffee purchasers

Age	Instant granules
15–24	57
25–34	61
35–44	59
45–54	55
55–64	52
65+	51

coffee granules. We therefore need to find the number of people in each age group, so that we can then work out how many people drink instant coffee granules. We could attempt to use the demographic data in the scenario, but the age groups do not match very well, so we have used some equivalent data from published government figures (in this case from a useful booklet called *Key Data*).

Table 2.15

Age	Instant as %	Female population	No. of coffee drinkers
15–24	57	4 389 300	2 501 901
25–34	61	4 160 500	2 537 905
35–44	59	3 920 100	2 312 859
45–54	55	3 135 000	1 724 250
55–64	52	3 056 500	1 589 380
65+	51	5 350 800	2 728 908

Using this data, you could find the figures given in Table 2.15. In order to work out the average age of users, we need to find the mid-point of each group (to represent the group) and then multiply this by the number of users. This is done in Table 2.16. (Remember that the age groups are age at last birthday, so the mid-point of 15–24 is half-way between 15 and 25, i.e. 20 years. We have also made the assumption that the last age group goes up to 85 years.) So the average age of those drinking instant granules is the sum of the fX column divided by the sum of the f column:

$$\overline{X} = \frac{604\ 932\ 930}{13\ 395\ 203} = 45.160\ 42$$

Table 2.16

Age	Instant granules (f)	Mid-point (X)	fX
15–24	2 501 901	20	50 038 020
25–34	2 537 905	30	76 137 150
35–44	2 312 859	40	92 514 360
45–54	1 724 250	50	86 212 500
55–64	1 589 380	60	95 362 800
65+	2 728 908	75	204 668 100
Total	13 395 203		604 932 930

which we would usually round to 45.16 years, or about 45 years and 2 months. (Note that the numbers here are rather large, because we are dealing with the whole population, but the method is just the same as that used earlier in this section.)

The median

To illustrate calculating the median, we will again use the data on the age of people using instant granules. The data is repeated in Table 2.17, but note that we have already worked out the cumulative frequency column. (If you can't remember how to draw an ogive, look back to p. 16).

Table 2.17

Age	Instant granules (f)	Cumulative frequency
15–24	2 501 901	2 501 901
25–34	2 537 905	5 039 806
35–44	2 312 859	7 352 665
45–54	1 724 250	9 076 915
55–64	1 589 380	10 666 295
65+	2 728 908	13 395 203

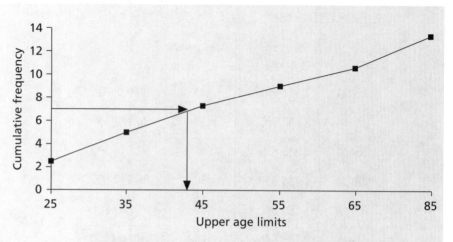

Figure 2.14   Ogive of female coffee drinkers.

Note that we have divided the total frequency by 2 to get 6 697 601.5 and marked this point on the vertical axis on Figure 2.14. We have then gone across horizontally until we hit the ogive and then down vertically until we hit the X-axis. Reading the value from here, we get the median to be approximately 43 years. The median is rarely equal to the mean (there is a difference of about 2 years in this case), but it would be very strange if there were a massive difference between them.

TASK

> **CAN YOU THINK OF AN EXAMPLE WHERE THE MEAN AND THE MEDIAN ARE UNLIKELY TO BE EQUAL TO EACH OTHER?**
> **HINT: WHAT WOULD HAPPEN IF MOST OF THE DATA WAS BETWEEN 5 AND 10, BUT THERE WERE A FEW VALUES OF 1000?**

The mode

There is little we can say about the mode in this case, except to note that the age group with the highest frequency is 25–34 years. (There are methods for calculating a value for the mode from such data, but the value of the result probably makes the effort not worthwhile!)

Interpretation of the numerical answers

So far we have been able to establish that the average age of female instant coffee drinkers in the UK is around about 45 years. We also know that the majority of coffee drinkers use mainstream instant coffee, but that there are significant minorities who use powder, decaffeinated and filter coffee, and we have been able to illustrate this in a variety of ways. Finally, we have identified the need to draw in data from other sources to give more detail to our results. There are several other diagrams and calculations which you could do from the data provided in the scenario.

SCENARIO 3: comparison of hotel room occupancy rates

You are working at the headquarters of a hotel group and your boss has been asked to draw up a comparison of the group's performance in relation to UK hotels in general. The performance measure which she has decided to use relates to demand for rooms and occupancy rates and you have been asked to collect appropriate data to allow this comparison to be made.

There are nine hotels in the group, and you have obtained basic information from the company files on each of them. This is summarized in Table 2.18. (Note that occupancy rate is the number of rooms occupied per night as a percentage of the total number of rooms in the hotel.)

Table 2.18   Number of rooms and average occupancy

| | Hotel | | | | | | | | |
	A	B	C	D	E	F	G	H	I
No. of rooms	30	40	25	36	50	62	28	40	70
Rooms occupied									
January	15	23	22	21	34	41	10	22	51
July	28	38	25	34	43	59	26	34	65

You have also been able to obtain sight of the results of a survey of 100 hotels which gives their occupancy rates in January and July. These results are shown in Table 2.19. Unfortunately, your boss is now away for a week, but the report has to be submitted by Friday, and it is up to you to produce it.

Table 2.19   Occupancy rates survey

Percentage of beds occupied	January	July
Under 20	8	1
20 but under 30	14	2
30 but under 40	18	2
40 but under 50	21	8
50 but under 60	15	15
60 but under 70	10	33
70 but under 80	8	24
80 but under 90	4	10
90 to 100	2	5

What do we need to measure?

The management is interested in the overall average occupancy rate for the hotel group and a comparison with the national average, but it is also concerned about the differences in occupancy rates between its own hotels. We therefore need to be able to describe this variability. A key point is to be able to measure and describe things about our particular hotel group, and then to be able to make comparisons with the hotel industry in general.

Which parts can we describe?

The first task will be to calculate the actual occupancy rate for each hotel, and to work out the average for the group, for January and for July. We then need to find a way of showing the variability in these occupancy rates.

In a similar way we can calculate the average occupancy rates for the hotels included in the survey, and measure the variability within this sample. We might also wish to identify the sort of occupancy rates for the 'top' hotels, and to see what percentage of hotels are doing better or worse than our group.

STATISTICAL BACKGROUND: *dispersion* (part 1)

Range

The **range** is simply defined as being the largest value minus the smallest value in the data. This is not a particularly useful measure, in general, since we may well have an extreme value in the data which distorts the value of the range. What tends to be more useful is to state the largest and smallest values.

Standard deviation

The **standard deviation** is a measure of spread or dispersion in the data. Unfortunately, it does not have an immediate intuitive meaning beyond the fact that a bigger number represents more spread. (Even this is not comparable between different data sets when the size of the original numbers differs considerably.) It is a measure that is used with the arithmetic mean, and looks for the variation of each individual bit of data from this value.

The formula for working it out for a simple list of numbers is

$$s = \sqrt{\left[\frac{\sum X^2}{n} - \left(\frac{\sum X}{n} \right)^2 \right]}$$

If we were to start with data that was presented in the form of a frequency table, then we would use the formula

$$s = \sqrt{\left[\frac{\sum fX^2}{\sum f} - \left(\frac{\sum fX}{\sum f} \right)^2 \right]}$$

Calculating an answer by hand

As with averages earlier in this section, we will look at some examples using simple data before we return to the scenario. If we use the same data on people served in a bar, which is repeated below, then we can use the first formula to find the standard deviation:

     15,   30,   35,   34,   30,   45,   40,   38,   50,   44

Table 2.20

X	X²
15	225
30	900
35	1 225
34	1 156
30	900
45	2 025
40	1 600
38	1 444
50	2 500
44	1 936
Total 361	13 911

Putting these numbers into a table will allow us to work out the sums that we require (Table 2.20). Now we can use the formula to get the value for the standard deviation:

$$s = \sqrt{\left[\frac{13\,911}{10} - \left(\frac{361}{10}\right)^2\right]}$$

$$= \sqrt{(1391.1 - 36.1^2)}$$

$$= \sqrt{(1391.1 - 1303.21)}$$

$$= \sqrt{87.89}$$

$$= 9.374\,966$$

Thus our measure of variation is 9.37 people. This does not have an immediate intuitive meaning(!) but from other parts of statistics, we can use it to make statements such as: 'Approximately 68% of the time, the number of people served was between 26.73 and 45.47 (i.e. the mean ± the standard deviation).'

 MICROSTATS   If you put the 10 numbers into the first column of MICROSTATS and type in DESCRIBE C1 you will get this answer. Try it!

Table 2.21

Number of people served (X)	Frequency (f)	fX	fXX
15	1	15	225
29	8	232	6 728
30	25	750	22 500
32	31	992	31 744
34	35	1 190	40 460
35	32	1 120	39 200
36	37	1 332	47 952
37	34	1 258	46 546
38	32	1 216	46 208
39	29	1 131	44 109
40	24	960	38 400
42	20	840	35 280
44	15	660	29 040
45	14	630	28 350
48	10	480	23 040
50	2	100	5 000
53	1	53	2 809
Total	350	12 959	487 591

Where we have rather more data, it would probably be arranged into a frequency distribution, so if we use the data given earlier as part of a much larger survey, shown in Table 2.21, we can use the second formula to work out the standard deviation. The formula that we need to use is

$$s = \sqrt{\left[\frac{\sum fX^2}{\sum f} - \left(\frac{\sum fX}{\sum f} \right)^2 \right]}$$

$$s = \sqrt{\left[\frac{487\ 591}{350} - \left(\frac{12\ 959}{350} \right)^2 \right]}$$

$$= \sqrt{(1393.117\ 143 - (37.025\ 71)^2}$$

$$= \sqrt{(1393.117\ 143 - 1370.904)}$$

$$= \sqrt{22.213\ 624\ 49}$$

$$= 4.713\ 133\ 192$$

Thus our measure of variation is 4.71 people. This still does not have an immediate intuitive meaning (!) but from other parts of statistics, we can use it to make statements such as: 'Approximately 68% of the time, the number of people served was between 32.31 and 41.73 (i.e. the mean ± the standard deviation).'

Return to Scenario 3

Our hotel group

The occupancy rate for each hotel in the group can be found by dividing the average number of rooms occupied by the number of rooms in the hotel and then multiplying the result by 100. This gives us the results given in Table 2.22.

Table 2.22

					Hotel				
	A	*B*	*C*	*D*	*E*	*F*	*G*	*H*	*I*
No. of rooms	30	40	25	36	50	62	28	40	70
Rooms occupied									
January	15	23	22	21	34	41	10	22	51
July	28	38	25	34	43	59	26	34	65
Occupancy rate (%)									
January	50.00	57.50	88.00	58.33	68.00	66.13	35.71	55.00	72.86
July	93.33	95.00	100.00	94.44	86.00	95.16	92.86	85.00	92.86

This shows two things immediately:

- The hotel group is doing rather better than average in terms of occupancy rate when compared with other hotels.

- The occupancy rate is higher in July than it is in January (a not very surprising fact!).

The range

For January, the hotel with the highest occupancy rate is C at 88% and the lowest is G with 35.71% thus the range is

$$88.00 - 35.71 = 52.29\%$$

TASK

> **WORK OUT THE RANGE FOR JULY.**

The standard deviation

Here we can use the first formula for standard deviation. We will put the data for January into a table to make it easier to see the calculations (Table 2.23). Therefore

$$s = \sqrt{\left[\frac{35\,558.5995}{9} - \left(\frac{551.53}{9}\right)^2\right]}$$

$$= \sqrt{(3950.9555) - 61.281\,111\,11^2)}$$

$$= \sqrt{(3950.9555 - 3755.374\,57)}$$

$$= \sqrt{195.580\,93}$$

$$= 13.985$$

TASK

> **WORK OUT THE STANDARD DEVIATION FOR THE HOTEL DATA IN JULY.**

Table 2.23

Hotel	X	X²
A	50.00	2 500.0000
B	57.50	3 306.2500
C	88.00	7 744.0000
D	58.33	3 402.3889
E	68.00	4 624.0000
F	66.13	4 373.1769
G	35.71	1 275.2041
H	55.00	3 025.0000
I	72.86	5 308.5796
Total	551.53	35 558.5995

The answer to this task is shown on the printout from a LOTUS 1-2-3™ spreadsheet (2.3). Notice that we get quite different answers to the standard

SPREADSHEET 2.3   PRINTOUT OF LOTUS 1-2-3™ SPREADSHEET

Number of Rooms and Average Occupancy

Hotel	A	B	C	D	E	F	G	H	I	
Rooms	30	40	25	36	50	62	28	40	70	
January	15	23	22	21	34	41	10	22	51	
July	28	38	25	34	43	59	26	34	65	

Occupancy Rate										Sums
January	50.00	57.50	88.00	58.33	68.00	66.13	35.71	55.00	72.86	551.53
July	93.33	95.00	100.00	94.44	86.00	95.16	92.86	85.00	92.86	834.65
	2500	3306.25	7744	3402.77	4624	4373.04	1275.51	3025	5308.16	35558.7
	8711.11	9025	10000	8919.75	7396	9055.67	8622.44	7225	8622.44	77577.4

Variance (January)	195.545	St. Deviation (January)	13.9837
Variance (July)	19.1441	St. Deviation (July)	4.37540

deviation for January and July. The larger value is for January when, if you look back at the original data, you will see that there is more variation from hotel to hotel. The lower figure is for July when there is less variation from hotel to hotel.

Hotels in the survey

Here we already have occupancy rates, and again, it is obvious that the level of occupancy is somewhat higher in July than it is in January.

The range

In this case it is not at all easy to find the range from the data, since, although we know that the maximum occupancy rate is 100%, we only know that the minimum occupancy rate is 'below 20%'. All we can say is that the range is at least 80.

The standard deviation

Here we will need to use the second formula, since the data is presented as a frequency distribution. Our first task is to find a mid-point for each of the groupings of occupancy rates. (This is done by adding the two ends of the group together and dividing the answer by 2.) The results are shown in Table 2.24.

Table 2.24   Occupancy rates survey

Percentage of beds occupied	f1 January	f2 July	X Mid-point
Under 20*	8	1	15
20 but under 30	14	2	25
30 but under 40	18	2	35
40 but under 50	21	8	45
50 but under 60	15	15	55
60 but under 70	10	33	65
70 but under 80	8	24	75
80 but under 90	4	10	85
90 to 100	2	5	95

*Assumed lower limit of 10

Table 2.25

Percentage of beds occupied	f January	X Mid-point	fX	fX²
Under 20	8	15	120	1 800
20 but under 30	14	25	350	8 750
30 but under 40	18	35	630	22 050
40 but under 50	21	45	945	42 525
50 but under 60	15	55	825	45 375
60 but under 70	10	65	650	42 250
70 but under 80	8	75	600	45 000
80 but under 90	4	85	340	28 900
90 to 100	2	95	190	18 050
Total	100		4 650	254 700

We now need to find the values for fX and fX^2 and we show this in Table 2.25. Remember that the fX^2 column consists of the frequency (f) times the mid-point (X) times the mid-point (X). We are now in a position to calculate the standard deviation for the January figures. Using

$$s = \sqrt{\left[\frac{\Sigma fX^2}{\Sigma f} - \left(\frac{\Sigma fX}{\Sigma f}\right)^2\right]}$$

we have

$$s = \sqrt{\left[\frac{254\ 700}{100} - \left(\frac{4650}{100}\right)^2\right]}$$

$$= \sqrt{(2547 - 46.5^2)}$$

$$= \sqrt{(2547 - 2162.25)}$$

$$= \sqrt{384.75}$$

$$= 19.615\ 05$$

TASK

> **WORK OUT THE STANDARD DEVIATION FOR THE SURVEY DATA IN JULY.**

The answer is given in the printout (Spreadsheet 2.4).

SPREADSHEET 2.4   PRINTOUT OF LOTUS 1-2-3™ SPREADSHEET

Occupancy rates survey

	f1	upper	f2	X	f1X	f1XX	f2X	f2XX
Percentage of beds occupied	January	limit	July	midpt				
Under 20%	8	20	1	15	120	1800	15	225
20% but under 30%	14	30	2	25	350	8750	50	1250
30% but under 40%	18	40	2	35	630	22050	70	2450
40% but under 50%	21	50	8	45	945	42525	360	16200
50% but under 60%	15	60	15	55	825	45375	825	45375
60% but under 70%	10	70	33	65	650	42250	2145	139425
70% but under 80%	8	80	24	75	600	45000	1800	135000
80 but under 90%	4	90	10	85	340	28900	850	72250
90% to 100%	2	100	5	95	190	18050	475	45125
	100		100		4650	254700	6590	457300

	January	July
Mean	46.5	65.9
St. deviation	19.61505	15.1720

STATISTICAL BACKGROUND: dispersion (part 2)

Quartile deviation

This is part of a set of statistics which are known as **position measures** (or order statistics) because they look at the data when it is arranged in numerical order and then find the particular value at a certain position in the list. (We have already come across a special case, when we looked at the median, which was half-way through the data.) To find the **quartiles** and quartile deviation (or semi-quartile range) we find the value 25% of the way through the data and call it Q_1; then find the value at a position 75% of the way through the data and call it Q_3. (What value would be called Q_2?)

The **quartile deviation** is defined as

$$QD = \frac{Q_3 - Q_1}{2}$$

where Q_1 is a reference to the lower quartile and Q_3 is a reference to the upper quartile.

Some people prefer to use the **quartile range** which is the difference between the upper and lower quartiles.

Percentiles

A **percentile** is a positional measure for any value between 1 and 100% of the way through the data, and can be worked out in a similar way to the quartiles. (Note: Although these position measures can be worked out for simple data, they are of much more value when we are faced by a grouped frequency distribution.)

Quartile deviation

From the frequency distribution, we could construct an ogive, as we did for Scenario 2, and this will allow us to estimate the percentage of hotels with given occupancy rate or less. To construct the ogive, we must first of all find the cumulative frequency table from the data. This is shown in Table 2.26. The ogive is shown in Figure 2.15. (Remember that in plotting an ogive, you plot the cumulative frequency against the upper limit of the group.) We can see that the median for this data is approximately 44%. In the same way we can find the lower quartile at 25% of the way through the data and the upper quartile at 75% of the way through the data. Should we want any other position measure, we can also use the ogive to find its value.

Table 2.26

Percentage of beds occupied	*f* January	CF
Under 20	8	8
20 but under 30	14	22
30 but under 40	18	40
40 but under 50	21	61
50 but under 60	15	76
60 but under 70	10	86
70 but under 80	8	94
80 but under 90	4	98
90 to 100	2	100

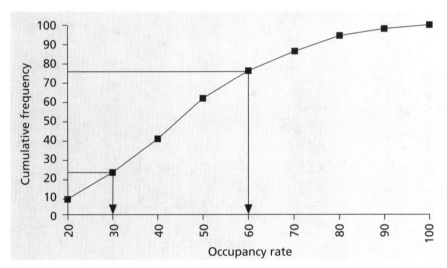

Figure 2.15 Ogive of occupancy rates for January.

Working from the ogive, we can see that Q_1 is approximately 30, Q_3 is approximately 60, so the quartile deviation is

$$QD = \frac{60 - 30}{2}$$
$$= \frac{30}{2}$$
$$= 15\%$$

Thus we can see that approximately 50% of the hotels in the survey have occupancy rates between 30% and 60%. If we want a single figure to represent dispersion in the data, then we can quote the quartile deviation as being equal to 15%. (The quartile range in this case is 30%.)

TASK

> **WORK OUT THE QUARTILE DEVIATION FOR THE SURVEYED HOTELS IN JULY.**

Percentiles

If we wanted to know the minimum occupancy rate for the 10% most successful hotels (in terms of occupancy), then we can go to the 90% mark on the Y-axis (Figure 2.16), go horizontally across to the ogive, and then vertically down to the X-axis. This gives a figure of approximately 75%, so we can say that 10% of hotels in the survey had occupancy rates above 75%.

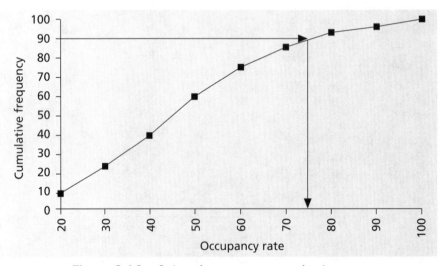

Figure 2.16 Ogive of occupancy rates for January.

A further application

Similarly, we know that for our hotel group, the average occupancy rate in January was 61.28%, so we can use the graph (Figure 2.17) to estimate how many hotels have higher occupancy rates than us. We do this by marking the value of the X-axis, and then going vertically until we hit the ogive, then horizontally until we meet the Y-axis. It is then possible to read off the figure. This gives us a figure of approximately 79%, so we are doing better than 79% of hotels.

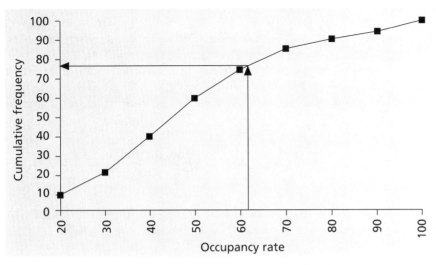

Figure 2.17 Ogive of occupancy rates for January.

Interpretation of the numerical answers

Looking at the answers that we have obtained, we can see that the amount of variability in occupancy rates in July is much less than it is in January, and that the average occupancy rate is also higher. This is good news for the hotel group! Ideally they would want to push up the occupancy rates in January in order to increase profitability. But what can we actually say about variability from our calculations?

First of all we can bring all the results together in Table 2.27. This gives us some good news to tell the board; our hotel group has higher

Table 2.27

Our hotel group	January	July
Average (%)	61.28	92.74
Range (%)	52.29	15
Standard deviation	13.985	4.3754
Surveyed hotels		
Average (%)	46.5	65.9
Range (%)	Over 80	Over 80
Standard deviation	19.61505	15.17201

occupancy rates than hotels in the survey (which we assume are typical of all hotels in the UK). Also, the variation in occupancy rates seems to be less (in other words, we do not seem to have any very poor rates).

We could work out a further statistic called the **coefficient of variation** which would allow us to make a direct comparison between the variability of our hotel group and those in the survey. This is worked out using the formula

$$\text{Coefficient of variation} = \frac{\text{Standard deviation}}{\text{Mean}} \times 100$$

and this gives us the figures shown in Table 2.28. These figures confirm that our hotel group is doing rather better than hotels in general.

Table 2.28

Coefficient of variation	January (%)	July (%)
Our hotel group	22.82	4.72
Surveyed hotels	42.18	23.02

SCENARIO 3 (postscript)

Your boss has now returned, and when the board comment on the report you produced, but submitted under her name, she receives considerable praise.

SCENARIO 4: Northbridge District Council – urban renewal spending in a local authority

A local authority has to monitor its spending from year to year, and to make some predictions about the likely level of expenditure in the coming year in order to set council tax levels. The increase in the level of tax is limited from central government, and thus the overall budget for the local authority is also limited. However, individual departments may be able to make a case that their spending should not be restricted to the size of the overall increase.

You are working for the Urban Renewal Department of the local authority and have been asked to produce a short report which shows how the costs of the department have changed over the last 3 years in comparison to the general level of inflation in the economy and the increases in the overall spending budget for the local authority. You have also been asked to include diagrams which show total spending by the department over a somewhat longer time span.

By looking back at the annual reports of the council, you have been able to obtain figures on overall spending by both the council and the department for a 12-year period, and these are summarized in Table 2.29.

Table 2.29

Year	Total council spending	Urban renewal spending	Retail prices index
19V1	£5 200 400	£229 087	147.8
19V2	£5 725 000	£324 900	156.6
19V3	£6 345 000	£356 000	166.3
19V4	£6 542 000	£378 690	173.8
19V5	£7 100 000	£400 834	189.1
19V6	£7 542 000	£450 988	197.9
19V7	£8 342 000	£485 990	215.7
19V8	£9 245 000	£499 871	231.7
19V9	£9 990 000	£530 678	254.4
19X0	£10 356 000	£550 800	271.2
19X1	£10 899 000	£564 868	286.6
19X2	£11 425 000	£587 324	301.7

Copious notes have been kept by the supplies manager for 3 years on the amounts of materials used by the department, and the costs that have been incurred. The Personnel Department have also been able to provide data for the same period on the number of people employed and their salary levels. These are shown in Table 2.30.

Table 2.30

Item	Prices			Quantities		
	19X0	19X1	19X2	19X0	19X1	19X2
Materials						
Bricks	£185.00	£189.00	£196.00	135	137	134
Sand	£33.00	£38.00	£42.00	80	90	94
Cement	£247.00	£251.00	£255.60	45	65	60
Timber	£25.50	£26.88	£26.90	500	500	540
Plants	£2.40	£2.40	£2.50	1200	1500	1400
Soils	£10.00	£11.00	£11.00	200	200	250

Table 2.30 *contd*

Item	*Prices*			*Quantities*		
	19X0	19X1	19X2	19X0	19X1	19X2
Staff						
Office	£13 890	£14 380	£14 680	6	5	5
Foremen	£14 350	£14 900	£15 300	4	5	4
Site	£13 100	£13 600	£13 800	27	26	28

What do we need to measure?

There is a lot of information in this scenario! We need to find some measure of the way in which prices and costs have increased for the Urban Renewal Department and to be able to compare these with the budgets for the council as a whole. It might also be useful to measure the increases in costs, not only overall, but for materials and staff separately.

Looking at the trend data in Table 2.29, we want to be able to compare the increases in spending between the council as a whole and the Urban Renewal Department. It would also be useful to compare these spending increases with the level of price inflation in the economy as a whole, in order to tell if the resources allocated from the council are increasing in real terms.

Which parts can we describe?

By converting the figures in Table 2.29 into index numbers and using a technique called **rebasing**, we can produce a graph which will allow a direct comparison between the three sets of figures. We could look at each of the individual items for materials and staff costs as used by the Urban Renewal Department and the way in which these have changed over the 3 years, but this would still be a very detailed picture of resource use. By using the basic ideas of index numbers, we can describe and summarize the price rises experienced by the department over all of the resources used. Adapting these ideas, we can also describe the quantity changes and the overall change in the cost of running the department.

STATISTICAL BACKGROUND: index numbers (part 1)

Index numbers

You must already have come across index numbers in one form or another, if only from reading newspapers or listening to the television news reports. The most frequently quoted is the **index of retail prices** which is used by economists to measure the level of inflation in the economy. (We will look at this index in more detail in the case study later in this section.)

Concept

Index numbers show the percentage change from a given point in time, called the **base year**. This base year is set to be equal to 100 to enable quick and easy comparisons to be made. At its simplest, an index number consists of the current value of something, often price, and its value in the base year. For example, if the price of a CD is £13 now and was £11 in our base year, then the index is given by dividing the price now by the price in the base year and multiplying the result by 100:

$$\frac{13}{11} \times 100 = 118.1818$$

More generally, we can write the formula

$$\text{Index} = \frac{P_n}{P_0} \times 100$$

Rebasing

This idea allows us to change the base year of an index series to one that is more convenient. It is useful if we want to show the way in which two or more sets of data have changed over time. To make the change we need to know the value of the index for the year which we want to make into the new base year (let us call this value P_*). We then divide each value of the index series by this value and multiply the result by 100. If we need a formula, we have

$$\text{Rebased index} = \frac{P_n}{P_*} \times 100$$

Calculating an answer by hand

First of all we will look at the figures in Table 2.29 on spending over a 12-year period. If we take the figures for total council spending we can see that spending in year 19V1 was £5 200 400. We will use this as the base year for our index number. Applying the formula given in the statistical background, we can work out the index number for year 19V2 as follows:

$$\text{Index} = \frac{P_n}{P_0} \times 100$$

$$= \frac{\pounds 5\ 725\ 000}{\pounds 5\ 200\ 400} \times 100$$

$$= 110.09 \quad \text{(rounded to two decimal places)}$$

Carrying out the same operation for year 19V3, we have

$$\text{Index} = \frac{\pounds 6\ 345\ 000}{\pounds 5\ 200\ 400} \times 100$$

$$= 122.01 \quad \text{(rounded to two decimal places)}$$

By continuing with this method, we can create Table 2.31.

Table 2.31		
Year	*Total council spending*	*Index number Base year = 19V1*
19V1	£5 200 400	100.00
19V2	£5 725 000	110.09
19V3	£6 345 000	122.01
19V4	£6 542 000	125.80
19V5	£7 100 000	136.53
19V6	£7 542 000	145.03
19V7	£8 342 000	160.41
19V8	£9 245 000	177.77
19V9	£9 990 000	192.10
19X0	£10 356 000	199.14
19X1	£10 899 000	209.58
19X2	£11 425 000	219.69

TASK

> **WORK OUT THE INDEX SERIES FOR THE SPENDING OF THE URBAN RENEWAL DEPARTMENT WITH A BASE YEAR OF 19V1.**

The answer to this task is shown in the LOTUS 1-2-3™ spreadsheet (2.5).

SPREADSHEET 2.5   PRINTOUT OF LOTUS 1-2-3™ SPREADSHEET

	A	B	C	D	E	F
1	Year	Total Council	Urban Renewal	Index	Index	
2		Spending	Spending	Total Sp	UR Sp	
3	19V1	£5,200,400.00	£299,087.00	100.00	100.00	
4	19V2	£5,725,000.00	£324,900.00	110.09	108.63	
5	19V3	£6,345,000.00	£356,000.00	122.01	119.03	
6	19V4	£6,542,000.00	£378,690.00	125.80	126.62	
7	19V5	£7,100,000.00	£400,834.00	136.53	134.02	
8	19V6	£7,542,000.00	£450,988.00	145.03	150.79	
9	19V7	£8,342,000.00	£485,990.00	160.41	162.49	
10	19V8	£9,245,000.00	£499,871.00	177.77	167.13	
11	19V9	£9,990,000.00	£530,678.00	192.10	177.43	
12	19X0	£10,356,000.00	£550,800.00	199.14	184.16	
13	19X1	£10,899,000.00	£564,868.00	209.58	188.86	
14	19X2	£11,425,000.00	£587,324.00	219.69	196.37	
15						

We now have a basis for comparing the growth in spending by the council as a whole with the spending by the Urban Renewal Department. As you can see, the spending by the council has risen to an index value of 219.69 (a rise of 119.69%) over the 12 years, whilst the spending by the department has only risen to an index value of 196.37 (a rise of 96.37%).

It would be useful to now compare these rises with the level of price inflation in the whole economy over the same period, and to do this we can use the index of retail prices. Currently, however, this has a base year before year 19V1, so to make comparisons easier, we need to rebase it to 19V1 (i.e. so that 19V1 = 100). Using the formula in the statistical background, we have

$$\text{Rebased index} = \frac{P_n}{P_*} \times 100$$

For 19V1 this will be

$$\text{Rebased index} = \frac{147.80}{147.80} \times 100 = 100.00$$

For 19V2, it will be

$$\text{Rebased index} = \frac{156.60}{147.80} \times 100 = 105.95$$

Carrying on this process, we get the answers shown in Table 2.32. Thus there has been a 104.13% rise in inflation over the 12 years.

Table 2.32

RPI	RPI rebased
147.80	100.00
156.60	105.95
166.30	112.52
173.80	117.59
189.10	127.94
197.90	133.90
215.70	145.94
231.70	156.77
254.40	172.12
271.20	183.49
286.60	193.91
301.70	204.13

We can now use the three index numbers with a base year of 19V1 to construct a graph, and thus make comparisons between the increases

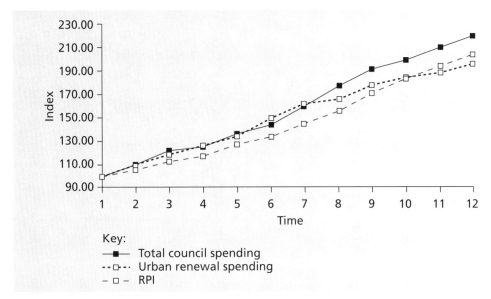

Figure 2.18

(Figure 2.18). Whilst this diagram is useful for long-term comparisons, it does not really tell us very much about year-to-year changes. It is fairly easy to work out these changes by taking the index number for one year and looking at the percentage rise from the previous year. Writing this down as a formula looks complicated, but is really very easy to do!

$$\text{Percentage change} = \left(\frac{P_n}{P_{n-1}} \times 100 \right) - 100$$

Doing this for 19V1 to 19V2 for the index of total spending of the council, we have

$$\text{Percentage change} = \left(\frac{110.09}{100.00} \times 100 \right) - 100$$
$$= 110.09 - 100 = 10.09\%$$

And for year 19V2 to 19V3 of the same series, we have

$$\text{Percentage change} = \left(\frac{122.01}{110.09} \times 100 \right) - 100$$
$$= 110.83 - 100 = 10.83\%$$

Using the same method, we can get the figures given in Table 2.33. (Notice that there is no figure for 19V1.)

Table 2.33	
Year	*% Rise (Total)*
19V1	
19V2	10.09
19V3	10.83
19V4	3.10
19V5	8.53
19V6	6.23
19V7	10.61
19V8	10.82
19V9	8.06
19X0	3.66
19X1	5.24
19X2	4.83

TASK

> **WORK OUT THE PERCENTAGE CHANGE FROM YEAR TO YEAR FOR THE SPENDING OF THE URBAN RENEWAL DEPARTMENT AND FOR THE RETAIL PRICES INDEX.**

The results you should obtain are shown on the LOTUS 1-2-3™ spreadsheet (2.6).

SPREADSHEET 2.6   PRINTOUT OF LOTUS 1-2-3™ SPREADSHEET

Spreadsheet 2.6 makes it easier to see in which years the department has done relatively well, and in which years it has been unable to increase its spending at the same rate as the council. We can now draw a diagram (Figure 2.19) to represent this situation. This is really as far as we can go with the data from the first part of Scenario 4.

	A	B	C	D	E
1	Year	Percent	Percent	Percent	
2		Rise (Tot)	Rise (UR)	RPI	
3	19V1				
4	19V2	10.09	8.63	5.9	
5	19V3	10.83	9.57	6.19	
6	19V4	3.10	6.37	4.51	
7	19V5	8.53	5.85	8.80	
8	19V6	6.23	12.51	4.65	
9	19V7	10.61	7.76	8.99	
10	19V8	10.82	2.86	7.42	
11	19V9	8.06	6.16	9.80	
12	19X0	3.66	3.79	6.60	
13	19X1	5.24	2.55	5.68	
14	19X2	4.83	3.98	5.27	
15					

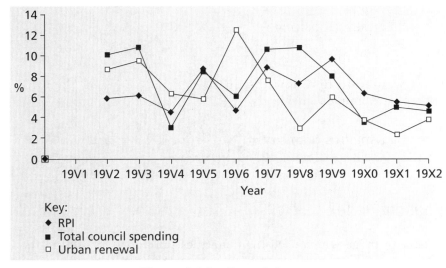

Key:
♦ RPI
■ Total council spending
□ Urban renewal

Figure 2.19 Rate of change.

Turning now to the more detailed figures in Table 2.30, we want to be able to measure the change in the prices we are paying for materials, staff, and the overall cost of running the department. Before we can do this, we need a little more statistical background.

STATISTICAL BACKGROUND: *index numbers (part 2)*

Multi-item indices

So far we have only dealt with an index for a single item. Whilst this is useful, as we have seen, we also need to combine varying price effects for several items into a single index number. This type of index is known as a **multi-item index**. The problem we face is how to combine the changes for the different items! An example would be your weekly 'shopping basket'; you could monitor inflation by pricing the same goods and quantities each week and noting the rise in their total price.

A major point to note is that combining the various items into an index without some form of weighting would mean that we assume that they all have equal importance – this is generally not the case!

Laspeyres index

This is an index which uses the quantities purchased or used in the base year to weight the various items contained in the index when calculating a price index. (Laspeyres indices are also known as **base-weighted indices**.) This is OK if the purchasing behaviour is fairly stable. The appropriate formula is

$$\text{Laspeyres price} = \frac{\sum(P_n Q_0)}{\sum(P_0 Q_0)} \times 100$$

If we wanted to find how the quantities had changed, then the appropriate formula would be

$$\text{Laspeyres quantity} = \frac{\sum(P_0 Q_n)}{\sum(P_0 Q_0)} \times 100$$

Paasche index

This is an index which used the quantities purchased or used in the current year to weight the various items contained in the index when calculating a price index. (Paasche indices are also known as **current-weighted indices**.) This is OK if the relative importance of the items is changing rapidly, but it is more costly to collect the data and there are questions about the validity of year-to-year comparisons. The appropriate formula is

$$\text{Paasche price} = \frac{\sum (P_n Q_n)}{\sum (P_0 Q_n)} \times 100$$

If we wanted to find how the quantities had changed, then the appropriate formula would be

$$\text{Paasche quantity} = \frac{\sum (P_n Q_n)}{\sum (P_n Q_0)} \times 100$$

Value index

Sometimes we want to reflect the overall change in the cost or revenue involved, so that we need to show the effects of both the price and quantity changes. This is known as a value index, and the appropriate formula is

$$\text{Value index} = \frac{\sum (P_n Q_n)}{\sum (P_0 Q_0)} \times 100$$

Return to Scenario 4

Here we are interested in the costs of both materials and staff to the Urban Renewal Department, and how these compare with the increases borne by the council as a whole and the funding levels for our department. We could, of course, just compare each item in the expenditure of the department with the figures for the whole council, but this would be a long, tedious, and boring process! Item-by-item comparisons would not allow any overall discrepancy to emerge. What we really need is a way of summarizing the changes, so that we can talk about the rise in cost of materials or staff.

It was suggested earlier (in the statistical background) that just looking at the changes in prices or costs would not be very productive, since this would assume that each item was equally important, and this is clearly not the case here! We have seen that there are two types of index number which can cope with groups of items, and we will use these to look at how costs have changed.

Laspeyres price index

This is a base-weighted index, that is, it assumes that the relative importance of the items remains the same throughout. We work with the 'basket of goods' purchased in the base year.

To illustrate the calculations we will use the data on materials purchased by the Urban Renewal Department in the 3 years. For convenience, the data is repeated in Table 2.34. Notice that we have now labelled the columns as P_0 and Q_0 for the base year price and quantity data respectively, and labelled the subsequent years' price data as P_1 and P_2. (Note: We did not necessarily have to take the first year's data as the base year, but this typifies the type of example we would generally work with.)

Table 2.34

Item	Prices			Quantities
	19X0	19X1	19X2	19X0
	P_0	P_1	P_2	Q_0
Materials				
Bricks	£185.00	£189.00	£196.00	135
Sand	£33.00	£38.00	£42.00	80
Cement	£247.00	£251.00	£255.60	45
Timber	£25.50	£26.88	£26.90	500
Plants	£2.40	£2.40	£2.50	1200
Soils	£10.00	£11.00	£11.00	200

Looking back at the formula, we have

$$\text{Laspeyres price} = \frac{\Sigma(P_nQ_0)}{\Sigma(P_0Q_0)} \times 100$$

where n will be 0, 1 or 2, depending upon which particular year we are trying to describe. We therefore need to work out some extra columns and then total them, so that we can work out the index numbers.

Doing this for year 19X1, we have the data shown in Table 2.35. So the Laspeyres price index for 19X1 (with 19X0 as the base year) is

$$L_p = \frac{58\ 370}{56\ 360} \times 100 = 103.57$$

Table 2.35

Item	Prices 19X0 P_0	19X1 P_1	Quantities 19X0 Q_0	$P_0 Q_0$	$P_1 Q_0$
Materials					
Bricks	£185.00	£189.00	135	24 975	25 515
Sand	£33.00	£38.00	80	2 640	3 040
Cement	£247.00	£251.00	45	11 115	11 295
Timber	£25.50	£26.88	500	12 750	13 440
Plants	£2.40	£2.40	1200	2 880	2 880
Soils	£10.00	£11.00	200	2 000	2 200
Total				56 360	58 370

Thus there has been a 3.57% increase in the cost of materials from year 19X0 to year 19X1.

Table 2.36

Item	Prices 19X0 P_0	Quantities 19X2 P_2	19X0 Q_0	$P_0 Q_0$	$P_2 Q_0$
Materials					
Bricks	£185.00	£196.00	135	24 975	26 460
Sand	£33.00	£42.00	80	2 640	3 360
Cement	£247.00	£255.60	45	11 115	11 502
Timber	£25.50	£26.90	500	12 750	13 450
Plants	£2.40	£2.50	1200	2 880	3 000
Soils	£10.00	£11.00	200	2 000	2 200
Total				56 360	59 972

We can do the same for 19X2 (Table 2.36). So the Laspeyres price index for 19X2 (with 19X0 as the base year) is

$$L_p = \frac{59\,972}{56\,360} \times 100 = 106.41$$

Thus there has been a 6.41% increase in the cost of materials from year 19X0 to year 19X2. Notice that we cannot say anything immediately about the rise in cost of materials from year 19X1 to year 19X2. If we wanted this information we would have to do another calculation – see earlier part of this section.

Paasche price index

The alternative method of constructing an index number uses the quantities in each year as the measure of relative importance, so we need more data to work this one out. Again the data is reproduced in Table 2.37.

Table 2.37

Item	Prices			Quantities		
	19X0 P_0	19X1 P_1	19X2 P_2	19X0 Q_0	19X1 Q_1	19X2 Q_2
Materials						
Bricks	£185.00	£189.00	£196.00	135	137	134
Sand	£33.00	£38.00	£42.00	80	90	94
Cement	£247.00	£251.00	£255.60	45	65	60
Timber	£25.50	£26.88	£26.90	500	500	540
Plants	£2.40	£2.40	£2.50	1200	1500	1400
Soils	£10.00	£11.00	£11.00	200	200	250

The formula we require is

$$\text{Paasche price} = \frac{\sum(P_n Q_n)}{\sum(P_0 Q_n)} \times 100$$

where n will be 0, 1 or 2, depending upon which particular year we are trying to describe. Taking year 19X1 first, our data give Table 2.38. So the Paasche price index for 19X1 (with 19X0 as the base year) is

$$P_p = \frac{64\ 868}{62\ 720} \times 100 = 103.42$$

Thus there has been a 3.42% increase in the cost of materials from year 19X0 to year 19X1.

Table 2.38

Item	Prices 19X0 P_0	19X1 P_1	Quantities 19X1 Q_1	P_1Q_1	P_0Q_1
Materials					
Bricks	£185.00	£189.00	137	25 893	25 345
Sand	£33.00	£38.00	90	3 420	2 970
Cement	£247.00	£251.00	65	16 315	16 055
Timber	£25.50	£26.88	500	13 440	12 750
Plants	£2.40	£2.40	1500	3 600	3 600
Soils	£10.00	£11.00	200	2 200	2 000
Total				64 868	62 720

Table 2.39

Item	Prices 19X0 P_0	19X2 P_2	Quantities 19X2 Q_2	P_2Q_2	P_0Q_2
Materials					
Bricks	£185.00	£196.00	134	26 264	24 790
Sand	£33.00	£42.00	94	3 948	3 102
Cement	£247.00	£255.60	60	15 336	14 820
Timber	£25.50	£26.90	540	14 526	13 770
Plants	£2.40	£2.50	1400	3 500	3 360
Soils	£10.00	£11.00	250	2 750	2 500
Total				66 324	62 342

We can do the same for 19X2 (Table 2.39). So the Paasche price index for 19X2 (with 19X0 as the base year) is

$$P_p = \frac{66\ 324}{62\ 342} \times 100 = 106.39$$

Thus there has been a 6.39% increase in the cost of materials from year 19X0 to year 19X2. Notice that again we cannot say anything immediately about the rise in cost of materials from year 19X1 to year 19X2.

TASK

> **WORK OUT THE LASPEYRES AND PAASCHE PRICES INDICES FOR THE STAFF COSTS OF THE DEPARTMENT.**

The answers appear in Spreadsheet 2.7.

Value index

Here we are reflecting the changes in both the costs and amounts that have faced the department. The formula was

$$\text{Value index} = \frac{\sum(P_n Q_n)}{\sum(P_0 Q_0)} \times 100$$

Table 2.40

Item	Prices 19X0 P_0	19X1 P_1	Quantities 19X0 Q_0	19X1 Q_1	$P_0 Q_0$	$P_1 Q_1$
Materials						
Bricks	£185.00	£189.00	135	137	24 975	25 893
Sand	£33.00	£38.00	80	90	2 640	3 420
Cement	£247.00	£251.00	45	65	11 115	16 315
Timber	£25.50	£26.88	500	500	12 750	13 440
Plants	£2.40	£2.40	1200	1500	2 880	3 600
Soils	£10.00	£11.00	200	200	2 000	2 200

Table 2.40   *contd*

Item	Prices 19X0 P_0	19X1 P_1	Quantities 19X0 Q_0	19X1 Q_1	P_0Q_0	P_1Q_1
Staff						
Office	£13 890	£14 380	6	5	83 340	71 900
Foremen	£14 350	£14 900	4	5	57 400	74 500
Site	£13 100	£13 600	27	26	353 700	353 600
Total					550 800	564 868

Taking both the materials costs and the staff costs, we can work out the appropriate figures for 19X1. The basic data we need is repeated in Table 2.40. So the value index for 19X1 (with 19X0 as the base year) is

$$\text{Value} = \frac{564\ 868}{550\ 800} \times 100 = 102.55$$

Thus there has been a 2.55% increase in the overall costs of the Urban Renewal Department from year 19X0 to year 19X1.

TASK

WORK OUT THE VALUE INDEX FOR 19X2 WITH 19X0 AS THE BASE YEAR.

Quantity indices

The process for calculating quantity indices, which show the changes in the amounts of materials or staff (or both) used, is very similar to that we have used so far. The only point to note is that you need to be very careful in labelling your columns, so that you actually multiply the correct numbers together. This whole process can become very tedious, and is ideally suited to work on a spreadsheet. See a spreadsheet printout for the data contained in this scenario (Spreadsheet 2.7).

SPREADSHEET 2.7   PRINTOUT OF LOTUS 1-2-3™ SPREADSHEET

Item	Prices 19X0	19X1	19X2	Quantities 19X0	19X1	19X2	P0Q0	P1Q0	P2Q0	P1Q1	P2Q2	P0Q1	P0Q2
Materials:													
Bricks	£185.00	£189.00	£196.00	135	137	134	24975	25515	26460	25893	26264	25345	24790
Sand	£33.00	£38.00	£42.00	80	90	94	2640	3040	3360	3420	3948	2970	3102
Cement	£247.00	£251.00	£255.60	45	65	60	11115	11295	11502	16315	15336	16055	14820
Timber	£25.50	£26.88	£26.90	500	500	540	12750	13440	13450	13440	14526	12750	13770
Plants	£2.40	£2.40	£2.50	1200	1500	1400	2880	2880	3000	3600	3500	3600	3360
Soils	£10.00	£11.00	£11.00	200	200	250	2000	2200	2200	2200	2750	2000	2500
Staff:													
Office	£13,890.00	£14,380.00	£14,680.00	6	5	5	83340	86280	88080	71900	73400	69450	69450
Foremen	£14,350.00	£14,900.00	£15,300.00	4	5	4	57400	59600	61200	74500	61200	71750	57400
Site	£13,100.00	£13,600.00	£13,800.00	27	26	28	353700	367200	372600	353600	386400	340600	366800
							550800	571450	581852	564868	587324	544520	555992
Materials							56360	58370	59972	64868	66324	62720	62342
Staff							494440	513080	521880	500000	521000	481800	493650

Laspeyres
Price

	Materials	Staff	Total
19X0	100.00	100.00	100.00
19X1	103.57	103.77	103.75
19X2	106.41	105.55	105.64

Paasche
Price

	Materials	Staff	Total
19X0	100.00	100.00	100.00
19X1	103.42	103.78	103.74
19X2	106.39	105.54	105.64

Laspeyres
Quantity

	Materials	Staff	Total
19X0	100.00	100.00	100.00
19X1	111.28	97.44	98.86
19X2	110.61	99.84	100.94

Paasche
Quantity

	Materials	Staff	Total
19X0	100.00	100.00	100.00
19X1	111.13	97.45	98.85
19X2	113.63	99.83	100.94

Value

	Materials	Staff	Total
19X0	100.00	100.00	100.00
19X1	115.10	101.12	102.55
19X2	117.68	105.37	106.63

Interpretation of the numerical answers

There are a lot of numerical answers to this scenario, and an overall summary is necessary. Looking at the percentage increases from the previous year that we can find from our index numbers, we have the data shown in Table 2.41. Overall, we can see that the Urban Renewal Department has done relatively badly when compared with the council as a whole. However, the council itself has not been allowed spending increases in line with inflation. The figures also highlight the reduction in staff within the department in 19X1 (–2.55%), but that these have been mostly recovered in 19X2 (+2.44%).

Table 2.41

	Annual percentage increase	
	Year 19X1	Year 19X2
Retail prices	5.68	5.27
Council spending	5.24	4.83
Urban renewal spending (total)	2.55	3.98
Urban renewal materials – cost	3.42	2.87
Urban renewal materials – quantity	11.13	2.25
Urban renewal staff – cost	3.78	1.70
Urban renewal staff – quantity	–2.55	2.44

As a final area in this section, we can look at a particular index number – see the case study below.

CASE STUDY: the general index of retail prices

This is one of the most widely quoted indices in the UK and for many years has formed the basis for the assessment of some government policies.

The first index, which started in 1914, attempted to measure changes in the prices of goods and in particular the 'cost of maintaining unchanged the standard of living of the working classes'. It did this by taking a 'basket of goods' which were purchased by a typical working-class family and monitoring their prices. Over the intervening years there have been many changes and revisions to the index. Many new goods and services have been added, the method of construction changed, and the scope of families covered vastly increased (although it still does not cover all households). The latest revisions took place in 1987.

Data for the index comes from two main sources:

- The weights are derived from the Family Expenditure Survey.
- The prices come from a survey conducted by 200 local offices.

The Family Expenditure Survey

This is a large-scale survey with an annual sample size of about 11 000 households. The survey continues throughout the year using a rotating, stratified random design (see Section 3). Each head of household completes two questionnaires relating to income and expenditure, and then each member of the household over 15 years of age keeps a diary of all purchases for a 2-week period. Considering the amount of information sought, the response rate of about 70% is fairly good.

Before data is used in the construction of weights for the retail prices index (RPI), returns relating to the highest income households and pensioner households are excluded, since it is expected that the expenditure patterns of these households will differ significantly from those of the general population (separate indices are produced). Other checks are also performed, since experience has shown that there tends to be an underestimation of the amount spent on betting, drinking and smoking, and an overestimation of the amount spent on electricity and gas in meter payments.

Expenditure patterns are summarized into over 300 groups and each is given a weight. The total of the weights is 1000. Comparisons of the weights attached to the major subgroups in the RPI give a social commentary; for example, the weight attached to food in 1956 was 350 (i.e. 35% of income was spent on food), whilst in 1987 the weight was only 213 (21.3% of income was spent on food). Since 1962 the weights have been revised each year.

Price information

This information is collected from 200 areas within the UK, in order to avoid a regional bias, and uses the prices charged, whether or not these include subsidies or discounts. Rents and rates (council tax) are taken gross, since allowances for these items are selective and not available to all consumers.

Weights

The weights attached to each of the subgroups in 1990 are shown in Table 2.42.

Table 2.42

Group	Weight
Food	158
Catering	47
Alcoholic drink	77

Table 2.42   *contd*

Group	Weight
Tobacco	34
Housing	185
Fuel and light	50
Household goods	71
Household services	40
Clothing and footwear	69
Personal goods and services	39
Motoring expenditure	131
Fares and travel costs	21
Leisure goods	48
Leisure services	30

Questions

1. Use your library to find the most recent copy of the *Monthly Digest of Statistics* (*MDS*) and find the weights for each group in the general index of retail prices (RPI) that are currently in force.
2. Also from the library, find a copy of the *MDS* from the 1960s and find the weights used for the RPI in 1956 and the early 1960s.
3. Use your findings from questions 1 and 2 to discuss the changes in the relative importance of each of the groups in the RPI. What would you suggest to be the reasons for these changes?
4. What would be the effect on the RPI of a rise in prices of 10% for alcoholic drinks?
5 What would be the effect of changing the weight of the food group from 158 to 213?

Further questions

1. A company has asked you to illustrate and summarize the age profile of their workforce. The personnel department have been able to give you the data shown in Table 2.43.

Table 2.43

Age group	Men	Women
Under 20	20	35
20 but under 25	40	44
25 but under 30	37	21
30 but under 35	35	18
35 but under 40	20	33
40 but under 45	9	34
45 but under 50	7	33
50 but under 55	12	18
55 but under 60	40	32
60 but under 65	36	0

(a) Choose appropriate diagrams to illustrate the age profile for men and for women.

(b) Calculate the average $(\overline{X})$ for each sex.

(c) Find the median and the quartiles for each group.

(d) What advice would you give to the personnel department on the basis of your findings?

2. The Baggins Hotel is concerned about staff turnover and has asked you to investigate. You have been able to obtain some information from the hotel records (Table 2.44).

(a) Calculate the average length of service for employees of the Baggins Hotel and the average for each of the groups identified in Table 2.44.

(b) Advise the hotel on where it has a problem with staff turnover and suggest reasons for these high turnover levels. What could the hotel do to decrease the turnover level amongst the groups of staff that you have identified?

Table 2.44

Position	Length of service at year end for all those employed during the year (months)
Receptionists	2, 3, 27, 4, 1, 2, 3, 1, 2
Porters	1, 2, 2, 1, 3, 12, 14, 1, 7, 2, 1, 1, 2, 2, 2, 1, 1
Cleaners	6, 12, 9, 4, 13, 27, 6, 36, 8, 10, 17, 19, 25, 1, 39, 6, 50, 24, 17, 23, 27, 19, 1, 2, 1
Waiters/waitresses	3, 6, 4, 9, 7, 2, 1, 10, 12, 9, 4, 17, 28, 14, 7, 2, 12, 10, 9, 8, 2, 6, 12, 1
Cooks	24, 39, 2
Managers	6, 27, 4, 90

 You may find it easiest to use MICROSTATS for this question.

3. The Borough of Eassington have been monitoring the use made of their facilities such as the library, the leisure complex and the Sundown Park area. They have provided you with details from their records which give average number of users per week (Table 2.45) and have asked you to provide illustrative diagrams and summary statistics to help them understand the current situation.

Table 2.45

Month	Library	Leisure complex	Sundown Park
		Facility	
January	252	665	401
February	268	851	305
March	304	843	359
April	245	735	453
May	220	648	518
June	194	504	678
July	164	778	944
August	208	1045	937
September	199	834	834
October	216	842	601
November	275	851	3054
December	299	734	372

Note: *The Sundown Park is used as a stage on the RAC Car Rally in November when approximately 10 000 people visit the park over a 2-day period.*

(a) Choose appropriate diagrams to illustrate this data.

(b) Calculate the average weekly attendance for the year (assuming for simplicity that there are four weeks in each month) for each of the facilities and argue a case against the use of such averages in this situation.

(c) Assuming that the averages are to be used, what could you say about the overall income to the borough if you are now told that the entry charge to each of the facilites was as follows?

Facility	Charge
Library	£0
Leisure complex	£1.50
Sundown Park	£1*

* Note that the entry charge is increased for the RAC Rally in November to £4.

4. A company for which you are working has experienced a fall in profits over the last few years and has asked you to investigate the possible reasons for this decline. The accounts department have been able to provide you with data from their records (Table 2.46).

Table 2.46

Year	Company price	Company unit sales (m.)	Company COGS (£m.)	Company expenses (£m.)	Industry price index (1980 = 100)	Retail prices index (1990 = 100)
19V5	15	14	145	35	159	69.3
19V6	16	15.2	170	38	169	75.6
19V7	18	15.1	185	45	174	83.7
19V8	20	16.2	205	60	180	90.2
19V9	21	16.1	220	72	186	95.4
19X0	21	16	225	80	193	100
19X1	23	15.4	235	94	200	105.3
19X2	24	14.9	235	101	205	107.2
19X3	25	14.8	240	111	209	109.1
19X4	25	15.2	249	120	211	111.3

Note: COGS = cost of goods sold.

(a) Calculate an index of company unit sales with 19X0 = 100.
(b) Calculate an index of company price with 19X0 = 100.
(c) Rebase the industry index of prices to 19X0 = 100.
(d) Rebase the retail prices index to 19X0 = 100.
(e) Construct a graph of these four indices on the same axes.
(f) Calculate the gross and net profit for the company in each year. Note:

Sales revenue = Unit sales * Price
Gross profit = Sales revenue – COGS
Net profit = Gross profit – Expenses

(g) Calculate the profit to sales ratio for each year. Note: this ratio is equal to

$$\frac{\text{Net profit}}{\text{Sales revenue}} \times 100$$

(h) Create a graph to show the profit to sales ratio over time.

(i) On the basis of the calculations that you have made, and the graphs you have created, suggest reasons for the fall in profits for your company.

5. You are working for the Sandymann Hotel Group and have been asked to investigate the rise in the food bill at one of the hotels. Having looked through the accounts records for the hotel you have been able to find the information given in Table 2.47.

Choosing appropriate index numbers calculate:
(a) a price index for each food group for each year;
(b) a quantity index for each food group for each year;
(c) a value index for each food group for each year;
(d) an overall price index for each year;

Table 2.47

Item	19X1		19X2		19X3	
	Price	Quantity	Price	Quantity	Price	Quantity
Vegetables						
Potatoes	£0.12	500	£0.15	520	£0.15	525
Broccoli	£0.85	300	£0.80	320	£0.90	310
Courgettes	£0.56	290	£0.68	310	£0.64	320
Swede	£0.20	150	£0.18	120	£0.19	110
Cauliflower	£0.88	250	£0.94	280	£0.98	290
Salad						
Tomatoes	£0.40	305	£0.45	325	£0.48	315
Water cress	£0.75	60	£0.95	65	£1.05	66
Lettuce	£0.50	288	£0.60	312	£0.60	355
Cucumber	£0.49	604	£0.55	582	£0.60	577
Peppers	£0.88	602	£0.94	642	£0.93	665
Fruit						
Apples	£0.45	155	£0.48	165	£0.49	165
Oranges	£0.66	194	£0.68	250	£0.72	246
Bananas	£0.99	205	£0.92	241	£0.86	231

Table 2.47   *contd*

Item	19X1 Price	Quantity	19X2 Price	Quantity	19X3 Price	Quantity
Meat						
Beef – prime	£4.50	110	£4.60	130	£4.55	140
Beef – other	£2.55	185	£2.58	180	£2.61	160
Lamb	£2.86	241	£2.95	234	£2.99	230
Pork	£2.46	253	£2.48	231	£2.58	224
Fish						
Salmon	£5.99	50	£6.24	70	£6.99	90
Squid	£2.15	20	£2.81	60	£2.76	110
Cod	£1.88	105	£1.96	96	£2.55	90
Plaice	£2.55	64	£2.64	85	£2.88	103
Basics						
Bread	£0.50	250	£0.55	260	£0.61	265
Butter	£1.22	200	£1.25	250	£1.26	230
Margarine	£0.89	300	£0.91	240	£0.91	210
Lard	£0.75	60	£0.78	65	£0.81	50
Herbs	£0.75	300	£0.78	320	£0.99	350
Spices	£0.65	200	£0.85	240	£0.80	260
Milk	£0.29	1050	£0.31	1160	£0.31	1240
Cream	£1.25	640	£1.35	680	£1.40	710

(e)   an overall quantity index for each year;

(f)   an overall value index for each year;

(g)   Write a brief report suggesting reasons (based on your calculations) for the increase in the food bill at this hotel.

Note: There could be a very large number of calculations to do in answering this question. If you have to do these calculations by hand, then it is suggested that you only calculate the indices for one or two of the food groups.

You could do this question using MICROSTATS.

6. You have been lucky enough to gain a work placement with Northbridge District Council and are working in the community services section of the social services department. As a project you have been asked to illustrate the changes in the wage cost of running the section, and have been able to obtain from council records the data given in Table 2.48.

Table 2.48

People	19X1		19X2	
	Average wage	Number	Average wage	Number
Manual	£12 000	135	£13 000	98
Supervisor	£15 000	18	£16 200	16
Middle manager	£20 000	8	£21 000	7
Senior manager	£30 000	3	£35 000	3

(a) Calculate an overall wage index for each year with 19X1 = 100.
(b) Calculate an overall labour quantity index for each year with 19X1 = 100.
(c) Calculate an index to represent the overall wage bill for each year with 19X1 = 100.

Further information now becomes available. The section is to be further reduced in size due to the failure of a compulsory competitive tendering bid and the new numbers of people at each level are shown in Table 2.49. Following negotiations with the appropriate unions, wage increases have been agreed for 19X3, and these are also shown in Table 2.49.

Table 2.49

Number	19X3 % Wage Rise
75	2
10	2
4	1
1	3

(d) Given this extra information, calculate the three indices in parts (a) – (c) for 19X3.

Section 3
Collecting data

Objectives

After studying this section you should be able to:

- identify and describe the different methods of data collection;

- explain the difference between primary and secondary data collection;

- explain the need for sampling;

- describe the difference between random and non-random methods of sample selection;

- appreciate the use of a sampling frame;

- critically appraise the various data collection methods;

- be able to recommend a data collection method for a given situation;

- criticize a questionnaire;

- design a questionnaire;

- use MICROSTATS to analyse questionnaire data.

Introduction

Any data, whether or not it is purely numerical, must be collected by someone, somewhere, at some time. What we are aiming to do in this section is to introduce methods of data collection that are used by various organizations to produce data which is actually representative of the real situation and does not contain avoidable bias.

Collecting data does not necessarily mean going out on the street and asking people questions, although this can be particularly important in a market research context. For example, a small business would not have the resources to finance such an activity, but this does not mean that they cannot use data to manage the business more effectively. Considerable amounts of data are available free of charge! Other data may be collected by simply observing what is happening.

What we need to do is to select the appropriate method for the situation we face, rather than having a standard method which we try to apply to every situation. We should not be confused by sheer quantity of data. Large amounts of data, on their own, do not help in the solution of problems; the data needs to be organized and analysed so that it becomes information.

BACKGROUND

Data	Facts or opinions which have been collected
Information	Data organized in such a way that it will help in decision making

SCENARIO 5: Reale Brewery – market size calculations

You are working for the marketing department of the Reale Brewery which wishes to estimate the likely profit from sales of a particular type of lager during the next year. Due to recent mismanagement of funds within the department, it will not be possible to commission a market research exercise of asking consumers about their drinking habits, nor to buy into an omnibus survey.

The task of estimating the likely profit has fallen to you, and you have been able to find some past data from within the company accounts. Showing your usual flair, you have also visited the local university library (you can still pass yourself off as a student when necessary) and obtained some data from publications of the Central Statistical Office. At the last minute you also discover a market report to the company from 1985.

The results of your data collection are summarized below:

Company accounts of Reale Brewery:

Market share of the total lager market	17% by volume
Retail price per pint	£1.65
Net price per pint	£0.90
Average production cost per pint	£0.27
Overhead cost per pint	£0.36

Results of library search:

Number of 18–25 year old males	4 587 900
Number of 18–25 year old females	4 389 300
Number of over 25 year old males	15 482 300
Number of over 25 year old females	17 482 300

Market report (1985)

Average weekly lager consumption of 18–25 year old males	6 pints
Average weekly lager consumption of 18–25 year old females	4 pints
Average weekly lager consumption of over 25 year old males	1 pint
Average weekly lager consumption of over 25 year old females	2 pints
Percentage drinking lager 18–25 year old males	50%
Percentage drinking lager 18–25 year old females	45%
Percentage drinking lager over 25 year old males	20%
Percentage drinking lager over 25 year old females	25%

The numerical task of estimating the likely profit to the Reale Brewery from sales of lager in the next year only involves a few, simple calculations. We can break this task down into stages to make the job even easier.

The total volume of lager likely to be consumed is as follows:

	No.	*	Per cent drinking	*	Average Consumption	Total Consumption
18–25 year olds (males)	4 587 900	*	50	*	6 pints	13 763 700
18–25 year olds (females)	4 389 300	*	45	*	4 pints	7 900 740
Over 25 year olds (males)	15 482 300	*	20	*	1 pint	3 096 460
Over 25 year olds (females)	17 482 300	*	25	*	2 pints	8 741 150

Total market by volume = 33 502 050 pints per week
Total market by volume = 1 742 106 600 pints per year

Since the brewery has a 17% share of the market (by volume), its sales are likely to be

1 742 106 600 pints * 17% = 296 158 122 pints per year

The retail price is irrelevant to the brewery in relation to this exercise; what matters is the net price (90p). We need, however, to subtract from this the production cost (27p) and the overhead charges (36p). This will give us a contribution to profit of

90 – 27 – 36 = £0.27p per pint

So the expected profit to the brewery from this lager is

296 158 122 * £0.27 = £35 538 974.64

Since the brewery gets £0.90p per pint, its turnover will be

296 158 122 * £0.90 = £222 118 591.50

So the Profit Ratio is

$$\frac{\text{Profit}}{\text{Turnover}} * 100$$

$$\frac{£35\ 538\ 974.64}{£222\ 118\ 591.50} * 100 = 16\%$$

and this represents a good return to the brewery.

As we said earlier, the calculations are relatively simple, but is the answer of any real use to the brewery?

TASK

WHERE MIGHT WE HAVE MADE ERRORS IN RELATION TO THE DATA WE HAVE USED?

STATISTICAL BACKGROUND: *secondary data*

Secondary data is data which has already been collected by someone else, usually for another purpose, or at another time. Using data which has been collected for another purpose is sometimes termed **by-product statistics**.

There are several dangers with using secondary data:

- It may be out of date.
- It may refer to a population or group that does not match your needs.
- It may not measure exactly what you want to measure.
- It may not be representative – poor sample design.

Each of these points must be considered before such data is used.

The big advantages of using secondary data are that:

- It is available immediately.
- It costs much less to obtain (often it is free).

When using secondary data the following questions need to be asked, and only satisfactory answers should mean that we actually make use of it.

Questions

- Who collected it?
- What was the purpose of collection?
- Was it a census or a sample?
- When was it collected?
- How was it collected?
- Is there an accuracy or reliability rating?
- How closely does it match your requirements?

Return to Scenario 5

The first question we might raise in relation to the calculations we have made would be in relation to the market report. In the scenario, it says that the report comes from 1985, and even if we were to accept that it was valid for that date, it seems likely that the market may have changed significantly since then. There is no indication of how the data in the report was obtained, and therefore we cannot draw any conclusions about how representative of the general population of lager drinkers it may have been at the time.

Having said this, it is the only data which we have to work with, but its use does raise serious questions about the usefulness of the profit figure which we have calculated.

The second area which we might question is the use of data from the company accounts. If these were the management accounts of the business, which they would have to be to give this much detail, then their major purpose is to help manage the business. The figure for overhead charge per pint is open to some question, as there are various ways of allocating overheads, and a different method may have given very different results. (This will be a policy decision on the part of the firm's accountants and managers.)

The third area we could question is the library data. Such data is derived from the 10-yearly Census of Population and statistics on births and deaths. It can never be totally up to date, and is only an estimate. In this case, the fact that it may be 6 months out of date should not cause too many problems.

Having said all this, providing the management of the brewery understands the limitations of the figures that you have used in compiling the report, they have some basis on which to make a decision. What is really needed is some more up-to-date information of the sort contained in the market report, but to obtain this, it would be necessary to conduct some primary data collection and collect some attitudinal data. Such methods are the subject of the next scenario.

SCENARIO 6: Reale Brewery

Your report from Scenario 5 (the Reale Brewery) has been accepted by management, and they recognize the severe limitations of using secondary data, especially when it is so out of date. They have asked you to design a survey in order to collect some primary data on the lager market (A market research company has been given the brief to design the questionnaire that will be used.)

In particular they want you to decide between using a random or non-random sample, and the likely cost of conducting the survey.

Data you have been able to obtain:

Cost of interview:	random sample	£5 per interview
		£1.50 per non-response
	non-random sample	£3 per interview
		£0.50 per non-response
Printing of a questionnaire:		£0.50 per questionnaire
Response rate:	random sample	65%
	non-random sample	35%
Acceptable error:		2%

In order to take this scenario forward, we need to find some more information about types of sample design (see Statistical background: sample design, p. 79) and we also need to decide how to make sure that we are asking the 'right' people the various questions. Another issue is to decide is how many people we should ask. When we have done this, we can calculate the likely cost of conducting a survey, and make a recommendation to management.

If we take the issue of size of the sample first, we can put some obvious limits on the exercise. We do not want to try to ask everyone about their lager-drinking habits since this would take far too long and cost far too much! On the other hand, there seems little point in going into the local pub and asking the first five people that we meet how much lager they drink (this, in any case, might be quite difficult at 11.00 o'clock at night!). What we need is some method of determining the size, based on what we are trying to achieve.

We need to define more closely what we are trying to do. In this case we want to estimate the percentage of people who drink lager, and how much they drink, and we know that we can have up to a 2% acceptable error in our answer. Next we need to take a formula from statistical theory (see Statistical background: sample size, p. 77).

STATISTICAL BACKGROUND: *sample size*

Sample size to estimate a percentage from a random sample can be determined by using the formula

$$\text{Size} = \frac{z^2}{e^2} \times p \times (100 - p)$$

where z is a value from a normal distribution, p is the sample percentage and e is the acceptable error size in the final result.

This is a definition, but is rather less than helpful! To simplify things, and make it usable, we will take the value of z to be 1.96 which is the value used in most cases. This means that we have a 1 in 20 chance of getting the 'wrong' answer, but for most purposes this is an acceptable risk. We will also take p to be 50% because you can work out that this will give the maximum sample size necessary. (We are assuming that 50% of people drink lager in our example, but even if they do not, we will have taken a big enough sample to make an estimate of what percentage of people do drink lager.)

An alternative is to look up the appropriate values in a table. Two tables are shown, Table 3.1 at the 95% confidence level (where there is a 1 in 20 chance of getting the 'wrong' answer) and Table 3.2 at the 99% confidence level (where there is a 1 in 100 chance of such an error).

Table 3.1   Sample sizes for 95% confidence

Acceptable error (%)	Estimated percentage				
	10 or 90	20 or 80	30 or 70	40 or 60	50
1	3457.44	6146.56	8067.36	9219.84	9604.00
2	864.36	1536.64	2016.84	2304.96	2401.00
3	384.16	682.95	896.37	1024.43	1067.11
4	216.09	384.16	504.21	576.24	600.25
5	138.30	245.86	322.69	368.79	384.16
6	96.04	170.74	224.09	256.11	266.78
7	70.56	125.44	164.64	188.16	196.00
8	54.02	96.04	126.05	144.06	150.06
9	42.68	75.88	99.60	113.83	118.57
10	34.57	61.47	80.67	92.20	96.04

Table 3.2   Sample sizes for 99% confidence

Acceptable error (%)	Estimated percentage				
	10 or 90	*20 or 80*	*30 or 70*	*40 or 60*	*50*
1	5 990.76	10 650.24	13 978.44	15 975.36	16 641.00
2	1 497.69	2 662.56	3 494.61	3 993.84	4 160.25
3	665.64	1 183.36	1 553.16	1 775.04	1 849.00
4	374.42	665.64	873.65	998.46	1 040.06
5	239.63	426.01	559.14	639.01	665.64
6	166.41	295.84	388.29	443.76	462.25
7	122.26	217.35	285.27	326.03	339.61
8	93.61	166.41	218.41	249.62	260.02
9	73.96	131.48	172.57	197.23	205.44
10	59.91	106.50	139.78	159.75	166.41

N.B. This is a very selective extract from statistical theory, and if you need more detail and background, you should go to a textbook which deals more formally with statistics.

The formula we need is

$$\text{Size} = \frac{z^2}{e^2} \times p \times (100 - p)$$

and we know that $z = 1.96$, $p = 50\%$ and that $e = 2\%$ from the scenario. Putting these into the formula, we get

$$\text{Size} = \frac{1.96^2}{2^2} \times 50 \times (100 - 50)$$

This works out to be 2401 people. This confirms the result shown in Table 3.1.

STATISTICAL BACKGROUND: sample design

Population is the complete group of interest. In many cases this may be the total adult population of the country, but it can also be a subgroup, for example, all mothers.

Sample design is the process of deciding how to select the sample (whether this consists of people or things), and may be extended to include the method used to contact human populations.

A census: this is a complete enumeration of the relevant population. In this case you have to contact everyone – the best example is the population census which is held every 10 years in the UK.

A sample: this is a subset (a part) of the total relevant population. Samples are usually taken to save time and money. Ideally we should be able to generalize the results from the sample to the whole population. In some cases, it will only be possible to take a sample, for example, if we were testing components to destruction, if we test them all, we will have nothing to sell!

A random sample: a random sample is one where each member of the population has some (calculable) chance of being selected. The simplest example would be if you had a population of 10 people, you could put all of the names into a hat and pick one – this would be a **simple random sample**. In practice, random designs can become somewhat more complex than this because we are dealing with much larger populations (and there is not a hat big enough!). What we need to do is to get a list of the population (the **sampling frame**) and give each one a number. We then generate random numbers (usually using a computer) and the numbers which come out are those selected for the sample. This method can be further developed to a **multi-stage design** where we split the population into groups (e.g. areas of the country) and pick a sample of these; then for each group selected we pick a random sample. This would be a two-stage design, but there is no reason why you cannot go to many levels before you finally select the people to be interviewed. (The main point is that at each stage, a random sample is selected.)

A non-random sample: such a sample means that individuals in the population do not have a calculable chance of being selected. The most common example is a quota sample where the sample is designed to match the sizes of various groups in the population; for example, if 51% of the population is female, then 51% of the sample will be female. Interviewers are simply given instructions to collect data from a certain number of people with particular characteristics; they are not told whom to interview.

Return to Scenario 6

Looking now at the design we want to use, we can say that the random design will give a more 'statistically valid' result (because everyone has a chance of being selected), but it will cost more in terms of time and money.

The quota sample will give results more quickly, but some people may be excluded because the interviewers decide not to interview them. (This could be just because they do not happen to be around when the interviewer is there, or it may be that the interviewer, inadvertently or deliberately, avoids interviewing certain types of people.)

Taking a random sample

This will mean that we want 2401 responses, and we know that the likely response rate is 65%, so our total sample size would need to be

$$\frac{2401 \times 100}{65} = 3693.8 \quad \text{(say 3694 people)}$$

We will assume that it is possible to get a list of all the population (people usually use the Electoral Register) and we can then draw up a random sample of 3694 people from this. Note that if this is from the whole of the UK, then we could end up interviewing people from almost anywhere, so the costs of travelling could prove to be very high.

Obviously we cannot go through the whole sample selection process here, but we will give a short example of selecting a random sample from a sampling frame. To do this we need two things – a list of people (usually the Electoral Register), and a way of choosing who to include in the survey. The method of selecting people is to use a set of **random number tables**; a small extract from such a table is given in Table 3.3.

Table 3.3   Extract from random number tables

22	72	00	22	76	95	91	89	93	47
50	49	28	5	30	49	18	7	86	84
87	42	84	44	41	21	11	26	60	56
32	10	48	60	99	9	67	6	92	73

Note: these numbers were generated using a spreadsheet random number generator; you will find that many calculators will also generate random numbers, or there are lists of such numbers available in many textbooks.

Table 3.4   Extract from an electoral register

No.	Name	Address
75	Sally Ann Ireton	38, Shawell Road
76	Paul Arthur Ireton	38, Shawell Road
77	Janet Fox	39, Shawell Road
78	George Osbourne	41, Shawell Road
79	Mary Louise Osbourne	41, Shawell Road
80	Alan Ian Buttery	42, Shawell Road
81	Brenda Mary Buttery	42, Shawell Road
82	John Kevin Buttery	42, Shawell Road
83	Krishna Sidhu	43, Shawell Road
84	Amiya Sidhu	43, Shawell Road
85	Sandra Margaret Pegg	47, Shawell Road
86	Peter Thomas Pegg	47, Shawell Road
87	Oliver John Pegg	47, Shawell Road
88	Anthony James Huckett	1a, Doddington Drive
89	Nigel Ian Huckett	1a, Doddington Drive
90	Cynthia Mary Huckett	1a, Doddington Drive
91	Paula Samantha Ford	1b, Doddington Drive
92	Peter George Cartwright	3, Doddington Drive
93	Evelyn Allen	3, Doddington Drive
94	Alan Arthur Lewis	5, Doddington Drive
95	Fiona Julia Lewis	5, Doddington Drive
96	Joseph Collins	7, Doddington Drive
97	Anna Margaret Robinson	7, Doddington Drive
98	Graham Alan Viney	9, Doddington Drive

Table 3.4   *contd*

No.	Name	Address
99	Clare Kiran Viney	9, Doddington Drive
00	Alexander Long Penny	11, Doddington Drive
01	Simon Kay	13, Doddington Drive
02	Gordon Bennet	15, Doddington Drive
03	Sheila Linda Bennet	15, Doddington Drive
04	Donna Mullins	17, Doddington Drive
05	Petra Louise Green	17, Doddington Drive
06	Andrew John Beech	19, Doddington Drive
07	Jean Hopkins	21, Doddington Drive
08	Martin Alan Quinn	21, Doddington Drive

Notice that each line from the Electoral Register (Table 3.4) has been given a two-digit number (but they do not start at 1 since this is only an extract). Suppose that we want to select a sample of 10 people from this part of the register by using the random number table, the process is as follows. Starting at the top left-hand corner of the table of random numbers

Table 3.5

No.	Name	Address
00	Alexander Long Penny	11, Doddington Drive
76	Paul Arthur Ireton	38, Shawell Road
95	Fiona Julia Lewis	5, Doddington Drive
91	Paula Samantha Ford	1b, Doddington Drive
89	Nigel Ian Huckett	1a, Doddington Drive
93	Evelyn Allen	3, Doddington Drive
86	Peter Thomas Pegg	47, Shawell Road
84	Aniya Sidhu	43, Shawell Road
87	Oliver John Pegg	47, Shawell Road
84	Amiya Sidhu	43, Shawell Road

(Table 3.3), the first number is 22, but since this does not appear in our sampling frame (but only an extract is given), we need to move on. Going across the table, 72 does not appear either, but the next number (00) does appear, so Alexander Long Penny is the first person in our sample. The next number is 22 which does not come into the extract, so we use the following number which is 76. This means that Paul Arthur Ireton is the second person selected. Carrying on with this process, the sample of 10 people would be as shown in Table 3.5. However, line 84 (Amiya Sidhu) has been selected twice because we did not specify that our selections were to be made without replacement (that is, once someone has been selected, they cannot be selected again), so we might want to take the next random number (99) and make the sample consist of 10 different people. The final person will now be:

99	Clare Kiran Viney	9, Doddington Drive

This example is a bit contrived in order to make it manageable, but you should be able to see that the people selected for the sample do not depend on the interviewer, nor on the person designing the survey, they are selected at random.

It is now up to the interviewers to find these particular people and interview them. It will not be good enough to substitute next-door neighbours if a person is not in; with random sampling, the interviewers will need to call back two or three times.

TASK

> **SELECT ANOTHER RANDOM SAMPLE OF 10 USING THE FOLLOWING RANDOM NUMBERS.**

44	26	40	93	96	80	16	71	16	44
36	81	32	39	88	38	53	63	20	6
54	33	31	94	4	28	19	82	46	94
32	5	42	94	29	33	86	36	67	1

If you work without replacement, you should get the sample shown in Table 3.6.

Table 3.6

No.	Name	Address
93	Evelyn Allen	3, Doddington Drive
96	Joseph Collins	7, Doddington Drive
80	Alan Ian Buttery	42, Shawell Road
81	Brenda Mary Buttery	42, Shawell Road
88	Anthony James Huckett	1a, Doddington Drive
06	Andrew John Beech	19, Doddington Drive
94	Alan Arthur Lewis	5, Doddington Drive
04	Donna Mullins	17, Doddington Drive
82	John Kevin Buttery	42, Shawell Road
05	Petra Louise Green	17, Doddington Drive

Taking a non-random sample

We know that the likely response rate is 35%, so to get 2401 responses we need to talk to

$$\frac{2401 \times 100}{35} = 6860 \text{ people}$$

and we will need to set up the quotas for various groups in the population to make sure that the structure of the sample reflects the structure of the population. Our groups can be obtained from Scenario 5 where we are given the size of the population in terms of sex and age. This information is repeated below:

Number of 18–25 year old males	4 587 900
Number of 18–25 year old females	4 389 300
Number of over 25 year old males	15 482 300
Number of over 25 year old females	17 482 300

As they stand, these numbers cannot help, but if we turn them into percentages, they will allow us to determine the quotas for the sample. The total population is the sum of the four numbers, this is 41 941 800. The percentages are then:

18–25 year old males	10.94%
18–25 year old females	10.47%
over 25 year old males	36.91%
over 25 year old females	41.68%

so the number of people we need to contact in each group will be

Number of 18–25 year old males	750.5 (say 751)
Number of 18–25 year old females	718.2 (say 718)
Number of over 25 year old males	2532.0
Number of over 25 year old females	2859.2 (say 2859)

Note: we are assuming that the non-response rate for each of the groups will be the same and this is unlikely to be the case in practice.

Costs

We can now work out the cost of carrying out each type of survey.
    For a random sample:

Item	Cost
Print 2401 questionnaires at £0.50	£ 1 200.50
Interview 2401 people at £5	£12 005.00
Non-responses (1293) at £1.50	£ 1 939.50
Total cost of design	£15 145.00

For a non-random sample:

Item	Cost
Print 2401 questionnaires at £0.50	£ 1 200.50
Interview 2401 people at £3	£ 7 203.00
Non-responses (4459) at £0.50	£ 2 229.50
Total cost of design	£10 632.50

What this has shown is that it will be considerably cheaper to conduct a non-random sample, but there is more chance of 'human error' creeping in in terms of the selection of the respondents. Your report to the management of the Reale Brewery should point out the advantages and disadvantages of each method of sample selection.

SCENARIO 7: *Hortish Arms Hotel*

You have recently begun work for a small hotel chain as a trainee manager, and amongst the various duties which you are expected to carry out are staffing the reception desk, standing in for absent porters, serving at tables when necessary, taking telephone messages for guests, and assisting the general manager of the Hortish Arms Hotel. In this latter capacity, you are given a pile of questionnaires which have been collected from guests over the last 2 weeks and told to explain what they mean!

After an initial look at some of the questionnaires, you see that guests seem to be saying that they are satisfied with the service offered by the Hortish Arms Hotel, but this does not match your experience of dealing with clients when you have been staffing the reception desk, since you have received several complaints. You decide that you must analyse the survey more carefully.

The questionnaire that was used is shown below:

HORISH ARMS HOTEL
GUEST QUESTIONNAIRE

This short questionaire is design to allow you to give your views on the Hortish Arms Hotel. Please hand it into reception when you pay your bill.

1. Name:...

2. Dates of Stay: ....

3. How many nights did you say at the hotel? ....

4. How much did you enjoy your stay in the hotel and the City?

Very Much	Enjoyed a lot	Enjoyed	Not sure	didn't enjoy

                                                                          (Please tick box)

5. Was your room usualy clean and tidy when you returned to it?
                                                        YES/NO (Please circle.)

6. Were the meal-times acceptable to you?
                                                        YES/NO (Please circle.)

7. Did you find plenty of things to do in the City?
                                                        YES/NO (Please circle.)

8.   Did you visit for pleasure or business?

                                    PLEASURE/BUSINESS (Please circle.)

9.   Were the staff helpful?

Very Helpful	Reasonably Helpful	Helpful	Not too helpful	Unhelpful

10.   Would you recommend this hotel to your freinds?

                                    YES/NO (Please circle.)

Remember that you can get a 25% off your next stay here (or in any of our other hotels) if you introduce a new guest within six months of your stay.

Thank for your help in compliling this information which will be used to further enhance the quality of service provided by the Hortish Arms Hotel.

A.P. Smithers

(General Manager)

Responses to the questionnaire are contained in the file HOTELQU.MCS on the disk at the back of the book, and can be analyzed using MICROSTATS. (A second version of the data is in file HOTQU.WKS if you wish to analyse the data using Lotus 1-2-3™.)

Note that there are various typographical errors in this reproduction which were also present on the original!

Before looking at the data which has been collected using this questionnaire, it is important to consider the questionnaire itself. (We would like to stress that this particular questionnaire has not been used by any hotel chain!) There are many errors contained in the questionnaire, some of which are relatively minor, and should have been picked up before it was printed or distributed. Having said this, you do come across actual questionnaires with similar mistakes.

A questionnaire should be checked for spelling errors. Looking through the questionnaire, you should be able to find several spelling mistakes which not only put people off filling in the form, but also do not match the quality image that the hotel is trying to project.

A questionnaire should avoid the use of a 'selling line' at the end of the questionnaire. This is likely to bias the responses which are received since there is a considerable incentive to say that you have enjoyed your stay at the hotel, not only because you can get future discounts, but also because the respondents have to hand in the completed questionnaire as they pay their bill. The idea behind handing in the questionnaire before the guest leaves is probably a good one, as it is likely to increase the response rate (the number of completed questionnaires received), but it might be preferable to ask guests to leave it in their room or a 'post-box', rather than allow the receptionist to see the contents before the guest actually leaves.

Ideally an interview or questionnaire should flow in a logical manner, with one question following on from the previous one. This is not the case with this questionnaire.

STATISTICAL BACKGROUND: *questionnaire design*

Writing questions for a questionnaire is something which seems very easy until you try to do it! The objective is to get a series of questions which will mean the same thing to everyone, so that it will be possible to amalgamate the results and draw conclusions about the whole population from the overall results. Various social researchers and polling organizations have developed 'rules' for writing questionnaires, and some of the basics are set out below.

Types of question

For a formal questionnaire, there are two basic types of question:

- open questions
- pre-coded questions

An open question allows the respondent to say exactly what he/she wants, but places a considerable burden on the interviewer, since he/she is supposed to record everything that the respondent says!

A pre-coded question gives the respondents a choice of several different responses, and they are asked to choose the one which represents their view or opinion. This is easy for simple questions such as 'Are you currently in full time employment?' as just a yes/no response is required. When you move on to opinion questions, however, you often find that respondents say, 'Well, none of them are exactly how I feel.' The best way to get the pre-coded answers is to conduct a pilot survey (i.e. with a small number of people) using open questions, and then derive the answers from what is said.

Questions should not be biased; the Survey Research Centre have identified five major sources of bias in questions:

- *Two or more questions presented as one:* in this case the respondent may answer only one of the questions. An example may be:

  Do you shop at a supermarket because it is cheap and offers a wide variety of goods?

                                                                    YES / NO

You may think they are cheap, but the range is limited, how do you then answer the question?

- *Questions which contain difficult or unfamiliar words:* there are several ways of interpreting this problem. A difficult word could be one which is imprecise, such as 'usually' or 'normally' or 'always' (which is, in fact, exact but people tend not to treat it that way). It also incorporates the problem of using jargon or technical expressions which may mean something to 'experts' but are meaningless to the general public. This could be medical, such as using rubella rather than german measles, or it could be using abbreviations, such as GDP or RPI.
- *Questions which start with words meant to soften harshness:* such words are really redundant; if you are going to ask the question, ask it! A typical phrase might be 'I hope you don't mind me asking, but . . .'. This puts the respondent on his or her guard, expecting an awkward question. If the question is particularly personal, then you need to build up a rapport with the respondent before asking such questions, and then you do not need these softening words. Another phrase to avoid is 'Do you, like most people . . .', which biases the likely response, since people tend to agree to such suggestions.
- *Questions which contain conditional or hypothetical clauses:* in general, people are not very good at imagining situations, especially if they have been stopped on the street by an interviewer. Such a question might be 'How do you think that your life would be different if you had got married at 16?'
- *Questions which contain one or more instructions:* in general, people are not very good at carrying out instructions, for example 'If you take your annual income after tax, and subtract your living costs such as food and accommodation, how much do you have left per week to spend on yourself?' This is almost impossible to answer for most people. It is also much too long as a question.

The Gallup organization have classified opinion questions in terms of the depth to which they probe, and suggest five levels:

- to find if a respondent is aware of an issue;
- to get the general feelings on the issue;
- to get answers on specific parts of the issue;
- to get reasons for the respondent's views;
- to find how strongly these views are held.

The above does not constitute a complete list of what can go wrong in question writing, but should prove a useful guide.

Return to Scenario 7

Looking through the questionnaire used by the hotel, we can see that several of the questions are biased. For example, question 4 is two questions as one. Also the pre-coded questions which have five possible answers, have three which are positive and only one which is negative; again this is likely to bias the responses received.

TASK

> **WRITE A QUESTIONNAIRE CONTAINING AT LEAST 10 QUESTIONS TO FIND HOW MUCH PEOPLE ENJOY THE COURSE WHICH YOU ARE ON.**

If we now go back to the survey from the Hortish Arms Hotel, and make an assumption that the questions asked were not biased, then we can analyse the findings by using the data held on the disk at the back of the book. (The actual data is reproduced as Appendix 3A at the end of this section if you do not have access to a computer.)

 Using MICROSTATS to analyse this data, the first step is to do a simple frequency count on the responses to each of the questions. The columns in the file HOTELQU.MCS are as follows:

(*Hint*: use HISTOGRAM command)

Column	Contents
1	Questionnaire number
2	Nights stayed (Qu. 3)
3	Enjoyment of stay (Qu. 4)
4	Was the room clean? (Qu. 5)
5	Meal-times (Qu. 6)
6	Things to do in the city (Qu. 7)
7	Reason for stay (Qu. 8)
8	Helpfulness of staff (Qu. 9)
9	Would you recommend the hotel? (Qu. 10)
10	Recoded Qu. 2 as: 1, 2 or 3 nights = 1
	4–7 nights = 2
	8–14 nights = 3

For columns C3 to C9 on the disk you can do this by getting into MICROSTATS and, once the file (HOTELQU.MCS) has been retrieved, getting a histogram for each of the columns. (Note that this would not work for column C2 as there are more than 10 different responses.) Column C10 is a recoded version of column C2 which categorizes the number of nights stayed at the hotel into three groups, so you can get a histogram for C10. An example of these histograms is given in Figure 3.1.

Middle of interval	Number of observations	
1.0	10	**********
2.0	17	*****************
3.0	15	***************
4.0	11	***********
5.0	11	***********
6.0	0	
7.0	0	
8.0	0	
9.0	0	
10.0	0	

Figure 3.1   Histogram of C3.

TASK

IF YOU HAVE ACCESS TO A COMPUTER, OBTAIN HISTOGRAMS FOR EACH OF THE COLUMNS C3 TO C10.

The histograms given by MICROSTATS are technically speaking only bar charts since the width of each group is the same (see Section 2 for details of the differences between bar charts and histograms). They give us some useful information about the responses to the questionnaire, for example, that 10 people enjoyed their stay 'Very much' and a further 17 classified it as 'enjoyed a lot'. This seems to be good news for the Hortish Arms Hotel.

   A second step in the analysis of the survey results would be to calculate some descriptive statistics from the data. We can do this in MICROSTATS by using the DESCRIBE command. An example is given below:

Command?DESCRIBE C2

Count of	C2	=	64	line 1
Minimum of	C2	=	1.000	line 2
Maximum of	C2	=	14.000	line 3
Sum of	C2	=	326.000	line 4
Mean of	C2	=	5.094	line 5
Median of	C2	=	3.000	line 6
Standard dev-n	[pop] of C2	=	4.018	line 7
Standard dev-n	[samp] of C2	=	4.050	line 8

Looking through these figures, we can see that there were 64 responses (line 1), and that they ranged from 1 to 14 (lines 2 and 3). The average length of stay, as measured by the mean, was just over 5 days (line 5), but the median stay was just 3 days (line 6). The standard deviation was just over 4 days (line 7). These figures not only describe the data from the survey, but they also enable us to check on the representativeness of the sample, since we can compare them with the same statistics for the hotel (i.e. for all guests over a longer time period).

For some of the columns the descriptive statistics will not mean anything, for example, in column C3 we have the data relating to Question 4 on whether or not the guests enjoyed their stay at the hotel. This gives a mean value of 2.938, but the data is purely classificatory (i.e. people just selected a category) and therefore any average is only indicative of general opinion based on a coding of 1 to 5.

TASK

IF YOU HAVE ACCESS TO A COMPUTER, OBTAIN DESCRIPTIONS FOR EACH OF THE COLUMNS C3 TO C10. WHICH MAKE SENSE?

If you want to take the analysis a little further, we will need to break down the responses to the survey into groups. These groups are based on the data obtained from the survey; for example, we can split people into groups who stayed a certain number of nights, or those who stayed on business or pleasure. The next step is to look at the data on some other question, and find out if the responses of our groups differ from each other.

 Producing these **cross-tabulations** is easy in MICROSTATS, because all we need to do is use a command like

CONT C10 C3

which means create a table of values with the responses to C3 classified against the responses to C10. If we remember that C3 contains data on whether or not the guests enjoyed their stay and C10 contains recoded data on how many nights they stayed, we get the data shown in Table 3.7.

What this table seems to suggest is that those who stayed for a short time, enjoyed themselves, but, in general, the longer they stayed, the less they enjoyed their visit. This must have implications for the way in which the hotel is run.

There are many more cross-tabulations which could be produced using this data, some of which will give useful information to the managers, and some will not really mean much. It is left to you, as a task, to produce some more cross-tabulations and interpret the answers that you get.

Table 3.7

C10	C3 Enjoyed very much	Enjoyed a lot	Enjoyed	Not sure	Didn't enjoy	Total
1, 2 or 3 nights	10	13	4	4	3	34
4–7 nights	0	3	6	4	2	15
Over 7 nights	0	1	5	3	6	15
Total	10	17	15	11	11	64

STATISTICAL BACKGROUND: cross-tabulations

A cross-tabulation is usually done with classificatory data, that is, where people have classified themselves into a group. Common examples are sex, marital status, age group. These groups are then used to break down the results of the other questions in the survey to see if the responses to particular questions are influenced by (or associated with) the groupings. The technique is very widely used, especially in marketing research where it can be used to identify 'segments' in the market.

It is possible to go one step further in the analysis of cross-tabulations by performing a **test of statistical significance** called **chi squared**. Whilst this is beyond the scope of this publication, you will find that MICROSTATS can perform the arithmetic that is necessary. You will need to refer to a more traditional statistics textbook if you need to carry out such tests.

SCENARIO 7 (Postscript)

Looking at the data and the actual questionnaire, your report to the manager will have identified that the questionnaire itself could have been made considerably better. The results, whilst giving an initial impression that all is well, upon closer examination show that those who stay for longer periods, especially for pleasure, are not totally satisfied with the service that they receive.

SCENARIO 8: Northbridge District Council – leisure facilities monitoring

The Northbridge District Council has collected some data from members of the public on their use of council leisure facilities. The data is summarized below and is also available on the disk (file NORTH.MCS for MICROSTATS and NOR.WKS for Lotus 1-2-3™). The survey was conducted by interviewing people 'on the street' and thus no data is available for non-response. A total of 100 people were interviewed over a 4-day period.

Extracts from survey data:

People using the facilities:	Yes	73%
	No	27%

Number of different facilities:	0	27%
	1	38%
	2	30%
	3+	5%

Actual facilities used:	Library	30%
	Swimming	25%
	Track	9%
	Parks	28%
	Ice rink	8%
	Golf course	17%

N.B. Totals to more than 100% since some people use more than one facility.

Table 3.8   Times of use

	8.00–10.00	10.00–12.00	12.00–14.00	14.00–16.00	16.00–18.00	18.00–20.00
Library	1	2	5	4	8	10
Swimming	5	0	4	6	1	9
Track	2	1	2	0	4	0
Parks	3	5	5	8	5	2
Ice rink	2	1	1	1	3	0
Golf course	4	4	5	2	2	0

Table 3.9

	Number	% of users
Views of quality		
Very good	7	9.6
Good	49	67.1
Poor	17	23.3
Continue to use if price raised (users)		
Yes	29	39.7
No	44	60.3
Use or use more if price lowered		
Yes	50	
No	50	

You are working for Northbridge District Council on a placement, and have been asked to assess the value of this survey information and to suggest any possible alternative methods of collecting such data.

At the first sight, the data from the survey appears to give us useful information about the views of the general public on the leisure services facilities provided by Northbridge District Council. However, we need to ask a few questions about the way in which the survey was conducted. For example:

- How were the people selected?
- Where was the survey conducted?
- When was the survey conducted?
- How many people had to be asked before 100 questionnaires were completed?

To be useful, some form of non-random design would need to be used in order to ensure that those selected for interview were representative of the general public of the area. The scenario states that the interviews were conducted 'on the street', but if this was only in one location, it may bias the results. A survey which only questioned people between 2.00 p.m. to 5.00 p.m. would also be likely to produce biased results. For such a survey it is not usual to record non-response, but if large numbers of people refuse to be interviewed, then can we be sure that those who actually answer the questions are representative of the public?

We will assume that you have been able to obtain satisfactory answers to these questions as we look at the task you have been set on your placement.

Interpreting the results

From the results of the survey, we can see that 73% of the people of the area use some of the council leisure facilities. A majority of the users (38%) only use one particular facility, with a small number using three or more. Of the six facilities listed, the library is the most widely used, closely followed by the parks; whilst the ice rink is the least used. The pattern of usage varies considerably from one facility to another.

In general, the leisure facilities offered by Northbridge District Council are regarded as good, but a significant minority (23.3%) of users think the facilities are poor. Approximately 40% of users would continue to use the facilities if prices were raised. Of the whole sample, 50% would use the facilities more if prices were reduced.

TASK

WHAT ARE THE MOST LIKELY PROBLEMS IN INTERPRETING THESE RESULTS?

Likely problems

The most obvious problem with this survey relates to time. If people were just asked if they had ever used the leisure facilities, then the results are likely to overestimate current usage. It would be useful to pose the questions in a form which relates to a specific time period, say the last 3 months.

A second problem may be one of respondents' memory. This could be especially true of the time of use of the facilities. If it is some time since they used, say, the park, they may not be able to recall the exact time they were there.

Another issue is in relation to the questions on price. Asking people if they would pay more is much too open a question; do you mean 1 pence more, or 5% more, or 50% more, or what? The same problem arises over price reductions. Questions in this area need to make specific statements on pricing, and then get the respondent's reaction to these.

STATISTICAL BACKGROUND: alternative data collection methods

There are many different methods of collecting data, none of which is 'correct' in all circumstances. It is really a question of fitting the method to the situation and the resources available.

Postal survey

This is where questionnaires are sent by post to potential respondents, and they are then expected to return them after completing the answers. The 'conventional wisdom' is that such surveys have very low response rates, and this is probably true for general surveys on general issues. However, if you were researching a specific issue and could target those who receive the questionnaires, then response rates can be just as high as with an interviewer-based survey. Other things that help the response rate are sponsorship by a well-known organization and the provision of a stamped addressed envelope in which to return the questionnaire. One specific danger with postal questionnaires is that you can never be sure who actually filled it in.

Panels

A panel consists of a group of people who give their opinions several times over a period of time – this could be a few months or many years. The advantage of panels is that because you are asking the same people on several occasions, you look at the way in which behaviour and attitudes change over time. The dangers are that the group may not be representative, either at first (due to selection problems) or after a while (due to changing their behaviour just because they are on a panel – this is called **panel conditioning**). Keeping track of the panel members can also be a problem, because people move, or just lose interest – this is called **panel mortality**. Examples of panels are in TV viewing (especially for opinions on programmes), consumer research and political research, especially close to election times.

Diaries

This method asks people to keep a diary of their activities over a period of time. It has the advantage of giving considerable detail and a close insight into behaviour, but can you be sure of when it was actually completed, or if all details were actually entered? The best example of diaries is the Family Expenditure Survey – see p. 62.

Observation

This is exactly what it says, you watch and record what happens. You will have seen people sitting at the roadside counting the number of cars passing a certain point for a traffic survey. Two types of observation are identified: **non-participant observation** where the observer is passive, and **participant observation** where the observer takes part in the activities and probably has to record his or her observations at a later time. The danger with participant observation is that the observer can lose his or her objectivity.

Cohort or longitudinal studies

These are similar to panel studies, but go on for much longer. They are usually associated with studies of development; for example, there is one study, which is still going on, which took all babies born in the UK in the first week of March 1948 and has followed them ever since. It has checked on their family circumstances, their physical development and their educational progress.

Looking at the survey conducted on behalf of Northbridge District Council, we had some reservations about some of the results, especially in relation to use of the facilities. There are some alternative methods which may have given better results for some of the issues raised by the report. For example, it would be possible to monitor the number of people at the swimming pool at certain times of the day for, say, a 2-week period, and this may give a clearer picture of actual current usage.

If the council want the views of users, then interviews could be conducted at the facilities, but this would not be able to address the question of why people do not use them! It seems unlikely that the other alternative methods shown in the statistical background would be appropriate in this case.

STATISTICAL BACKGROUND: non-response

Non-response is where those selected to take part in a survey, do not, for some reason, actually take part. It is normally only recorded for probability (or random) samples, since these are the ones which pre-select respondents. (In a non-random sample, you can just select someone else if a person refuses to co-operate.)

Reasons for non-response vary. The most obvious is when someone totally refuses, but this is a surprisingly small percentage of the population (about 5%). Respondents may be out at the time of the interviewer's call – and they should be visited again, or they may be away for an extended period and miss the survey altogether. Because a random sample selects respondents before going out to interview them you may find people have moved. For this reason it may be better to select addresses rather than individuals from the sampling frame (houses move rather less often than people!). Some people may not be able to co-operate if they are too infirm or inarticulate.

Conclusions

After reading through this section and completing the tasks you should be in a position to assess other people's surveys and data. These results should not just be taken on face value; we need to question how the data was actually collected before we can use the results and make decisions.

Further questions and scenarios

1. Use the data from Northbridge District Council (Scenario 4) to obtain frequency counts for each of the columns. Continue your analysis by finding cross-tabulations of:
   (a) facilities used by satisfaction with quality;
   (b) facilities used by usage if prices rise;
   (c) facilities used by usage if prices are reduced;
   (d) satisfaction with quality by usage if prices rise;
   (e) satisfaction with quality by usage if prices are reduced.

2. *Policing: satisfaction survey.* The local police force are concerned with their 'image' and have asked you to design a short questionnaire to find out from members of the local community how their role is seen. You will be able to conduct the survey on a personal interview basis, but have been given a limitation that any interview should not last for more than 10 minutes.

3. *BPICS survey.* The British Production and Inventory Control Society (BPICS) is a professional association with groups in the various regions of the country. A questionnaire was used in the Midlands region to look at what members actually wanted from their branch.

   The questionnaire used is given below, and the results are on the disk – BPICS.MCS for MICROSTATS and BPICS.WKS for Lotus 1-2-3™.

   Critically assess the questionnaire and use the results to make recommendations to the branch on the sort of activities which they might consider putting on for members.

   We would like to acknowledge the kind permission of BPICS (West Midlands Branch) for use of this questionnaire and data.

West Midlands Branch
Membership Questionnaire

Dear Member,

Your Branch committee became very concerned during 1992/93 at the very limited attendance at Branch events. This has improved considerably in the current year but we still feel very ill informed as to what you as members expect us to be doing. We are also keen to retain and expand membership by making the West Midlands Branch a lively and participative one. The attached questionnaire is intended to fill some of the gaps in our understanding of your needs. I know that filling out and returning questionnaires is a nuisance but we do need the widest possible response both from those who do attend current events and from those who are not attracted by our current efforts.

Please make the effort and complete and return the attached questionnaire now.

Many thanks in anticipation of your help.

John Alexander
Vice President

Return Address:

John Alexander
UCEBS,
Department of Management,
Perry Barr,
Birmingham,
B42 2SU.

West Midlands Branch
Membership Questionnaire

For each of the following questions please tick the box or boxes which represent your answer and if requested give brief explanatory comments. All responses will be treated as confidential. Thank you.

1. What class of membership do you hold?

   Member ☐   Graduate ☐

   Fellow ☐   Student ☐

   Associate ☐   Company ☐

2. Were you introduced to BPICS by:

   Friend or colleague ☐   Other ☐
                               Please specify
   Employer ☐   -
                               -
   Advertising ☐   -

3. Which functions do you attend:

	Often	Occasionally	Never
National Conference	☐	☐	☐
National Seminars	☐	☐	☐
BPICS Certificate or Diploma Course	☐	☐	☐
Branch Events	☐	☐	☐
Branch AGM	☐	☐	☐

4. What are the benefits to you of belonging to BPICS?

   ....

   ....

   ....

   ....

5. Do you find the 'Control' magazine

Useful ☐   Not very useful ☐   Do not read it ☐

6. How do you value your area branch?

Excellent ☐   Good ☐   Satisfactory ☐   Poor ☐

7. Do you understand the role of the branch?

Yes ☐   No ☐

If yes what briefly do you believe its role to be?

....

....

....

8. Do you find the JIT notes informative?

Yes ☐   Not very ☐   No ☐

9. How many branch events have you attended in the last 12 months?

None ☐   1–2 ☐   3–4 ☐   All ☐

10. In general how do you rate the following aspects of Branch events?

	Poor	Satisfactory	Good	Excellent
a. Location (i.e. convenient to reach)	☐	☐	☐	☐
b. Start time	☐	☐	☐	☐
c. Duration	☐	☐	☐	☐
d. Subject matter	☐	☐	☐	☐
e. Quality of presentation	☐	☐	☐	☐
f. Organisation of event	☐	☐	☐	☐

11. Which is your nearest large town? ....

12. Would you be prepared, with help from the Branch, to organise an event?

Yes ☐   No ☐

Please put forward your suggestion

....

....

13. How interested would you be in attending any of the following events if organised?

(Please circle a number for each event)	Not interested				Very interested	
Factory Visit	1	2	3	4	5	
Guest Speaker	1	2	3	4	5	
Social Event	1	2	3	4	5	
Seminar/Conference	1	2	3	4	5	
Other	1	2	3	4	5	Please specify:

14. How well do the following event times meet your needs?

(Please circle a number for each time)	Not likely to attend				Very likely to attend
Weekend	1	2	3	4	5
Weekday daytime	1	2	3	4	5
Weekday evening	1	2	3	4	5

15. Do you feel you receive sufficient notice of forthcoming events?

Yes ☐   No ☐

If No how much notice would you like?...

16. Does the branch currently offer:

Sufficient Events ☐   Too Many Events ☐   Too Few Events ☐

17. Is there anything you feel the Branch could do for you that it is not doing at present?

Please state:

....

....

....

....

....

....

....

18. Are you currently:

Employed ☐   A Student ☐   Unemployed ☐   Retired ☐

If you are unemployed or retired please answer the following questions on the basis of your last employment. If you are employed please answer for your current job.

19. What is the title of your post? ....

20. Please indicate which of the following best describes your job role:

Shop Floor ☐   Office ☐   Management ☐

Other ☐   Please specify:......................................

21. Does your company provide a product or a service?

Product ☐   Service ☐

22. Which of the following best describes the area in which you work?

Agriculture, forestry and fisheries	
Energy and water supply industry	
Extraction of minerals and ores	
Smelting and rolling of metals	
Chemical production including plastic and rubber compounds	
General metal goods and engineering	
Vehicle and vehicle component manufacture	
Other manufacturing (please state)	
Construction	
Distribution and freight handling	
Communications and computer systems	
Banking, finance, business services	
Education	
Other services (please state)	

23. Do you have a supervisory/management role?

Yes ☐   No ☐

If Yes please specify the number of people you supervise:

Under 10 ☐ 10–20 ☐ 26–50 ☐ Over 50 ☐

24. Are you able to make financial decisions on behalf of your organisation (e.g. order stock, authorise overtime, purchase equipment)?

Yes ☐   No ☐

If Yes please give brief details

....
....

25. Does your job role allow you to introduce colleagues to the society?

Yes ☐   No ☐

If Yes have you brought them to Branch events?

Yes ☐   No ☐

26. To help us categorise your responses we would like to know:
Gender:

Male ☐   Female ☐

Age

Under 25 ☐ 25–35 ☐ 35–45 ☐ Over 45 ☐

27. Would you be prepared to answer additional questions on the telephone if we need more help? If so please provide your name and phone number. Thank you.

....

Many thanks for your valuable help in completing this question-naire. Please do remember to post it to:

John Alexander, UCEBS, Department of Management, Perry Barr, Birmingham B42 2SU.

Appendix 3A   Data from BPICS questionnaire

SPREADSHEET 3.1

	A	B	C	D	E	F	G	H	I	J	K	L	M	N	O	P	Q	R	S
1	1	1	1	2	3	3	3	1	1	3	2	99	2	1	99	99	99	99
2	1	3	2	99	99	2	99	2	1	2	2	6	1	1	2	2	2	2
3	1	2	3	3	99	3	3	3	1	3	2	99	1	1	1	1	2	2
4	1	2	2	2	3	3	3	2	1	3	1	1	1	1	3	3	99	2
5	1	3	99	99	99	1	99	99	2	2	2	99	1	3	2	1	2	2
6	3	1	99	99	99	2	99	99	1	3	1	99	1	1	2	1	2	2
7	1	3	3	3	3	2	3	2	2	3	1	2	1	2	3	3	3	2
8	1	1	2	2	2	2	2	2	1	3	1	99	1	1	1	2	2	2
9	1	3	3	3	3	2	3	2	1	3	1	5	2	1	3	2	2	1
10	1	3	3	3	99	2	3	99	1	3	1	99	1	2	3	3	2	4
11	1	3	1	99	99	2	99	4	1	2	1	5	1	2	2	3	3	4
12	1	1	2	2	2	1	2	2	1	3	1	5	1	3	2	1	3	3
13	1	2	3	3	2	2	3	3	1	3	2	99	1	1	3	3	99	99
14	6	1	3	2	3	1	3	4	1	2	1	5	1	3	3	2	3	3
15	5	3	2	99	1	1	3	2	1	1	1	5	1	3	4	3	3	4
16	2	1	1	99	99	2	2	2	1	3	1	5		1	2	1	2	2
17	3	2	3	2	2	3	3	2	1	3	2	99	1	1	2	2	2	2
18	1	1	3	3	3	2	3	5	3	3	1	4	2	2	2	3	3	3
19	1	2	99	99	1	99	99	2	1	3	2	99	1	1	2	2	2	2
20	1	3	3	3	3	2	3	4	2	3	2	99	99	1	3	2	2	3
21	1	3	3	2	3	3	3	3	1	3	1	99	1	1	1	3	3	4

SPREADSHEET 3.1   *contd*

T	Y	V	W	X	Y	Z	AA	AB	AC	AD	AE	AF	AG	AH	AI	AJ	AK	AL
99	99	2	1	99	1	4	3	5	99	1	3	5	1	99	1	99	1	2
2	2	1	1	99	3	4	3	3	99	2	3	5	1	99	1	99	1	2
99	99	3	2	99	5	4	1	3	99	1	2	3	2	8	1	1	1	2
99	99	1	2	99	2	4	1	4	99	1	1	4	1	99	1	99	1	2
2	3	4	2	99	5	4	3	3	99	1	1	5	1	99	1	99	1	3
2	2	5	1	99	4	99	99	99	99	1	1	5	1	99	1	99	1	2
3	3	1	1	99	3	3	2	2	99	1	3	4	1	99	1	99	1	4
2	2	5	1	99	5	5	99	5	99	1	1	5	1	99	99	99	1	2
2	2	4	1	99	4	4	2	3	99	1	2	4	1	99	3	99	1	1
4	4	4	2	99	5	5	1	2	1	3	2	1	1	99	1	2	1	3
3	4	3	1	1	5	5	3	5	99	3	3	4	1	99	1	99	1	2
2	3	4	1	99	5	5	2	4	99	3	2	5	1	99	3	1	1	3
99	99	1	2	99	4	4	1	3	99	1	2	4	1	99	1	99	1	4
2	3	1	99	99	4	4	2	4	99	3	1	5	1	99	1	3	1	2
3	4	6	2	99	5	5	1	3	99	5	3	4	1	99	1	99	1	1
2	2	4	2	99	5	4	99	4	99	3	2	4	1	99	1	99	1	4
2	2	1	2	99	4	4	2	4	1	1	4	4	2	6	1	99	1	3
3	3	1	2	99	4	5	1	1	99	1	1	4	1	99	1	99	1	2
2	2	4	2	99	1	1	1	1	1	1	1	2	1	99	1	99	1	2
99	99	1	2	99	5	4	2	3	99	1	3	4	2	3	3	1	1	2
3	3	3	2	99	5	4	1	4	3	1	5	1	1	99	1	1	1	2

SPREADSHEET 3.1 *contd*

AM	AN	AO	AP	AQ	AR	AS	AT	AU	AV	AW
3	3	14	1	2	1	1	2	1	2	2
3	1	11	1	2	1	1	1	1	3	99
3	1	8	1	2	1	1	2	1	2	1
3	1	6	1	1	1	1	2	1	2	99
3	1	8	1	1	1	2	99	1	4	99
3	1	8	1	4	1	1	2	1	3	1
4	2	13	2	99	2	1	2	1	4	1
3	1	7	1	4	1	1	2	99	99	1
3	2	11	1	1	1	1	2	1	2	1
2	1	6	2	99	1	2	99	1	3	1
3	1	4	1	3	1	1	2	1	2	1
3	1	8	2	99	1	1	1	1	2	1
3	2	14	1	1	1	1	2	1	2	1
3	1	6	1	1	2	1	1	1	2	1
3	2	14	1	1	1	1	1	1	4	1
4	1	5	2	99	2	1	2	1	4	1
2	1	8	1	2	1	1	2	1	3	1
3	1	8	1	3	1	1	2	1	4	1
3	1	6	1	2	1	1	2	1	3	99
3	3	11	1	1	1	1	1	1	3	1
3	3	8	1	1	2	1	2	1	2	1

SPREADSHEET 3.1   contd

A	B	C	D	E	F	G	H	I	J	K	L	M	N	O	P	Q	R	S
22	5	4	99	99	1	99	99	99	2	3	2	99	1	1	2	2	2	2
23	4	3	3	2	2	2	2	1	1	3	1	5	8	2	2	3	3	2
24	1	4	3	3	2	1	99	3	1	2	1	5	1	4	3	2	2	2
25	1	1	2	3	3	1	1	2	1	2	1	5	1	2	3	3	3	3
26	1	3	2	2	3	2	3	2	1	3	2	99	2	2	2	1	2	2
27	1	1	2	2	99	99	99	2	99	99	99	99	99	99	99	99	99	99
28	2	4	2	2	99	2	3	1	1	3	99	1	1	1	99	99	99	99
29	2	2	2	2	3	1	2	2	1	2	1	6	1	3	2	2	3	3
30	1	1	99	99	99	2	99	1	1	2	1	5	1	2	3	3	3	3
31	5	1	3	3	1	3	3	2	1	2	1	6	2	1	2	3	99	2
32	1	1	1	99	99	99	99	5	1	3	2	99	2	1	2	2	2	2
33	6	2	3	3	3	3	3	4	2	4	2	99	2	1	1	1	1	1
34	1	4	2	2	3	2	2	2	2	2	1	6	1	3	2	2	2	3
35	5	4	3	3	1	3	3	1	1	99	1	6	1	1	99	99	99	99
36	1	1	99	99	99	2	99	2	1	2	2	99	2	2	2	2	2	2
37	6	2	3	3	3	2	3	2	1	2	1	5	1	2	2	2	3	3
38	1	1	2	2	3	1	1	2	1	2	99	5	1	3	3	3	2	3
39	6	3	2	99	99	2	99	4	1	3	2	99	1	2	2	2	3	3
40	1	1	2	2	99	99	99	2	1	99	2	99	1	1	99	99	99	99
41	1	1	2	99	99	2	99	3	1	99	99	99	1	1	1	3	3	3
42	1	1	99	2	99	1	2	1	1	1	1	3	1	3	3	3	3	3

SPREADSHEET 3.1   contd

T	Y	V	W	X	Y	Z	AA	AB	AC	AD	AE	AF	AG	AH	AI	AJ	AK	AL
2	2	3	2	99	3	3	3	3	3	1	3	3	1	99	1	99	1	2
2	3	4	1	99	5	4	3	4	5	3	3	5	1	99	3	1	1	2
2	2	6	2	2	5	5	1	1	5	99	99	99	1	99	1	4	3	99
3	3	4	1	99	5	3	3	3	3	1	4	4	1	99	1	99	1	2
3	2	3	1	3	1	5	5	5	99	2	5	2	2	26	3	99	3	2
99	99	99	99	99	99	99	99	99	99	99	99	99	99	99	99	99	1	1
99	99	4	1	99	3	3	99	3	99	4	1	4	1	99	99	5	1	1
2	2	6	1	1	3	4	4	4	99	1	2	4	1	99	1	5	1	4
3	3	7	2	99	4	4	3	5	99	5	5	3	1	99	1	99	1	1
99	99	5	2	99	5	5	1	4	99	1	3	5	1	99	1	6	3	2
2	2	1	2	99	4	3	2	4	99	4	1	2	1	99	1	99	1	4
1	1	1	2	99	5	5	5	4	99	3	5	3	2	4	3	99	1	3
3	3	1	99	99	3	3	2	3	99	1	2	3	1	99	1	99	1	2
99	99	5	2	99	4	4	4	3	4	4	1	3	1	99	1	99	1	3
3	1	3	1	3	5	3	1	1	99	1	4	4	1	99	1	1	1	2
2	2	3	2	99	4	5	1	4	99	1	4	4	2	4	1	5	1	1
3	3	5	1	99	5	4	3	3	99	1	2	4	1	99	1	99	1	4
2	2	1	1	99	5	3	3	4	99	1	3	4	2	6	3	99	1	2
99	99	1	2	99	1	1	2	1	1	1	3	1	1	99	1	7	1	2
99	99	7	2	99	4	4	1	3	99	2	1	3	1	99	1	99	1	1
2	4	8	2	99	5	4	2	3	99	3	5	5	1	99	1	99	1	2

SPREADSHEET 3.1   *contd*

AM	AN	AO	AP	AQ	AR	AS	AT	AU	AV	AW
4	1	8	1	1	1	1	2	1	2	99
3	3	6	1	1	1	1	1	1	2	99
3	1	7	1	3	1	1	2	1	3	1
4	2	14	1	1	1	1	1	1	3	99
3	3	7	1	4	1	1	1	1	4	1
3	2	14	1	3	1	1	1	1	4	2
3	2	14	99	99	1	1	2	2	4	1
4	2	11	2	99	2	1	2	1	3	1
3	1	8	1	4	1	1	2	1	3	1
2	1	8	2	99	2	2	99	2	2	2
3	2	12	1	1	2	1	2	1	2	99
3	1	7	2	99	2	2	99	1	2	2
3	1	7	1	1	1	1	1	1	2	2
3	1	8	1	1	1	1	2	1	2	2
3	2	6	1	4	1	1	1	1	4	1
3	1	8	1	3	1	1	1	1	2	2
4	2	11	1	1	2	1	1	1	3	1
3	1	8	1	2	1	1	1	1	99	
3	1	6	1	1	1	1	2	1	3	1
4	2	14	2	99	1	1	2	1	4	1
3	1	11	1	2	1	1	1	2	2	1

SPREADSHEET 3.1 contd

	B	C	D	E	F	G	H	I	J	K	L	M	N	O	P	Q	R	S
43	2	4	2	3	3	2	3	5	2	2	1	6	1	2	3	99	3	99
44	1	1	2	3	3	2	2	1	1	2	1	1	2	2	2	2	2	2
45	1	1	2	3	3	2	2	1	1	3	1	3	1	1	2	1	2	3
46	1	4	3	3	3	3	3	2	1	3	2	99	2	1	1	1	2	2
47	1	3	99	99	99	2	99	2	1	2	2	99	1	3	3	1	3	3
48	1	1	3	2	3	2	3	2	1	2	1	4	1	1	3	2	3	3
49	3	1	3	1	3	2	3	2	1	2	1	1	1	1	2	2	2	2
50	1	4	99	2	99	2	2	2	1	2	1	4	1	2	3	3	3	3
51	3	2	3	3	3	3	3	4	1	2	2	99	1	1	2	2	2	1
52	1	3	99	99	99	99	99	3	1	99	2	99	1	1	99	99	99	99
53	1	1	2	3	3	2	2	1	1	99	1	99	1	1	99	99	99	99
54	1	1	99	99	99	99	99	2	2	99	2	99	2	1	3	2	3	2
55	1	3	3	3	3	3	3	2	1	3	1	5	1	1	3	3	3	99
56	1	1	2	3	3	2	3	2	1	99	2	99	99	1	2	1	99	99
57	1	2	3	3	1	2	3	3	1	3	2	99	2	2	99	99	99	99
58	3	4	99	99	99	2	99	3	1	1	1	5	1	2	2	3	3	4
59	1	1	3	3	3	2	3	3	1	3	2	99	99	1	3	2	2	2
60	3	1	3	3	3	2	3	3	1	4	2	99	2	1	99	99	99	99
61	1	3	3	3	3	3	3	3	1	2	1	5	1	1	3	1	2	3
62	1	1	2	2	3	99	99	5	1	3	1	99	1	1	3	3	3	3
63	1	2	2	2	99	2	3	2	1	2	1	99	1	2	3	3	3	2
64	6	2	2	99	99	1	3	2	1	2	1	5	99	3	2	2	3	3

SPREADSHEET 3.1   *contd*

T	Y	V	W	X	Y	Z	AA	AB	AC	AD	AE	AF	AG	AH	AI	AJ	AK	AL
99	2	6	2	99	5	4	1	99	99	1	1	5	1	99	1	1	1	4
2	2	1	1	3	4	4	2	3	99	1	3	4	1	99	3	5	1	4
99	99	4	1	3	4	4	3	3	99	2	3	4	1	99	1	1	1	2
2	2	4	2	99	4	3	1	2	99	4	1	3	1	99	1	1	1	2
3	3	5	2	99	5	3	4	3	99	5	2	4	1	99	3	5	3	2
2	3	1	1	3	4	4	4	4	4	5	1	3	1	99	1	99	1	4
3	3	5	2	99	3	3	2	4	99	1	3	4	1	99	1	99	1	2
2	3	1	2	99	3	5	5	3	5	99	99	5	1	99	1	5	3	4
2	2	4	2	99	5	99	4	1	99	4	2	4	1	99	1	99	1	2
99	99	1	1	3	3	99	4	3	99	4	4	2	1	99	99	99	1	1
99	99	4	99	99	4	99	2	3	99	3	2	4	1	99	1	99	1	4
99	99	1	2	99	5	3	1	2	99	3	1	4	1	99	99	99	1	2
99	99	1	1	3	4	2	5	5	99	4	4	1	1	99	1	6	1	2
99	99	3	2	99	2	3	1	4	99	1	3	1	2	8	99	99	1	4
99	99	1	1	99	2	3	3	3	99	1	2	4	1	99	1	99	1	2
2	4	6	2	99	2	5	1	1	1	3	2	5	1	2	1	99	1	3
3	3	1	2	99	3	2	1	3	99	1	2	3	1	99	1	99	1	4
99	99	1	2	99	5	4	1	3	99	1	3	5	2	4	3	5	1	2
99	99	1	2	1	5	3	1	3	99	1	4	1	1	99	1	1	1	3
3	3	1	1	99	4	4	4	4	4	1	3	3	1	99	1	99	1	1
3	3	4	2	99	5	3	1	3	99	1	4	3	2	5	1	5	1	2
3	2	1	99	99	5	4	1	3	99	1	5	5	2	2	1	99	1	4

SPREADSHEET 3.1 *contd*

AM	AN	AO	AP	AQ	AR	AS	AT	AU	AV	AW
4	3	7	2	99	2	1	1	1	4	1
4	2	14	1	1	1	1	2	1	3	1
3	2	14	1	1	1	1	1	1	4	1
3	1	8	1	2	1	1	2	1	2	1
3	2	11	1	3	1	1	1	1	3	1
4	2	14	1	1	1	1	1	1	2	1
3	1	6	1	2	2	1	2	1	1	2
3	1	7	1	1	1	2		1	3	1
3	1	11	1	3	1	1	2	1	3	2
3	1	7	1	3	1	1	2	1	2	1
4	2	14	1	1	1	1	2	1	4	1
3	1	7	1	4	1	1	2	1	2	1
3	3	11	1	1	1	1	2	1	2	1
4	2	11	2	99	2	1	2	1	4	1
3	1	11	1	1	2	1	2	2	2	99
2	1	6	2	99	2	1	2	1	4	1
2	2	11	1	1	1	1	2	1	2	99
3	1	11	1	1	2	1	2	1	2	99
4	2	11	2	99	2	1	2	1	3	1
4	3	6	1	3	1	1	2	1	3	99
3	1	8	1	1	1	1	2	1	3	99
4	2	11	2	99	2	1	1	1	4	1

Table 3.10   BPICS questionnaire – codebook

Column	Area	Codes
A	Questionnaire number	1 to 64
B	Class of membership	1 – Member 2 – Fellow 3 – Associate 4 – Graduate 5 – Student 6 – Company
C	Introduction to BPICS	1 – Friend or colleague 2 – Employer 3 – Advertising 4 – Other
	Functions	
D	National conference	1 – Often 2 – Occasionally 3 – Never
E	National seminars	1 – Often 2 – Occasionally 3 – Never
F	BPICS Certificate or diploma course	1 – Often 2 – Occasionally 3 – Never
G	Branch events	1 – Often 2 – Occasionally 3 – Never
H	Branch AGM	1 – Often 2 – Occasionally 3 – Never
I	Benefits of belonging	1 – Contacts 2 – Information, new developments 3 – Newsletter, books 4 – Qualification, education 5 – Conferences
J	*Control* magazine	1 – Useful 2 – Not very useful 3 – Do not read it
K	Value of area branch	1 – Excellent 2 – Good 3 – Satisfactory 4 – Poor

Table 3.10   *contd*

Column	Area	Codes
L	Understand role of branch	1 – Yes 2 – No
M	What is the role?	1 – Local knowledge 2 – Communication 3 – Promotion 4 – Represent members 5 – Meetings, awareness 6 – Support, advisory
N	JIT notes informative	1 – Yes 2 – Not very 3 – No
O	Branch events attended in last 12 months	1 – None 2 – 1–2 3 – 3–4 4 – All
	Branch events	
P	Location	1 – Poor 2 – Satisfactory 3 – Good 4 – Excellent
Q	Start time	1 – Poor 2 – Satisfactory 3 – Good 4 – Excellent
R	Duration	1 – Poor 2 – Satisfactory 3 – Good 4 – Excellent
S	Subject matter	1 – Poor 2 – Satisfactory 3 – Good 4 – Excellent
T	Quality of presentation	1 – Poor 2 – Satisfactory 3 – Good 4 – Excellent
U	Organization	1 – Poor 2 – Satisfactory 3 – Good 4 – Excellent

Table 3.10   *contd*

Column	Area	Codes
V	Nearest town	1 – Birmingham 2 – Oxford 3 – Stoke, Telford, Shrewsbury 4 – Coventry, Warwick, Leamington 5 – Wolverhampton, Walsall, Dudley 6 – Redditch, Stratford, Worcester 7 – Northampton 8 – Leicester
W	Help organize event	1 – Yes 2 – No
X	Suggestion	1 – Visit 2 – 3 – Workshop
	Interested in attending	
Y	Factory visit	1 – Not very 2 – 3 – 4 – 5 – Very
Z	Guest speaker	1 – Not very 2 – 3 – 4 – 5 – Very
AA	Social event	1 – Not very 2– 3 – 4 – 5 – Very
AB	Seminar/conference	1 – Not very 2 – 3 – 4– 5 – Very
AC	Other	1 – Not very 2– 3 – 4 – 5 – Very

Table 3.10 *contd*

Column	Area	Codes
	Times	
AD	Weekend	1 – Not very likely to attend 2 – 3 – 4 – 5 – Very likely to attend
AE	Weekday daytime	1 – Not very likely to attend 2 – 3 – 4 – 5 – Very likely to attend
AF	Weekday evening	1 – Not very likely to attend 2 – 3 – 4 – 5 – Very likely to attend
AG	Sufficient notice	1 – Yes 2 – No
AH	If no, how long?	In weeks
AI	How many events?	1 – Sufficient events 2 – Too many 3 – Too few
AJ	Other things to do	1 – Local events 2 – Recruitment 3 – More technical details 4 – Courses (low cost) 5 – Notice board, calendar, library 6 – Lower fees 7 – Parts acquisition
AK	Employed	1 – Employed 2 – Student 3 – Unemployed 4 – Retired
AL	Job title	1 – Director 2 – Manager 3 – Education, other 4 – Consultant

Table 3.10 *contd*

Column	Area	Codes
AM	Job role	1 – Shop floor 2 – Office 3 – Management 4 – Other
AN	Company product/service	1 – Product 2 – Service 3 – Both
AO	SIC code	1 – Agriculture 2 – Energy 3 – Extraction 4 – Smelting 5 – Chemical 6 – General metal 7 – Vehicle 8 – Other manufacture 9 – Construction 10 – Distribution 11 – Computers 12 – Banking 13 – Education 14 – Other services
AP	Management role	1 – Yes 2 – No
AQ	Number supervised	1 – Under 10 2 – 10–20 3 – 20–50 4 – Over 50
AR	Financial decisions	1 – Yes 2 – No
AS	Job allows introductions	1 – Yes 2 – No
AT	Brought to branch events	1 – Yes 2 – No
AU	Sex	1 – Male 2 – Female
AV	Age	1 – under 25 3 – 35–45 2 – 25–35 4 – Over 45
AW	Answer telephone	1 – Yes 2 – No

99 used throughout for missing data.

Appendix 3B Data from the Hortish Arms Hotel questionnaire

Data has only been included from questions 3 to 10 so that confidentially can be maintained.

Each question has been coded such that YES = 1 and NO = 2 for questions 5, 6, 7, and 10. For question 8 PLEASURE = 1 and BUSINESS = 2. The actual number of nights is given as a response to question 3. For questions 4 and 9, the scale is coded from 1, the most favourable response, to 5, the least favourable response.

SPREADSHEET 3.2 DATA FROM THE HORTISH ARMS HOTEL QUESTIONNAIRE

C1	C2	C3	C4	C5	C6	C7	C8	C9
LABEL	Q3	Q4	Q5	Q6	Q7	Q8	Q9	Q10
1	2	2	1	1	2	2	2	1
2	3	3	1	1	2	2	2	1
3	7	3	1	2	1	1	4	1
4	5	4	2	1	1	1	2	1
5	2	1	2	1	2	1	1	1
6	2	2	1	1	2	2	1	1
7	1	1	1	1	1	2	2	1
8	7	3	2	2	1	1	1	1
9	5	2	1	1	2	2	2	1
10	1	1	1	1	1	2	2	1
11	1	2	2	2	2	2	3	1
12	2	1	1	1	2	2	1	1
13	1	2	2	1	1	2	1	1
14	3	3	1	1	2	1	2	1
15	2	2	2	1	1	2	3	1
16	4	3	2	2	2	1	3	1
17	3	1	1	1	1	1	1	1

SPREADSHEET 3.2   contd

C1	C2	C3	C4	C5	C6	C7	C8	C9
LABEL	Q3	Q4	Q5	Q6	Q7	Q8	Q9	Q10
18	5	4	2	1	2	1	5	2
19	2	3	1	1	1	2	4	1
20	3	5	2	2	1	2	5	2
21	1	2	1	2	2	2	3	1
22	7	4	2	2	2	1	4	1
23	7	3	1	1	2	1	2	1
24	14	5	2	2	1	1	5	2
25	14	4	2	1	1	1	5	2
26	2	4	1	1	1	2	5	2
27	14	5	2	2	2	1	4	2
28	10	5	2	1	1	1	4	2
29	9	3	1	1	1	1	4	1
30	3	2	1	1	1	2	1	1
31	14	3	2	1	2	1	1	1
32	12	5	2	2	2	1	3	2
33	10	4	1	1	2	1	3	1
34	8	3	2	1	2	1	2	1
35	3	4	2	1	1	1	4	1
36	1	2	1	1	1	1	2	1
37	12	5	2	1	2	1	4	2
38	1	2	1	1	1	2	3	1
39	14	3	1	2	2	1	3	1
40	3	3	1	1	1	2	3	1
41	2	4	2	1	2	2	2	1
42	5	5	2	1	1	2	4	2

SPREADSHEET 3.2 contd

C1	C2	C3	C4	C5	C6	C7	C8	C9
LABEL	Q3	Q4	Q5	Q6	Q7	Q8	Q9	Q10
43	5	3	2	2	1	1	4	1
44	3	1	1	1	2	2	1	1
45	2	1	1	1	1	2	1	1
46	12	5	2	2	2	1	5	2
47	12	3	1	1	2	1	2	1
48	10	2	1	1	1	1	3	1
49	8	4	1	2	1	2	3	1
50	5	2	1	1	1	1	4	1
51	4	5	1	2	1	1	5	2
52	6	2	2	1	2	2	2	1
53	4	4	1	1	1	2	4	1
54	3	2	2	1	1	2	4	1
55	3	4	2	1	1	2	2	1
56	2	1	1	1	1	1	1	1
57	3	2	1	1	2	2	1	1
58	1	1	1	1	1	2	1	1
59	2	5	1	2	2	2	4	2
60	3	2	2	1	1	1	3	1
61	1	5	2	2	1	2	2	1
62	3	1	1	1	1	2	1	1
63	2	2	1	1	2	2	3	1
64	5	3	1	1	1	1	2	1

Note that the file also contains a column C10 which is the number of nights stayed at the hotel recoded such that 1, 2 or 3 nights is coded as 1; 4, 5, 6 or 7 nights are recoded as 2; and more than 7 nights are recoded as 3.

This data is available on the disk, as a MICROSTATS file under the name HOTELQU.MCS (it also uses the file HOTELQU. NAM) and as a Lotus 1-2-3™ file under the name HOTQU.WKS.

Appendix 3C   Data from Northbridge District Council survey

Questions are coded as 1 for YES and 2 for NO except for the question on the number of facilities used which is the actual number used. A response coded as 0 can be assumed to be no answer and is taken as non-use of a particular facility.

SPREADSHEET 3.3   DATA FROM NORTHBRIDGE DISTRICT SURVEY

LABEL	USEANY	NOUSED	LIB	SWIM	TRACK	PARK	ICE	GOLF	QUAL	P UP	P DOWN
1	1	2	1	0	0	0	1	0	2	1	1
2	1	1	1	0	0	0	0	0	1	0	0
3	1	2	0	1	1	0	0	0	2	1	1
4	1	1	1	0	0	0	0	0	2	1	0
5	1	1	0	0	0	0	0	1	1	0	0
6	2	0	0	0	0	0	0	0	0	0	1
7	1	1	1	0	0	0	0	0	2	1	0
8	1	2	1	0	0	0	1	0	1	0	0
9	1	1	0	0	0	0	0	1	2	1	0
10	1	2	1	0	0	1	0	0	2	0	0
11	1	2	0	1	1	0	0	0	1	0	0
12	1	1	1	0	0	0	0	0	1	0	0
13	2	0	0	0	0	0	0	0	0	0	0
14	2	0	0	0	0	0	0	0	0	0	0
15	2	0	0	0	0	0	0	0	0	0	1
16	1	1	0	0	0	0	0	1	2	1	1

SPREADSHEET 3.3   contd

LABEL	USEANY	NOUSED	LIB	SWIM	TRACK	PARK	ICE	GOLF	QUAL	P UP	P DOWN
17	1	4	0	1	1	1	1	0	2	0	1
18	1	2	1	1	0	0	0	0	1	0	0
19	2	0	0	0	0	0	0	0	0	0	1
20	1	1	1	0	0	0	0	0	2	1	0
21	1	1	1	0	0	0	0	0	1	0	0
22	1	1	0	0	0	0	0	1	2	1	1
23	1	2	0	1	0	1	0	0	2	1	1
24	2	0	0	0	0	0	0	0	0	0	0
25	1	1	0	0	0	0	0	1	2	0	0
26	1	2	0	1	0	1	0	0	1	0	0
27	1	1	1	0	0	0	0	0	1	0	0
28	1	1	0	0	0	0	0	1	2	1	0
29	2	0	0	0	0	0	0	0	0	0	1
30	2	0	0	0	0	0	0	0	0	0	0
31	1	2	0	1	0	1	0	0	2	1	0
32	1	1	1	0	0	0	0	0	2	0	0
33	2	0	0	0	0	0	0	0	0	0	1
34	1	2	0	1	0	1	0	0	1	0	0
35	1	1	1	0	0	0	0	0	1	0	0
36	1	2	1	0	0	1	0	0	2	1	0
37	1	1	0	0	0	0	1	0	2	0	0
38	1	2	0	1	0	1	0	0	1	0	0
39	1	2	0	1	0	1	0	0	2	1	0
40	1	2	0	1	0	1	0	0	2	0	0
41	1	2	0	1	0	1	0	0	1	0	0
42	2	0	0	0	0	0	0	0	0	0	0

SPREADSHEET 3.3   contd

LABEL	USEANY	NOUSED	LIB	SWIM	TRACK	PARK	ICE	GOLF	QUAL	P UP	P DOWN
43	1	2	0	1	0	1	0	0	2	0	1
44	1	1	0	0	0	0	0	1	3	1	1
45	1	5	0	1	1	1	1	1	2	1	1
46	1	1	0	0	0	1	0	0	2	0	1
47	1	1	1	0	0	0	0	0	2	1	1
48	1	1	0	1	0	0	0	0	1	0	1
49	1	1	1	0	0	0	0	0	2	0	1
50	2	0	0	0	0	0	0	0	0	0	0
51	1	1	0	1	0	0	0	0	2	1	1
52	1	1	1	0	0	0	0	0	3	1	1
53	2	0	0	0	0	0	0	0	0	0	1
54	1	1	0	1	0	0	0	0	2	1	1
55	2	0	0	0	0	0	0	0	0	0	1
56	1	1	0	0	0	1	0	0	2	0	1
57	1	1	1	0	0	0	0	0	2	1	1
58	2	0	0	0	0	0	0	0	0	0	0
59	1	2	0	0	0	1	0	1	1	0	1
60	1	2	0	1	1	0	0	0	2	1	1
61	2	0	0	0	0	0	0	0	0	0	0
62	1	3	0	1	0	1	0	1	3	1	0
63	1	2	0	1	0	1	0	0	2	0	1
64	1	1	1	0	0	0	0	0	2	0	1
65	1	1	1	0	0	0	0	0	2	0	1
66	1	1	0	0	0	0	0	1	2	1	0
67	1	2	0	1	0	1	0	0	2	0	0
68	1	2	1	0	0	1	0	0	3	1	1

SPREADSHEET 3.3   contd

LABEL	USEANY	NOUSED	LIB	SWIM	TRACK	PARK	ICE	GOLF	QUAL	P UP	P DOWN
69	1	1	0	0	0	0	0	1	2	0	1
70	1	1	1	0	0	0	0	0	1	0	0
71	1	2	0	0	0	1	1	0	2	0	1
72	2	0	0	0	0	0	0	0	0	0	0
73	2	0	0	0	0	0	0	0	0	0	1
74	1	1	0	0	0	1	0	0	2	0	1
75	2	0	0	0	0	0	0	0	0	0	1
76	2	0	0	0	0	0	0	0	0	0	1
77	1	2	0	0	1	1	0	0	2	0	1
78	2	0	0	0	0	0	0	0	0	0	0
79	2	0	0	0	0	0	0	0	0	0	0
80	1	2	0	1	0	1	0	0	2	0	1
81	2	0	0	0	0	0	0	0	0	0	0
82	1	3	1	1	0	1	0	0	2	0	0
83	1	1	0	0	0	0	0	1	2	0	1
84	1	1	1	0	0	0	0	0	3	1	1
85	1	4	1	0	1	1	0	1	1	1	1
86	2	0	0	0	0	0	0	0	0	0	0
87	1	1	0	0	0	0	0	1	2	0	1
88	1	1	1	0	0	0	0	0	2	0	1
89	2	0	0	0	0	0	0	0	0	0	0
90	1	2	0	1	1	0	0	0	3	1	1
91	2	0	0	0	0	0	0	0	0	0	1
92	1	2	1	1	0	0	0	0	2	0	0
93	1	2	0	0	0	0	1	1	2	0	0
94	2	0	0	0	0	0	0	0	0	0	0

SPREADSHEET 3.3   *contd*

LABEL	USEANY	NOUSED	LIB	SWIM	TRACK	PARK	ICE	GOLF	QUAL	P UP	P DOWN
95	1	2	1	0	0	0	0	1	2	0	1
96	1	1	1	0	0	0	0	0	3	1	1
97	1	2	0	0	1	1	0	0	2	0	0
98	2	0	0	0	0	0	0	0	0	0	0
99	1	2	1	0	0	1	0	0	2	0	1
100	1	1	0	0	0	0	1	0	2	1	1

Section 4
Forecasting

Objectives

After studying this section you should be able to:

- explain the importance of forecasting;

- distinguish between statistical and judgemental methods of forecasting;

- select an appropriate method on the basis of available data;

- make all the necessary calculations for a chosen method;

- explain these calculations;

- make predictions from the chosen method;

- critically appraise the predictions made.

Introduction

Companies and individuals plan for the future. Decisions can be relatively short term, concerned with such matters as the availability of cash or production next week, or relatively long term, concerned with more strategic issues such as a major investment or a change in company marketing policy. Organizations of different kinds face a future that is far from certain and need to make decisions on the basis of the best information available. Some decisions with the value of hindsight are going to be judged bad decisions. In many cases, the factors that render a decision bad could not have been anticipated but in other cases the gathering of good quality information and analysis could have improved the decisions made. How many of the recent wars could have been anticipated and how many disasters could have been averted for example? To improve the quality of decisions can have immense benefits for companies and individuals alike. Providing a forecast of future trends or events will inform the decision maker about the likely consequences of any planned action and may also present choices that had not previously been recognized. A company, for example, that specializes in frozen foods will value a forecast of likely demand for their existing products in future years but will also be looking for new opportunities that new sectors of the market or changing attitudes generate. This section is concerned with using available information or resources to make predictions about the future and to appraise critically the usefulness of such predictions.

SCENARIO 9: Rugged Bikes – market forecast

A small business has been selling mountain bikes for the last 3 years. Sales have increased but shown a marked seasonal variation. At times the business has not been able to meet demand and at other times has been left with excessive stock. It was originally thought that the bikes would be sold mostly during the summer months as people pursue outdoor activities. However, sales have always increased before Christmas as the mountain bikes were bought by family and friends as gifts. The quarterly sales figures for the last 3 years are given in Table 4.1, where quarter 1 covers the months January to March, quarter 2 April to May, quarter 3 June to August and quarter 4 September to December.

You have been employed to assist with the marketing activities of the business and have been asked to describe the sales trend and make predictions for the next 2 years.

Table 4.1

Year	Quarter 1	Quarter 2	Quarter 3	Quarter 4
19X1	540	440	330	600
19X2	570	460	340	630
19X3	580	470	345	670

How do we make a forecast?

The information given in Table 4.1 shows clearly that the sales of mountain bikes from this small business have increased year by year. If we calculate the annual sales by adding the quarterly figures for each of the years, we can see that sales have increased from 1910 (540 + 440 + 330 + 600) in year 19X1 to 2000 in 19X2 to 2065 in 19X3. If we look at any of the columns, we can also see this consistent increase quarter by quarter: so, for example, sales in quarter 1 have increased from 540 in year 19X1 to 570 in 19X2 to 580 in 19X3. In this case, the historical trend is easy to describe but we are still left with the decision of how to predict future sales.

There are a number of ways of producing a forecast and the most appropriate needs to be chosen on the basis of the historical data available, the particular variables of interest and the time horizon for the particular forecast. The strategic plans of the company are also important as a forecast should support and inform these plans. The company may also want the forecast to allow for changes in the environment not reflected in historical figures.

In the scenario given, 3 years of quantitative data are available on a single variable, the number of mountain bikes sold, and the prediction required is for the next 2 years. The forecast could be based on your judgement, or the judgement of others as to what was likely to happen, referred to as **judgemental** forecasting, or the forecast could be based on the application of a particular statistical method to the numerical data, referred to as **statistical** forecasting. The quality of the forecast made will depend on the data or information available and the forecasting method selected.

BACKGROUND: judgemental forecasting

Subjectivity

The distinguishing feature of judgemental forecasting is subjectivity. The factors considered are chosen by the forecaster. The importance of these factors is weighted by the forecaster in a non-numeric way and finally the interpretation of events is made by the forecaster in a way he or she considers appropriate. The approaches to judgemental forecasting considered here are on the basis of personal experience (a personal forecast), the experience of others (expert opinion or the Delphi technique) or a summary of interview information (survey methods).

A personal forecast

We are all likely to have a view of the future. Our experience of a particular product or situation allows us to 'paint a picture' of the future that takes account of the factors that we consider important. A personal forecast is of particular value when quantitative data is limited or of limited value and the user has to weight a number of other complex factors.

Expert opinion

It can be argued that there are very few new problems. Whether the concern is over a national issue, such as the level of unemployment, or a company issue, such a responding to changing customer attitudes, it is likely that expertise does exist. It is, however, a matter of judgement when to seek the advice of experts and, when advice is forthcoming, whether to accept it.

The Delphi technique

The Delphi technique provides a method of working with a group of experts and has been described in a number of different ways. It was originally developed to draw together expert opinion on how many Soviet atomic bombs would be required to cause a specific level of damage on the United States. Essentially, a panel of experts is selected and individually questioned about the topic of interest. They do not meet as a group and are not put under a group pressure to conform. They may be asked to give relatively open responses to the question of interest or rank possible outcomes. The results of this process are then collated and circulated to the panel. The experts can consider the range of views generated and can be asked to consider further questions. The process is repeated until a consensus view emerges. The technique provides a particularly useful way to deal with business uncertainty and innovation. The use of experts can provide creative solutions that might not otherwise have emerged, such as the use of new materials, the movement to new markets and the change of organizational structure.

Survey methods

The use of survey methods has been considered in Section 3. As discussed, a survey requires a representative sample of appropriate people (or items) from a defined population. On the basis of answers received, we can make broad generalizations from the sample to the population. Clearly an improved knowledge of the opinions and behaviours of the current population will lead to a better understanding of future trends. However, the answers received will depend on the questions asked, the method of questioning, i.e. personal interview or postal interview, and the selection of the sample. The sample results will require a method of summary and interpretation. All of these factors require judgement and hence the method is included under judgement forecasting even though statistical methods are likely to be used to select the sample and summarize the data.

Return to Scenario 9

Looking at the figures given in the scenario, what would you predict for next year? If we were to accept the present trend, predictions like 590 for quarter 1, 480 for quarter 2, 350 for quarter 3 and 710 for quarter 4 would seem reasonable. To take the most recent increase quarter by quarter and project that forward one year is a method that is used and has the advantage of being easily understood. But why should the trend remain about the same? It could be argued that the job of a manager is to change the trend, e.g. increase sales above those expected and/or develop new products. Merely to add or subtract a figure is not using the knowledge the forecaster is likely to have. The forecaster may know for example that a competitive outlet will soon open near by, that interest is waning in mountain bikes and consumer spending is likely to increase. Some factors may lead to an increase and others to a decrease – the forecaster needs to make a judgement as to the overall effect.

The manager of the small business may have strong views on the sales trends of mountain bikes. He or she may be very committed to the concept of the mountain bike and believe that over time the number of people interested in ownership will continue to increase. Others might argue that it is just another fad, like skateboards, and that sales will begin to decline. If the concept of the **product life cycle** were applied then one would expect to see growth, followed by a period of stability and then eventual decline. A personal forecast would need to take account of the range of factors and, indeed, different theories. If the required forecast is relatively short term, say 3–6 months, then it can be assumed that many things will remain unchanged and that we only need to take account of those factors we know about. If the business has recently received good local publicity or it is known that a competitive store is to open nearby, then any personal forecast could be easily revised. However, in the longer term, say the next 5 years, there could be considerable changes to the products available, the structure of the local population and the road system. A personal forecast can respond to market opportunities or social change in a way that the mere projection of a statistical trend cannot. Who, for example, in the 1970s or 1980s would have predicted the popularity of the heavy framed mountain bike in the early 1990s? A personal forecast does allow the user to work with answers that appear to make 'common sense'.

So what are the drawbacks of such a personal forecast? Given that they are no more than a personal judgement on the relative importance of various factors, they are no different from an opinion. Like an opinion, no two people are necessarily going to agree on the future sales of mountain bikes or anything else. A forecast does imply a model or view of the world, implicitly or explicitly, which in turn implies the use of theories and assumptions. Discussion can often be most usefully focused on these theories and assumptions. Personal judgement can become distorted for all kinds of reasons and the process of questioning can clarify how the future is being perceived. However, it is important to be aware of the problem of bias in any such forecast.

The advice of others can be of considerable value and may bring a new perspective to any particular problem. Advice is typically sought on such matters as finance, production methods, design and marketing. Expertise and expert opinion are sometimes considered the domain of the larger organization solving the larger type of problem. However, evidence and experience suggest that good quality advice can be essential for the success of the smaller business. The smaller business, like Rugged Bikes, is less likely to have the range of necessary business expertise within the business and may need to seek external support. The small business described could benefit from advice on economic and market trends within the region. The business could also benefit from advice on how to make an appropriate forecast – perhaps from you!

The Delphi technique is generally seen as a method used by the larger type of organization. Resources are needed to recruit and manage a group of experts. These experts may be recognized internationally for their particular expertise and may not be interested in the sale of a few mountain bikes. However, like most techniques, the Delphi technique can be adapted to meet specific requirements. The basic principle of networking with a group of interested people can still apply. A consensus view of the future can bring a greater awareness to a particular problem than the views of an individual. The advent of new technologies means that for many, electronic mail and telephone conferencing are already available. Such exchange of information is going to enhance the decision-making process.

Survey methods generally seek information directly from those people (or items) of interest – the population. To know what past, existing or potential customers think of your product or service provides the type of information that a decision maker can use to formulate a business or organizational response. The definition of population is clearly important – the answers you get do depend on who you ask. The answers you get will also depend on the questions you ask, but of importance for Rugged Bikes described in Scenario 9, a survey can provide the understanding of why someone may or may not buy a mountain bike in the future. The outcome of a particular survey may indicate what the business can do to increase the chance of a sale.

There are a number of techniques that can be used to clarify the basis of such judgemental forecasting and provide a method of analysis. The techniques tend to extract the major issues and focus any discussion on the range of factors and assumptions that may be of importance.

BACKGROUND: *judgemental techniques*

The why technique

Many problems and many solutions are expressed in general terms. By probing these problems and solutions with the question why, a better understanding of the causes and effects can be achieved. The technique involves repeatedly asking the question why perhaps with probing statements such as 'Why did you say that?' or 'Why should that be the case?'

Five Ws and H technique

This technique is used to clarify the problem and approaches to the problem. The five Ws and H are the questions who, what, where, when, why and how. These questions provide a checklist that can be used on the whole problem or parts of the problem.

Force field analysis

Force field analysis is a way of representing the pressures for change in any situation. The current situation is represented by a line (which can be vertical or horizontal) with pressures for the same kind of change on one side of the line with opposite pressures on the other side of the line. Clearly if the pressures do not balance, then the situation is likely to change in response to the overwhelming force. The type of diagram produce is illustrated in Figure 4.1.

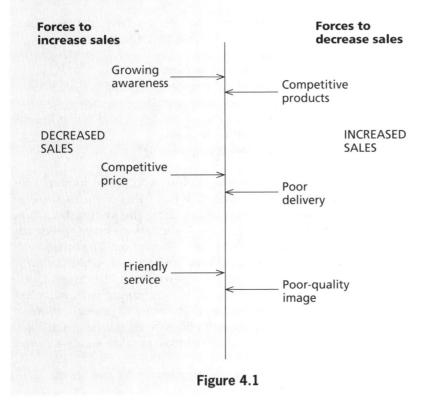

Figure 4.1

Return to Scenario 9

In the early stages of any investigation, it is important to clarify the nature of the problem being investigated and what others expect from the investigation. In this case, you have been asked to 'describe the sales trend and make predictions for the next 2 years'. It is not clear, however, from this problem statement whether it is the sales trend just from this small business or what predictions are required for the next 2 years. Sales trends could be at a local, regional or national level and apply to particular products or product groups. Predictions could be weekly, monthly, quarterly or annually. Predictions can be stated in mathematically precise terms or left rather vague. Whether you intend to clarify the problem yourself or through others it is worth asking the question why. Consider the following possible dialogue between you and the manager of this small business:

The manager	The sales of mountain bikes are likely to increase over the next 2 years.
You	Why are they likely to increase over the next 2 years?
The manager	The sales of mountain bikes have increased over the last 3 years and this increase is likely to continue.
You	Why is this likely to continue?
The manager	Mountain bikes have been popular.
You	Why have they been popular?
The manager	The kids like mountain bikes and our bikes are very competitively priced.
	(two statements to question)

This type of dialogue could continue to explore who the customers were, what they were prepared to pay and what other factors were of importance. The technique as described, is using the knowledge of the manager to explain the reasons for past sales. The reasons given will clearly relate to the manager's own experience and perception. The outcome of such a dialogue is therefore not without bias – the manager is still giving an opinion. A different manager in the same setting might present a very different set of arguments. The value of the technique is to move the respondent, the manager in this case, away from broad generalizations or opinions to specific reasons and the assumptions or models he or she might be using. A change of assumption or model may provide a very different view of the world.

We could ask the manager the who, what, where, why and how:

- Who are the customers?
- What do they want to purchase?
- Where do they want to purchase?
- Why do they want to purchase?
- When do they want to purchase?
- How do they purchase?

This technique will tend to clarify perceptions of the future and provide information that would not emerge by merely looking at past figures. To know that most customers would want to purchase a mountain bike using a credit card, for example, could make a significant difference to the conduct of future business. There are many variants of this technique and the use of such checklists is becoming more common. The use of such techniques highlights the complexity of business-related problems and the fact that there is rarely one explanatory variable. If we consider the sales of any product, for example, these are likely to be related to the product's price, the price of competitive products, quality, the quality of competitive products, advertising and so on. In the case of the small business selling mountain bikes, an understanding of customers and potential customers is clearly essential if future sales are to be sustained or increased.

A force field diagram can be drawn using factors identified using other techniques. It could be that the perceived fun element of mountain bikes and that cycling is accepted as healthy will exert a pressure to increase sales. However, cycling may also be seen as dangerous and this would exert a negative pressure. The force field diagram would include these factors (Figure 4.2) and others.

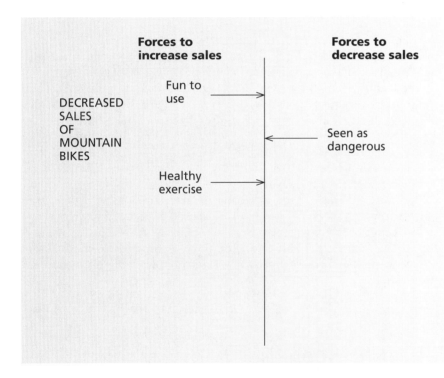

Figure 4.2   A partially completed force field diagram showing the forces affecting the sales of mountain bikes by Rugged Bikes.

Judgemental techniques can be used to exploit the knowledge of the manager and other interested groups. However, the quality of the decisions being made can improve if the available sales figures are understood and meaningful projections of future trends made.

STATISTICAL BACKGROUND: statistical forecasting

Statistical forecasting is based on the analysis of past data. A statistical method is used to describe that data in terms of an average or more complex formula and a prediction of future figures made. The data needs to be examined to decide which statistical method is most appropriate and this is normally done by means of a simple graph.

A **time series** is the set of observations collected at successive points in time or over successive periods of time. A series of readings taken on gas pressure within a pipeline at the end of each hour and a record of sales achieved each quarter are both examples of a time series.

A **time series model** considers the general factors that can explain the variation within a time series and provides a framework to analyse these factors. A time series model is built up in parts and will typically include a trend, a seasonal factor and a random factor.

A **moving average** is found by taking observations over a meaningful time period, i.e. a year, calculating the average and then moving on by one observation to calculate the next average.

The **trend** (denoted by T) is the general movement in the data. The trend may be increasing, decreasing or showing no change. The trend may be linear or non-linear. Whether the established trend will usefully predict the future will depend on how likely observed changes are to continue.

The **seasonal factor** (denoted by S) is the regular fluctuation associated with the time of the year. The increased sales of ice cream in the summer months or increased sales of gas in the winter months are both examples of seasonal variation we should expect and allow for.

The **random factor** (denoted by R) or residual factor is an allowance for all the factors that can affect the data. A time series model can allow for predictably hot weather but not unseasonably hot weather, for example.

Return to Scenario 9

It can be seen in the graph in Figure 4.3 that the sales of mountain bikes have increased over the 3 years from 19X1 to 19X3, and that there has been considerable seasonal variation. You should particularly note how sales peak in the fourth quarter of each year.

To build up an appropriate time series model, it will be necessary to identify the trend and the seasonal variation. The trend is concerned with the longer-term movement in the data and can be identified by averaging out the short-term fluctuations. The moving average is found by dividing an appropriate total by the number of observations included (like any simple average). The important decision at this stage is the number of observations to include. In this case, the sales of mountain bikes in 4

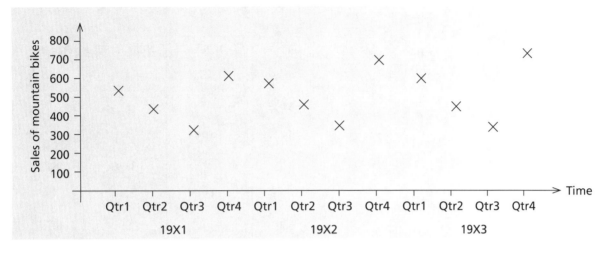

Figure 4.3

consecutive quarters would be added as this figure would give the meaningful total of sales in a year. In contrast, if the subject of investigation were the absenteeism rates during the 'normal' working week, Monday to Friday, then the weekly total, and an average based on the division by 5, would be most meaningful.

Before we proceed to calculate an average and continue to calculate a series of (moving) averages, we need to consider whether the number of observations is even or odd. If the number of observations is odd, the calculated average can be matched against a middle point. If the average is determined on the basis of 5 working days for example, then the average can be plotted against the third day. However, if the average is based on an even number, then the average will fall between the middle two points. In this scenario, the average is based on 4 quarters and the average will lie between the second and third quarter used. To overcome this problem with even numbers of observations, a process called **centring** is used. In this case, a 4-quarter total is first calculated, then an 8-quarter total by summing adjacent 4-quarter totals. This 8-quarter total is then divided by 8 to produce a **centred moving average**. The calculations are shown in Table 4.2.

TASK

> **EITHER BY HAND OR ON A SPREADSHEET, PRODUCE TABLE 4.2.**

> MICROSTATS   To obtain the 4-quarter moving average of the data in column C1 and place it in column C2 use the command:
>
>   MAVE C1 C2.

Table 4.2

Year	Quarter	Sales	4-qtr total	8-qtr total	Average
19X1	1	540			
	2	440			
			1910		
	3	330		3850	481.25
			1940		
	4	600		3900	487.5
			1960		
19X2	1	570		3930	491.25
			1970		
	2	460		3970	496.25
			2000		
	3	340		4010	501.25
			2010		
	4	630		4030	503.75
			2020		
19X3	1	580		4045	505.625
			2025		
	2	470		4090	511.25
			2065		
	3	345			
	4	670			

There are a number of points to note about Table 4.2. The first 4-quarter total was determined by summing the quarterly figures from year 19X1. The next quarterly total used the figures from quarters 2, 3 and 4 from year 19X1 and quarter 1 from year 19X2. The procedure continues by dropping off one quarterly figure and adding in a new one – producing a moving total and ultimately a moving average (to be centred in this case). Each total does include a quarter 1, 2, 3 and 4 but the order moves as follows:

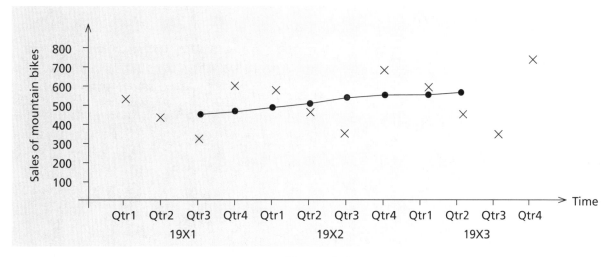

Figure 4.4

1234 then 2341 then 3412 then 4123 and back to 1234. Given that the sales of mountain bikes is typically high for 2 quarters (quarters 1 and 4) and low for the remaining 2 quarters, there will be a meaningful averaging-out in any calculation that includes all 4 consecutive quarters. Also, if you look closely at the table, you will see that the 4-quarter total is out of line. The first 4-quarter total lies between quarters 2 and 3 of year 19X1 and the next between quarters 3 and 4 of 19X1 and so on. But by summing pairs of 4-quarter totals and centring, the 8-quarter total is in line. The average given in the last column is found by dividing the 8-quarter total by 8. Check these calculations.

The trend can be plotted on the same graph as the original set of observations as shown in Figure 4.4. The difference between the original observations and the trend line values is, in part, explained by the seasonal variation. These differences are shown in Table 4.3. The seasonal difference shown in the last column of Table 4.3 can be summarized to give a measure of what the typical difference is for a particular time of the year, i.e. the seasonal factor. The method is again one of averaging, and in this case, the seasonal differences are averaged by quarter (Table 4.4). The average seasonal difference, quarter by quarter, provides a measure of the seasonal factor. It should be noted that there are other measures of the seasonal factor and that the figures calculated are an estimate rather than a precise measure of this factor. What these measures do tell the business is how many mountain bike sales they can expect (within limits) above or below trend at a particular time of the year.

Having established a trend and a seasonal factor, a mathematical model needs to be constructed to bring these together to allow the prediction of future sales of mountain bikes. The time series model being developed in this case is an **additive** model with three components: the trend (T), the seasonal factor (S) and the random factor (R). In this additive model, the components are added together to explain the actual observation (denoted by A):

$$A = T + S + R$$

Table 4.3

Year	Quarter	Sales	Moving average	Seasonal difference
19X1	1	540		
	2	440		
	3	330	481.25	−151.25
	4	600	487.5	112.5
19X2	1	570	491.25	78.75
	2	460	496.25	−36.25
	3	340	501.25	−161.25
	4	630	503.75	126.25
19X3	1	580	505.625	74.375
	2	470	511.25	−41.25
	3	345		
	4	670		

Table 4.4

Year	Quarter 1	Quarter 2	Quarter 3	Quarter 4
19X1			−151.25	112.5
19X2	78.75	−36.25	−161.25	126.25
19X3	74.375	−41.25		
Total	153.125	−77.5	−312.5	238.75
Average	76.5625	−38.75	−156.25	119.375

If we consider the third quarter of year 19X1 for example, we would get

$$330 = 481.25 + (-156.25) + R$$
$$330 = 325 + R$$

It should be noted that in this case the seasonal factor was negative, indicating that third quarter sales are typically below the trend. The random factor is 5 which is relatively small compared to actual sales of 330 but does indicate that actual sales were slightly better than the time series model would suggest. The difference between actual sales and the figure derived from summing the trend and seasonal factor $(T + S)$ can be explained in a number of ways, including the appropriateness of the time series model used and the number of important factors excluded. It could be found from further investigation, for example, that in this particular quarter the health benefits of cycling had received considerable publicity.

Having established a model which does seem to describe the data reasonably (the random factor is relatively small), we are now in a position to make predictions for the next 2 years based on this model. Given that the trend is calculated as a centred moving average, the trend values start at quarter 3 of year 19X1 and finish at quarter 2 of year 19X3. The trend needs to be extended forward for the quarters of years 19X4 and 19X5. This process is called **extrapolation**. An examination of the plotted trend values reveals a straight line or linear type of function which is easily extended by continuing the line on the graph with a steady hand (!) or in some other more mathematical way. A graph showing the extension of the trend line is given in Figure 4.5.

TASK

> **PRODUCE A GRAPH SHOWING THE ACTUAL SALES OF MOUNTAIN BIKES AND THE TREND. PROJECT THIS TREND FORWARD AND ESTIMATE TREND VALUES FOR QUARTERS 1, 2, 3 AND 4 FOR THE YEARS 19X4 AND 19X5.**

 MICROSTATS   The command:

> ADDN C1 C2 C3 C4

uses the data given in column 1 and places the trend values in column 2, seasonal differences in column 3 and residual values in column 4.

Projected sales are determined by taking the extrapolated trend values and adding (or subtracting if negative) the seasonal factor (Table 4.5). The projected trend given in Table 4.5 is likely to differ from the one you have or could determine graphically (unless you have used linear regression like the authors). Whatever method is used still implies a set of assumptions, and whether these are valid or not 'only time will tell'. The trend given increases by four sales each quarter and therefore assumes a straight line or linear relationship. There is a judgement about any trend projection and product or market knowledge can be used to improve a forecast. If, for example, a product is moving towards the end of its product life cycle – a marketing model which suggests a non-linear long-term sales pattern for most products which starts with a growth phase, then a phase of relative

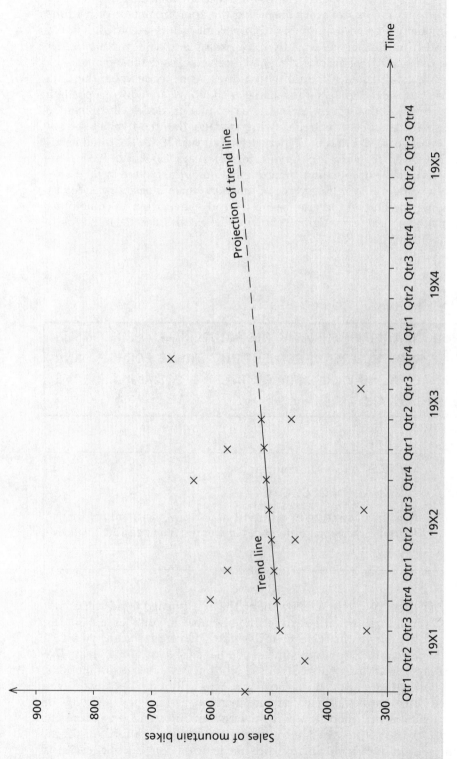

Figure 4.5

Table 4.5

Year	Quarter	Projected trend	Seasonal adjustment	Projected sales
19X4	1	524	+76.5625	601
	2	528	−38.75	489
	3	532	−156.25	376
	4	536	+119.375	655
19X5	1	540	+76.5625	617
	2	544	−38.75	505
	3	548	−156.25	392
	4	552	+119.375	671

stability and finally decline, e.g. vinyl records – then you may choose to represent this expected decline in the projected trend. It is possible to consider several possible trends or scenarios and examine the resultant sales projections.

All projections also require a management of the numbers involved. In this case, the projected trend figures are rounded to the nearest whole number. Mathematical approaches may give figures to many decimal places but this precision is meaningless within the context of this problem. You only sell complete mountain bikes! But also, the trend is only indicative of what is likely to happen and events may lead to very different sales figures. The trend is only there to guide and help the manager, not lead the manager. The seasonal adjustment uses the figures as calculated and the rounding takes place in the final column when projected sales are presented. As a general rule, rounding takes place at the end of any set of calculations, with the accuracy maintained within any workings.

Having approached a problem with judgemental and statistical methods, there is still a matter of judgement on what the outcomes of such analysis actually mean. Techniques, like the why technique and moving average plotting, are informative about the past but only provide a frame of reference for the future. Indeed, many managers would claim that their job is to change or manage the future and do better than trends would suggest. However, an understanding of the past trend will also enhance the understanding of the relationships involved and avoid the possible consequences of misunderstandings and simplification. In the introduction to this section we asked 'How many of the recent wars could have been anticipated and how many disasters could have been averted?'; the answer depends, in part, on how well the past is understood. How you project the future will depend on the models and assumptions you use. To clarify such models and assumptions will help produce a picture of the future.

SCENARIO 10: Bailey Group Hotels – usage rates of hotel leisure facilities

You have recently completed a report for your boss on hotel occupancy rates (if you have already forgotten, refer back to Scenario 3 in Section 2). Your boss was pleased with your work but did find the concept of standard deviation difficult to understand!

In one of the larger hotels within the hotel group, leisure facilities have been open to the public during daytime hours, Monday to Friday, on an experimental basis. The prices charged locally for similar facilities were found and a competitive price determined. The aim of the exercise was to make better use of such expensive facilities that were only used extensively by guests in the evening or at weekends. The maintenance of the leisure facilities are an accepted overhead and will not change with increased use. However, staff need to be in attendance during opening hours and this additional use will increase staff costs. To be viable, at least 200 paying customers would need to use these facilities each week.

The facilities have now been open for 3 weeks. You have been given the figures on usage rates shown in Table 4.6. You have been asked to examine these figures and make some provisional recommendations.

Table 4.6

Week	Monday	Tuesday	Wednesday	Thursday	Friday
1	28	27	40	56	63
2	26	25	38	52	60
3	29	25	36	50	58

You have been asked to examine the figures and this can be done effectively using the time series model. The main difference here, is that the cycle of variation is over 5 weekdays rather than the more usual 4 quarters. The moving average approach remains the same except that the average is based on five figures and we do not need to use the process of centring; if there are five sequential time periods, the third period is naturally at the centre.

Table 4.7 shows the determination of the 5-day moving average. The trend can be plotted on the same graph as the original data as shown in Figure 4.6. The trend is downwards in this case and there is substantial variation. The difference between the original observations and the trend line values is, in part, explained by the daily variation – Mondays seem relatively quiet and Fridays relatively busy. The daily differences are shown in Table 4.8.

Again we can summarize the daily differences by averaging (Table 4.9, p. 148). A clear downward trend emerges from the analysis of the data. The daily average has moved down to 40 and below giving a 5-day average of 200 or below. Monday, Tuesday and Wednesday are consistently low with the figures for Thursday and Friday much higher. To understand these

Table 4.7

Week	Day	Number of customers	5-day moving total	Moving average
1	Monday	28		
	Tuesday	27		
	Wednesday	40	214	42.8
	Thursday	56	212	42.4
	Friday	63	210	42.0
2	Monday	26	208	41.6
	Tuesday	25	204	40.8
	Wednesday	38	201	40.2
	Thursday	52	204	40.8
	Friday	60	204	40.8
3	Monday	29	202	40.4
	Tuesday	25	200	40.0
	Wednesday	36	198	39.6
	Thursday	50		
	Friday	58		

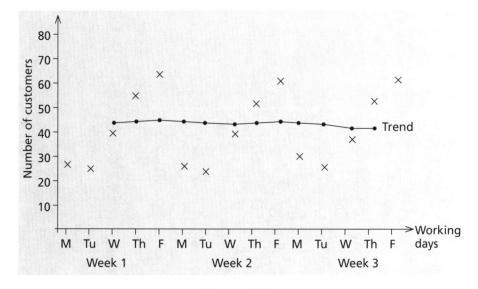

Figure 4.6

Table 4.8

Week	Day	Number of customers	Moving average	Daily difference
1	Monday	28		
	Tuesday	27		
	Wednesday	40	42.8	-2.8
	Thursday	56	42.4	13.6
	Friday	63	42.0	21.0
2	Monday	26	41.6	–15.6
	Tuesday	25	40.8	–15.8
	Wednesday	38	40.2	–2.2
	Thursday	52	40.8	11.2
	Friday	60	40.8	19.2
3	Monday	29	40.4	–11.4
	Tuesday	25	40.0	–15
	Wednesday	36	39.6	–3.6
	Thursday	50		
	Friday	58		

Table 4.9

Week	Monday	Tuesday	Wednesday	Thursday	Friday
1			–2.8	13.6	21.0
2	–15.6	–15.8	–2.2	11.2	19.2
3	–11.4	–15.0	–3.6		
Total	–27.0	–30.8	–8.6	24.8	40.2
Average	–13.5	–15.4	–2.9	12.4	20.1

figures requires more than statistical projection. A number of factors could explain these figures, such as:

- poor promotion and publicity;
- reduced prices elsewhere on Mondays, Tuesdays and Wednesdays;
- time of the year (e.g. school holidays).

Judgemental techniques can help develop a more complete picture once a set of facts has been established. The difficult part is often knowing what the 'facts' actually mean. Having established the present position, it could be worth undertaking another exercise, perhaps in the form of brainstorming, to identify possible options. One option, for example, would be to offer these facilities on a Saturday or Sunday, another option would be to improve promotion and indeed another option would be to offer special rates or packages on a Monday, Tuesday and Wednesday. Once you begin to look at a problem from a broader perspective, the number of possible responses can become quite extensive.

You have been asked to make some provisional recommendations. Clearly the leisure facilities have been able to attract numbers of customers in the right order of magnitude (a couple of hundred a week over the first 3 weeks) and must surely have potential. The interesting information that you need on customer attitudes and preferences is not available. In this case further research, perhaps using a questionnaire with existing users, would provide valuable information on why people actually pay the stated price and use the facilities.

There are a number of ways of projecting this trend forward and we will now consider one of them – **linear regression**.

STATISTICAL BACKGROUND: *linear regression*

A **linear** relationship is one that produces a straight line graph – see part 5, in Appendix A 'A refresher in numeracy skills'. A straight line graph is described by a equation of the form $y = a + bx$ where a is the intercept and b is the gradient.

Regression is the plotting of one factor against another. The factor we are attempting to explain or predict is y and this is plotted on a graph from the vertical or y-axis. The factor we are using for explanation is x and is plotted from the horizontal or x-axis.

Linear regression provides a method to estimate the equation $y = a + bx$. The gradient b is found using

$$b = \frac{n\Sigma xy - \Sigma x \Sigma y}{n\Sigma x^2 - (\Sigma x^2)}$$

and the intercept a is found using

$$a = \frac{\Sigma y}{n} - \frac{b\,\Sigma x}{n}$$

The calculations

In this case it is the trend that is being projected forward and not the original data. The first trend value is 42.8 and there are a total of 11 trend (moving average) values.

The formula for the gradients, b, and the intercept, a, involves some relatively tricky calculations. We need the sum of x, y, x^2 and xy. In this case, the x-variable is time starting on Wednesday of week 1. It is convenient to number the time periods 1, 2, 3, and so on but any equally spaced sequence of numbers is as valid. Corresponding to each of the numbered time periods is a trend (moving average) value. You can develop your answer on a spreadsheet or for smaller problems like this, using a table (Table 4.10).

Table 4.10

x	y	x^2	xy
1	42.8	1	42.8
2	42.4	4	84.8
3	42.0	9	126.0
4	41.6	16	166.4
5	40.8	25	204.0
6	40.2	36	241.2
7	40.8	49	285.6
8	40.8	64	326.4
9	40.4	81	363.6
10	40.0	100	400.0
11	39.6	121	435.6
Total 66	451.4	506	2676.4

By substitution, we can determine the gradient and intercept values:

$$b = \frac{11 * 2676.4 - 66 * 451.4}{11 * 506 - (66)^2}$$

$$= \frac{-352}{1210}$$

$$= -0.290\,9091$$

and

$$a = \frac{451.4}{11} - (-0.290\,9091) * \frac{66}{11}$$

$$= 42.781\,818$$

An accuracy of one decimal place is sufficient for this problem, and the result can be quoted as an equation:

$$y' = 42.8 - 0.3x$$

where y' denotes that the y-value is estimated.

If we wanted to estimate the number of customers on Monday and Tuesday of week 4 (a 'what if' type question), as a first step we would have to substitute the values 14 and 15 for x. The x-value of 11 took the series through to Wednesday of week 3 and weekends are excluded. We would then need to make a daily adjustment. When $x = 14$,

$$y' = 42.8 - 0.3 * 14$$

$$= 38.6$$

Typically Mondays are 13.5 below trend, so the adjusted prediction would be

$$38.6 - 13.5 = 25.1 \text{ people}$$

When $x = 15$

$$y' = 42.8 - 0.3 * 15$$

$$= 38.3$$

Typically Tuesdays are 15.4 below trend, so the adjusted prediction would be

$$38.3 - 15.4 = 22.9 \text{ people}$$

These results could have been obtained directly using a spreadsheet package like Lotus. You may even find that your calculator will give you the regression coefficients.

MICROSTATS   If the y values are placed in column 1 and the x values in column 2 then the command:

REGR C1 C2
will regress y on x.

SCENARIO 11: Northbridge District Council – urban renewal spending in a local authority (II)

You are still working for the urban renewal department of the local authority (see Scenario 4 in Section 2). You have recently produced a report using figures on the overall spending by both the council and the department for a 12-year period. There has been considerable interest in your report and you have been asked to respond to two specific questions from prominent councillors: 'What is the likely spending on urban renewal in 19X3 and 19X4 if the present spending trend continues?' and 'What is the relationship between urban renewal spending and council spending?' The figures for council spending are given in millions and the figures for urban renewal in thousands for computational convenience (Table 4.11).

Table 4.11

Year	Total council spending (£m.)	Urban renewal spending (£000s)
19V1	5.200 400	229.087
19V2	5.725 000	324.900
19V3	6.345 000	356.000
19V4	6.542 000	378.690
19V5	7.100 000	400.834
19V6	7.542 000	450.988
19V7	8.342 000	485.990
19V8	9.245 000	499.871
19V9	9.990 000	530.678
19X0	10.356 000	550.800
19X1	10.899 000	564.868
19X2	11.425 000	587.324

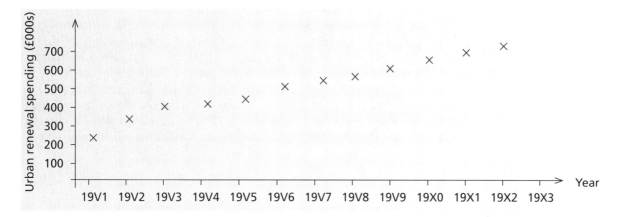

Figure 4.7

Each question will require its own analysis but there is a common issue – how to describe a relationship between two variables. The first question is concerned about a relationship against time and the second is concerned with a relationship between two measured factors. In each case, a graph plot would describe the relationship of interest and indicate whether or not it was linear. Although the more extreme examples of perfect linearity (all points on a straight line) or no relationship (a random scatter of points) would be evident from the graph, in many cases judgement is not so easy. In this section, we shall consider what inferences are possible from the graph and how a measure of the relationship can help us make a judgement about the data.

A graph of urban renewal spending (in £000s) against time is shown in Figure 4.7. The points do lie on a straight upward scatter. It is unlikely that data taken from the real world would ever lie exactly on a straight line even if an underlying linear relationship did exist. There are very few matters of interest that depend on a single factor, even though one or a few dominant factors may explain most of what we see. In this case, spending

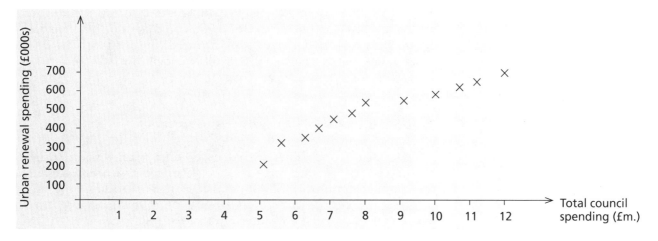

Figure 4.8

on urban renewal is likely to have many influences, but emerging historically is a straight line trend. Urban renewal spending is plotted against council spending in the graph in Figure 4.8. Again a linear-type relationship emerges. The fact that urban renewal spending is on the y-axis and council spending is on the x-axis does imply a cause and effect. In this case, the implied logic is that urban renewal spending depends on council spending and not the other way round. The choice of axes is important and does suggest that the problem is being thought about in a particular way.

STATISTICAL BACKGROUND: correlation

Relationships

Graphs are plotted for a purpose; either to describe or explore the relationship between y and x. The variable x is often referred to as the **independent** variable and can be thought of as the variable that is controlled or given, e.g. the agreed advertising budget or level of fertilizer applied. The variable y is often referred to as the **dependent** variable and can be thought of as the variable measuring the response to other factors, e.g. the sales given advertising or crop yield given fertilizer.

Association

By observing a graph or examining statistical measures, it may be possible to identify a way in which y relates to x for the data we have. This observed relationship can be referred to as an **association**. An association may exist because there is a relationship of some form between y and x or that for this particular set of data a pattern has emerged by chance. As an extreme example, if you were to look at rainfall readings around the world you would eventually find a set that would relate to the number of goals scored by your local football team. It is true that if you look at enough data you will find associations, but what is more difficult to establish is whether or not the association is meaningful.

Cause and effect

The fact that two variables are associated does not necessarily mean that the x-variable is the cause and the y-variable measures the effect. The interpretation of data depends on purpose, and as already suggested this could be to describe or explore relationships. If the purpose is to describe a relationship that we believe to exist (we are testing an idea for example), then the association found provides supportive evidence. If, on the other hand, we are exploring the data for possible relationships, then an association would indicate that there might be an idea worth exploring further, perhaps with further research. One purpose, therefore, is to test ideas and the other is to search for them.

Correlation

Correlation is a measure of association between two variables. Correlation lies in the range –1 to +1 where:

- –1 means all points lie on a straight line sloping downwards;
- +1 means all points lie on a straight line sloping upwards;
- 0 means the points are randomly scattered or a straight line could not be fitted.

Some illustrative examples are shown in the graphs in Figure 4.9, where r is the correlation coefficient.

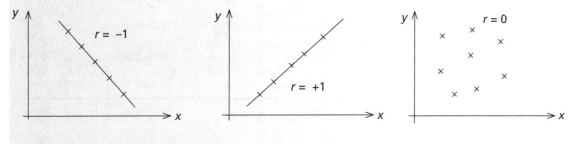

Figure 4.9

The correlation coefficient

The correlation coefficient (r) for measured data (e.g. time, income, height but not ranked data) is given:

$$r = \frac{n\Sigma xy - \Sigma x \Sigma y}{\sqrt{[(n\Sigma x^2 - (\Sigma x)^2)(n\Sigma y^2 - (\Sigma y)^2)]}}$$

Return to Scenario 11

As we have seen in the graph of urban renewal spending against time, there are no predictable cyclical variations that require time series modelling. We merely need to describe the trend. The graph suggests a linear association. The correlation coefficient provides a measure of that

Table 4.12

x (time)	Urban renewal (£000s)	x^2	y^2	xy
1	229.087	1	52480.854	229.087
2	324.900	3	105560.01	649.800
3	356.000	9	126736	1068
4	378.690	16	143406.12	1514.76
5	400.834	25	160667.9	2004.17
6	450.988	36	203390.18	2705.928
7	485.990	49	236186.28	3401.93
8	499.871	64	249871.02	3998.968
9	530.678	81	281619.14	4776.102
10	550.800	100	303380.64	5508
11	564.868	121	319075.86	6213.548
12	587.324	144	344949.48	7047.888
Total 78	5360.03	650	2527323.5	39118.181

association on a scale ranging from –1 to +1. The calculations will require a sequential series for time and it is easier to use 1, 2, 3 and so on, rather than a more complex series such as 1981, 1982, 1983. The calculations are shown in Table 4.12.

By substitution, the value for the correlation coefficient can be found:

$$r = \frac{12 * 39\,188.818 - 78 * 5360.03}{\sqrt{\{(12 * 650 - (78)^2) * (12 * 2\,527\,323.5 - (5360.03)^2)\}}}$$

$$= \frac{51\,335.832}{\sqrt{\{1716 * 1\,597\,960.4\}}}$$

$$= 0.980\,345$$

TASK

CHECK THESE CALCULATIONS.

If you have just completed the above task, we hope that your answer agrees with ours. As a quick check, you can check that the calculated value of r lies in the acceptable range of -1 to $+1$; this does not guarantee correctness but does detect any major errors. Also, the graph suggests a strong positive relationship, so we would expect a value close to $+1$.

MICROSTATS   The command:

CORR C1 C2

will determine the correlation between the data given in column 1 and the data given in column 2.

We could now calculate by hand the linear regression coefficients. The given formula (see formula sheet – Appendix G) could be used to calculate the value of the gradient, b, and the intercept, a. However, we think you will agree that this is all becoming rather tedious. Even the calculations based on 12 years' worth of data seem lengthy and in many cases we will need to deal with much larger and more complex sets of data.

Let us consider some of the options for the determination of the correlation coefficient and the linear regression coefficients. Many of you may own calculators that will determine these values – we suggest you try the procedures using the examples given. The Lotus spreadsheet and the MICROSTATS package (provided with this book) will both quickly do the necessary calculations. To illustrate the use of this software, Lotus will be used to determine the trend in urban renewal spending and MICROSTATS will be used to explore the relationship between urban renewal spending and council spending.

The output obtained from Lotus (using the DATA menu and REGRESSION) is shown in Spreadsheet 4.1. The Lotus printout does provide all the answers we want and some that we will not be using. This illustrates a typical problem we can expect when working with software packages, that the output may not necessarily be in a format familiar to us. Essentially we need to know the correlation coefficient and the coefficients of linear regression in the two-variable case ($y = a + bx$). Lotus offers the facility to calculate multiple regression (several x-variables) which is beyond the scope of this book but also produces the output of the simpler case in the same way. The R squared value of 0.961 076 is the correlation coefficient squared, so taking the square root will give $r = 0.980\ 3448$ or just $r = 0.98$ to two decimal places. The intercept value a is 252.2152 (given as the constant in the printout) and the gradient is 29.915 98. The linear equation would take the form

$$y = 252.2152 + 29.915\ 98x$$

SPREADSHEET 4.1

		Regression Output:	
1	229.087		
2	324.9	Constant	252.2152
3	356	Std Err of Y Est	22.76656
4	378.69	R Squared	0.961076
5	400.834	No. of Observations	12
6	450.988	Degrees of Freedom	10
7	485.99		
8	499.871	X Coefficient(s)	29.91598
9	530.678	Std Err of Coef.	1.903835
10	550.8		
11	564.868		
12	587.324		

Given the value of the correlation coefficient we first need to decide whether regression analysis is worthwhile. As a general rule of thumb:

- if $r > +0.9$ then we have a good positive relationship;
- if $r < -0.9$ then we have a good negative relationship.

More advanced textbooks will outline methods to test whether the relationship is good or not in statistical terms. In this case, regression does seem worthwhile and predictions can be made from the regression equation. To predict urban renewal spending in 19X3 and 19X4 we would let the series of x-values continue with $x = 13$ and $x = 14$.

When $x = 13$,

$$y = 252.2152 + 29.915\ 98 * 13$$

$$= 641.122\ 94\ (\text{\pounds}000s) \text{ or } \text{\pounds}\ 641\ 123\ (\text{to nearest \pounds})$$

When $x = 14$,

$$y = 252.2152 + 29.915\ 98 * 14$$

$$= 671.038\ 92\ (\text{\pounds}000s) \text{ or } \text{\pounds}671\ 039\ (\text{to nearest \pounds})$$

This analysis does provide the answer to the first specific question in the scenario which was seeking an estimate of likely spending on urban renewal if the present trend were to continue. This is, of course, a major assumption of all forecasting that historic trends as known will continue. In reality, you need to bring all available knowledge to such business-forecasting problems and use statistical analysis as part of that knowledge. It could be, for example, that you expect a product or service to follow a life cycle curve and would not expect a past trend to continue.

TASK

> **IF YOU HAVE ACCESS TO AN APPROPRIATE SPREADSHEET, REPRODUCE THE RESULTS GIVEN.**

We could again use Lotus to analyse the relationship between urban renewal spending and council spending. However, the MICROSTATS package also offers the facility to graph plot and determine correlation and linear regression coefficients. A package, like MICROSTATS, could be more effective for large data sets than a spreadsheet. In this case, the data for total council spending was entered into column C1 and urban renewal spending into column C2. Using the commands for correlation (CORR C2 C1) and the regression of C2 on C1 (REGR C2 C1) the following results were obtained:

$$r = 0.9694$$

and

$$y = 33.4958 + 50.2280x$$

 MICROSTATS   Use your copy of MICROSTATS to obtain these results

The results obtained from the analysis, and indeed the way budgets are managed, would suggest that there is an association between urban renewal spending and council spending. There is a strong positive correlation between the two factors and a visual inspection of the graph plot would support that view. In fact, we could go one step further and show that every time x increases by 1 unit (a £1m. increase of council spending) then y will increase by 50.2280 (a £50 228 increase in urban renewal spending).

TASK

> USING THE REGRESSION EQUATION GIVEN, LET X TAKE THE VALUES 1, 2, 3, 4, 5, 6, 7, 8, 9, 10 AND 11. WORK OUT THE CORRESPONDING Y VALUES. WORK OUT THE INCREASE IN Y FOR EACH UNIT INCREASE IN X, AND CHECK THAT IT CORRESPONDS TO THE REGRESSION COEFFICIENT FOR A GRADIENT.

Even though we can show evidence of association, this does not prove cause and effect. It is true, in this case, that historically, urban renewal spending has increased in line with more general council spending. However, both have increased at a similar rate over time and there could be a common third (or indeed fourth or fifth) variable. Statistical analysis alone is unlikely to prove the cause but it does supply necessary supportive evidence.

Conclusions

Most problems we deal with require a view of the future. The future will never be known with certainty but we can, at least, work through what might happen. The 'what might happen' arguments provide a picture of the future that can be challenged, discussed and developed. This putting together of a scenario is seen as a very useful way of exploring the future direction a business or any other kind of organization can take. The scenario allows assumptions, often implicit, to surface and the frameworks of analysis to be clarified. A scenario allows parameters to be changed and the consequences examined: a 'what if' analysis.

This section is intended to give you the tools to develop forecasts of the future. If the numerical data is of good quality, then statistical methods such as time series modelling or linear regression might be most appropriate. If the quantitative data is limited and a number of issues need to be clarified by those involved, the judgemental methods are likely to be most appropriate. In either case, the forecaster is likely to have to use a level of judgement when deciding on the best method and when deciding the information is complete enough and valid enough to be worth reporting.

Questions

1. The local police force have become concerned about the level of bicycle theft. The Chief Constable believes that this type of theft is on the increase and would like an independent investigation – by you. You

have been given the quarterly figures for reported bicycle theft from the records of the last 3 years (Table 4.13).

Table 4.13

Year	Quarter 1	Quarter 2	Quarter 3	Quarter 4
19X1	43	154	346	48
19X2	57	172	360	45
19X3	38	150	350	59

You have been advised that your report should include an analysis of the figures given and advice on how further information on the level of bicycle theft could be obtained. Make a prediction of likely bicycle theft in 19X4.

2. The figures given in Table 4.14 show the number of warranty claims against a particular product. Prepare a report describing any trend observed and explaining the importance of seasonal variation.

Table 4.14

Year	Quarter 1	Quarter 2	Quarter 3	Quarter 4
19X1	75	95	104	87
19X2	73	87	98	80
19X3	63	79	90	69

3. A friend of yours intends to open a pet shop in the local high street. She has no idea about the level of future demand and is seeking your advice. What advice would you give?

4. A headmaster friend of yours has decided to look at the number of pupils absent from school since the beginning of term (which started 4 weeks ago) (Table 4.15). You have agreed to try and identify any daily variation and trend.

Table 4.15

Week	Monday	Tuesday	Wednesday	Thursday	Friday
1	23	22	27	24	21
2	25	20	29	23	22
3	23	20	30	24	22
4	24	23	32	25	23

In addition to reporting on the statistical trends, you have agreed to suggest how further information could be obtained from teachers and pupils on the rates of absenteeism.

5. Your company has recently opened a telephone customer helpline during office hours. The number of calls over the 3-week trial period is given in Table 4.16. Determine the trend and daily variation. Using linear regression or another appropriate method extrapolate the trend into the fourth week, and make a prediction of likely daily demand.

Table 4.16

Week	Monday	Tuesday	Wednesday	Thursday	Friday
1	642	578	542	533	523
2	674	597	568	553	542
3	698	605	581	568	559

6. A small hotel has been reviewing the number of 'weekend breaks' taken over the last 3 years to ascertain whether there has been growth in this type of business activity. It is known that, for any one weekend, a number of factors can affect the figures such as the weather, sports

Table 4.17

Month	Year 19X1	Year 19X2	Year 19X3
January	5	6	6
February	7	7	9
March	11	13	16
April	9	14	15
May	13	16	17
June	17	21	22
July	18	19	22
August	20	22	24
September	20	26	28
October	16	18	20
November	8	8	10
December	4	4	6

events and the availability of the hotel facilities. To average out this effect the hotel has collated the figures on a monthly basis over the last 3 years (Table 4.17).

The hotel has recently bought a new computer and would like you to develop a spreadsheet model to explain the data. The manager has asked you to use a 12-month moving average and show this on a graph with the original data if possible. Impress your manager!

7. Your department is responsible for health and safety training within a large organization. The number of courses presented has declined over the past 5 years as shown in Table 4.18.

Table 4.18

Year	Number of course presentations
1989	130
1990	121
1991	105
1992	99
1993	92

(a) Graph this data and comment on the relationship.
(b) Calculate the correlation coefficient and explain what the calculated value means.
(c) Determine the linear regression coefficients for intercept and gradient.
(d) Using linear regression, predict the number of course presentations for 1994.
(e) If the number of presentations in 1994 turns out to be 95 how would you justify the prediction you made?
8. You are now working in a personnel department and have been asked to look at the relationship between the score achieved on an aptitude test and the scoring given for on-the-job performance. In both cases the score is out of 100 and a high score means better performance. Only 10 employees have been involved in this pilot scheme and you have been asked to report on the findings (Table 4.19).
(a) Graph job performance score against aptitude score and comment on the relationship.
(b) Calculate the correlation coefficient and explain the meaning of the calculated value.
(c) Determine the linear regression of job performance score against aptitude score and show this on your graph.
(d) Using linear regression, predict the job performance score on a new employee who has just achieved a score of 40 on the aptitude test.

Table 4.19

Employee	Aptitude score	Job performance score
A	33	78
B	48	78
C	22	37
D	59	92
E	53	96
F	75	90
G	32	55
H	24	38
I	18	21
J	45	87

(e) What reservations would you have about using linear regression in the way outlined in part (d)?

9. An importer of kitchen appliances has presented you with the figures shown in Table 4.20. Using MICROSTATS or some other appropriate computer package explore the data given and comment on your findings.

Table 4.20

Year	Sales (£m.)	Advertising (£000s)	Enquiries (000s)
19X1	36	49	50
19X2	34	49	60
19X3	48	52	66
19X4	54	54	67
19X5	57	56	69

Section 5
Models

Objectives

After studying this section you should be able to:

- explain the purpose of a mathematical model;

- identify different types of model used in a business or organizational setting;

- construct a model to describe some business and organizational situations;

- use a model to undertake a 'what if' analysis;

- make recommendations on the basis of the model constructed;

- critically appraise the use of models and modelling.

Introduction

A model is a representation of a real situation or system. It is unlikely ever to capture the complexity of the real thing but is intended to give an insight and understanding that would not otherwise exist. A new car would not go into production without experimentation on a prototype and a pilot would not be left to face difficult landing procedures without the training and experience of a flight simulation. A model can fulfil the same role for a business as the prototype for the car manufacturer or the simulator for the pilot. A model can be used to test ideas and experiment. A model allows the user to ask the question 'what if' and consider the possible outcomes from future situations. A model can be used to develop a view of the future and, perhaps of most importance, minimize risk. Things can always go wrong, but it can be of considerable benefit to any organization to avoid costly mistakes. A model may not provide all the answers but it can allow managers to develop a better judgement. The model used may be relatively simple, like predicting today's sales on the basis of yesterday's sales, or be relatively complex like predicting next year's growth in gross domestic product given a host of economic measures.

Whatever the model there are some common features:

- an understood or defined problem;
- a purpose or set of objectives;
- a set of assumptions implicitly or, preferably, explicitly stated;
- a set of relationships which could be in the form of equations;
- data describing the problem;
- the ability to generate a solution;
- the scope to experiment.

It is not possible in this text to consider a comprehensive list of models. Many models are very specialist in nature and are only worth pursuing in particular situations and others may need to be developed when a situation arises. In this section, five scenarios are presented to demonstrate the range of models available and some of the techniques of modelling. Each scenario is self-contained and develops a particular set of ideas. Scenarios 12 and 13 do draw on mathematical solutions but are more concerned with the ways a spreadsheet model can be developed. Scenario 14 is concerned with managing data derived from scoring criteria (e.g. 5 is good and 1 is bad) rather than measurement in quantities such as time, money or weight. Scenario 15 is concerned with financial analysis and Scenario 16 with the ways a visual presentation can help manage complex projects. By working through some of the scenarios, you will develop an appreciation of modelling and recognize some of the potential benefits.

SCENARIO 12: The Carkit Company – breakeven modelling

You have always loved cars (well the authors do!). You have always wanted to design and direct the manufacture of cars but the reality is that you do not have the money or experience to do this in any major way at the moment. However, you have impressed your friends with the way you have constructed kit cars. Assembling kit cars for others has presented you with a real business opportunity and you have collected some cost information.

It would cost about £200 per week to lease and maintain a suitable workshop over the full calendar year. The kits would cost between £2400 and £6800 and be paid for directly by your customers to the producer of the kit. However, you do accept an advisory role and may not be prepared to work with some kits for technical reasons. You intend to charge a standard £1600 to build a kit with customer-supplied components, providing construction time is no longer than 2 weeks. You know that each construction project will involve expenses such as paints, oils and fastenings and these can sum to £300 or more.

You would like to know how many kit cars you would need to build to break even and how many you would need to build to give you what you would see as a minimum acceptable profit of £18 000 per annum before deductions.

Approaching this problem

The problem in this case is clear, and just the information required to solve this problem is given. In most substantive business problems, there is the major task of establishing that the information provided is complete and consistent. You may need to add to the information you have been given by desk research, survey research or by other means or even accept that you will need to develop a model without all the information you would really like. You could find that you are given more information than you need and that the quantity of information does not help you solve the problem – there are may examples of eager managers requesting computer printouts that turn out to be several centimetres deep when received.

In this case, some figures are given on a weekly basis and others on an annual basis. In most business problems annual figures are used to be consistent with annual reporting and annual rates of interest. In this scenario it is meaningful to consider the profitability of the business over the period of one year.

It is important to know who the customer is. In this case you are the problem owner and, hopefully, the problem solver. In the larger organization, there is often a distinction between the problem owner and problem solver which needs to be carefully understood. Many problem owners are seeking recommendations on how to solve their problem, and require the problem solver to develop decision criteria.

BACKGROUND: modelling

A model

There are essentially three categories of model that we will consider (other authors may differ in their typology but the broad grouping will remain the same):

- A **physical model** generally involves a scaled or simplified representation of the real thing. Cardboard cut-outs can be used to represent office furniture or materials-handling equipment, for example.
- **Schematic models** are a more abstract representation of reality and include all forms of graphs and charts. They facilitate analysis through the manipulation of the data used to construct the graph or chart.
- **Mathematical models** use a range of numbers, letters, special characters and symbols in sets of equations. These models may be **deterministic**, giving exact and certain outcomes, or **probabalistic** where outcomes are uncertain (Section 6).

A problem

There can be an emphasis on problem solving without a real consideration of what the problem is. How many times have you heard people say that they have solved or are solving the wrong problem! There are a number of ways of defining a problem; we will use 'a situation where a gap is perceived to exist between what is and what should be'.

A variable

A **variable** represents a quantity or characteristic that is subject to change within any particular problem. The marks achieved by a group of students in a mathematics test are likely to vary and would typify the measurement of a variable.

A parameter

A **parameter** is fixed for a particular problem. When evaluating the cost of running a car for one year, the insurance may be fixed and hence is a parameter; in the longer term it may be subject to change and then becomes a variable.

Return to Scenario 12

This problem is amenable to analysis using schematic and mathematical models. The information presented can be described using graphs or equations. There are the given cost and price parameters:

Fixed cost	£10 400 per annum (£200 × 52)
Price	£1600 per car
Unit cost	£300 per car

and in this case the single variable, x, the number of cars built in a year. The terms 'fixed cost' and 'unit cost' may be new to you. What typifies problem solving is the use of given information, the search for new information and the application of knowledge. In many cases, you will need to accept that additional knowledge will be necessary to understand the solutions developed by other people and to develop more effective solutions of your own. **Fixed costs** are those costs that remain constant over a defined period and will include items such as rent, office salaries and insurance. **Unit costs** are those that are directly related to production and will include items such as material costs, contract labour and commission. The **break-even point** gives the level of production where profit is zero. At the break-even point of zero profit, the revenue from sales is equal to the cost of sales. A table can be used to show how revenue, and the **variable cost** (which is the unit

Table 5.1

Production x	Revenue 1600x	Fixed cost	Variable cost 300x	Total cost 10 400+300x	Profit
0	0	10 400	0	10 400	–10 400
1	1 600	10 400	300	10 700	–9 100
2	3 200	10 400	600	11 000	–7 800
3	4 800	10 400	900	11 300	–6 500
4	6 400	10 400	1 200	11 600	–5 200
5	8 000	10 400	1 500	11 900	–3 900
6	9 600	10 400	1 800	12 200	–2 600
7	11 200	10 400	2 100	12 500	–1 300
8	12 800	10 400	2 400	12 800	0
9	14 400	10 400	2 700	13 100	1 300
10	16 000	10 400	3 000	13 400	2 600

cost times the number of units) element, increase with production and how the fixed cost element remains the same (Table 5.1). Table 5.1 also shows **total cost** (which is the sum of the fixed cost and variable cost) and **profit** (which is the difference between revenue and total cost).

It can be seen from Table 5.1 that at low production levels the business can expect to make a loss. On the basis of the figures given, eight kit cars would need to be constructed each year to break even – produce a 0 profit. The difference between the price and unit cost (£1600 – £300 = £1300) is known as the **contribution to profit** and it can be seen that the completion of each additional kit car will add £1300 to profit (or reduce the loss if profit is negative). The graph plot of revenue and total cost against output levels in Figure 5.1 presents the schematic model.

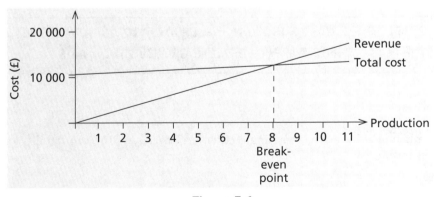

Figure 5.1

TASKS

1. IF YOU HAVE ACCESS TO SPREADSHEET SOFTWARE, PRODUCE TABLE 5.1.
2. IF YOU HAVE ACCESS TO GRAPHICS SOFTWARE, PRODUCE THE GRAPH PLOT SHOWN IN FIGURE 5.1.
3. DETERMINE THE PRODUCTION LEVEL THAT WOULD GIVE PROFITS OF £18 000.

The mathematical model can be built up in parts – an approach referred to as a **build-up model**. The parts are as follows:

Revenue (R): $R = 1600x$ (where x is the number of kit cars produced)

Fixed cost (FC): $FC = 10\ 400$

Variable cost (VC): $VC = 300x$

Total cost (TC): $TC = FC + VC$

$$= 10\ 400 + 300x$$

Profit (π): $\pi = R - TC$

$$= 1600x - (10\ 400 + 300x)$$

$$= 1600x - 300x - 10\ 400$$

$$= 1300x - 10\ 400$$

TASKS

GRAPH THE PROFIT FUNCTION $\pi = 1300x - 10\ 400$. INTERPRET THE POINT WHERE THE PLOTTED LINE CROSSES THE x-AXIS.

Mathematically we have a single equation describing the profitability of this business:

$$\pi = 1300x - 10\ 400$$

To determine the break-even point we can set profit (π) equal to 0 and solve. Hence

$$0 = 1300x - 10\ 400$$
$$1300x = 10\ 400$$
$$x = 8$$

Using the same approach, we can determine the production level giving an annual profit of £18 000:

$$18\ 000 = 1300x - 10\ 400$$
$$28\ 400 = 1300x$$
$$x = 21.85$$

To achieve an acceptable profit of £18 000, at least 22 cars would need to be produced.

If we return to the checklist given in the introduction to this section, we can again consider the general issues of model development:

- The problem was clearly defined and concerned with a knowledge gap. You only needed to know the levels of output necessary to break even and achieve a given level of profits. Problems are often more complex than this.
- The objective in this case was to complete the task. The objective could have been extended to consider how reliable the data was and how certain the outcomes were.
- A number of assumptions were made to model the problem. The cost of 'about £200' and 'can sum to £300' were treated as exact. All the relationships were assumed linear – gave straight line graphs. It is often the case in business that as the scale of operation changes the cost and the price of additional units change.
- The problem was easily described using either a graph or equations. In many problems, this cannot be done so precisely and other methods have to be used (for example simulation).
- It is unusual to have just the right data. Often the data needs to be generated using surveys or other methods, or found through desk research.
- In Scenario 12, a single equation was developed for profit with a single variable x. Most problems encountered in the working world include several variables and a number of equations.
- It is useful to consider a 'what if' analysis. A manager will remain better informed if a number of alternatives can be considered. We can ask a number 'what if' questions:
  (a) what if annual fixed cost increased to £11 700?

$$\pi = 1300x - 11\ 700$$

To find the break-even point $\pi = 0$, and

$$1300x = 11\ 700$$

$$x = 9$$

It can be noted that as the fixed cost element increased, the number of units necessary to break even also increases.

(b) What if unit cost per car fell from £300 to £100? Then

$$\pi = 1600x - (10\ 400 + 100x)$$
$$= 1600x - 100x - 10\ 400$$
$$= 1500x - 10\ 400$$

To break even, $\pi = 0$ and

$$1500x = 10\ 400$$
$$x = 6.9$$

If unit costs are reduced, a smaller number of units are needed to break even.

By changing the parameters of the problem, generally one at a time, it is possible to anticipate the effects of possible future events whether they are likely or unlikely.

SCENARIO 13: Mount Vision Hospital – stock control

The Mount Vision Hospital is looking for cost reductions in all areas of operation. It is an old and relatively small hospital compared to many, and tends to follow established procedures for most operational matters. It has been suggested that some cost reductions could be achieved by revising purchasing practices without affecting the service to patients. You have just been appointed to the post of senior purchasing officer. You know that it is not possible at this stage to consider the many items you are responsible for but you have agreed to look at a typical purchase and identify whether any improvement could be made in purchasing practice. You have decided to look more closely at the purchase of paper towels as this typifies a particular type of product group. The demand for paper towels is fairly constant and an order is placed each month for 400 cases. You have estimated that the cost of making this order is about £15 when all administrative time and expense are allowed for. It is known that some paper towels are lost through pilfering and damage; an amount you think is no more than 2%. In addition, the accounting department have advised you to allow for capital tied up in stock at the rate of 10% per year. The cost to the hospital of paper towels is £30 per case.

Approaching this problem

In this problem you will need to find a way to summarize the given information and you also need to look for a better solution. The problem is all about cost minimization subject to meeting the demand for paper towels. A starting point is clearly to establish the annual cost of the present practice and look for ways that this could be reduced.

In this case there are three components of cost: the **cost of ordering stock**, the **cost of holding stock** and the **purchase cost**.

Cost of ordering stock

An order is placed every month at an administrative cost of £15; the annual cost of ordering is therefore

£15 * 12 = £180

Cost of holding stock

The cost of holding cases of paper towels in stock needs to include the 2% lost through pilfering and damage, and the 10% attributed to the cost of capital. If this 12% is applied to the £30 cost of each case of paper towels then

£30 * 0.12 = £3.60

which is the cost of holding one case in stock for one year.

However, any one case is unlikely to be held in stock for one year (particularly if stock is managed on a 'first in first out', FIFO, basis). Stock in this case is more easily understood as a flow with a batch of 400 being delivered each month and gradually being depleted though the month. The system could be simply represented (given the available information) by a stock level of 400 at the beginning of the month, falling to 300 after 1 week, 200 after 2 weeks, 100 after 3 weeks and 0 after 4 weeks; the cycle then begins again. The stock levels do vary from 400 to 0 but will average out at 200. The stock costs could vary from

£3.60 * 400 = £1440 if a constant 400 cases were kept in stock

to

£3.60 * 0 = £0 if 0 cases were kept in stock

Holding costs average out to £720 (i.e. 200 * £3.60) per year.

The purchase cost

The annual purchase cost is the number of cases bought each year (400 * 12) multiplied by the purchase price of £30:

$$400 * 12 * £30 = £144\,000$$

In some cases, the price will depend on the quantities bought and the frequency of ordering. This calculation should reflect the actual annual cost and should allow for any price adjustment.

Total annual cost

The overall cost is found by summing the component parts:

Cost of ordering stock	£180
Cost of holding stock	£720
Purchase cost	<u>£144 000</u>
Total annual cost	£144 900

It is worth noting that the most significant part of the total annual cost, in this case, is the purchase cost even though attention may focus on order policy and the cost of holding. A 1% saving on purchase cost is £1400 which is greater than the cost of ordering stock (£180) plus the cost of holding stock (£720). To understand how these costs can be managed a stock control model can be developed.

BACKGROUND: modelling stock control

Economic order quantity

The **economic order quantity** (EOQ) or **economic batch quantity** (EBQ) both refer to the same model of stock control. The model is used to determine the order quantity that minimizes total cost.

Ordering cost

Ordering costs include all those costs associated with procurement, such as administration, selection of supplier, writing purchase orders, receiving and inspecting goods. If larger quantities are ordered, fewer orders will be made each year and the ordering cost will decrease.

Holding cost

Holding costs include all those costs associated with the storage of goods, such as handling, deterioration, insurance and tied-up capital. If larger quantities are ordered, the level of stock will increase and the holding cost will increase.

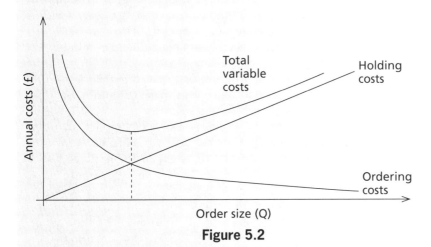

Figure 5.2

Total variable cost

Total variable cost (TVC) is the sum of the ordering cost and holding cost. If the purchase cost is constant, then the minimum total variable cost will also be the minimum overall cost and give the EOQ. The graph in Figure 5.2 illustrates the typical cost structure.

EOQ formula

The following formula will give the economic order quantity:

$$\text{EOQ} = \sqrt{\frac{2 \times C_O \times D}{C_H}}$$

where D is annual demand, C_O is the ordering cost and C_H is the cost of holding one unit for one year.

A number of assumptions are made in the derivation of this formula including constant demand. The formula therefore is only really valid if the assumption of constant demand, zero lead time and other assumptions are sufficiently correct.

Return to Scenario 13

To model the stock costs of paper towels outlined in Scenario 13, an illustrative spreadsheet with eight columns has been constructed (Spreadsheet 5.1). The columns represent the following:

- Column A is the ordering frequency. Given an annual demand for 4800 cases, we could make one order a year (order frequency) of 4800, or two orders a year of 2400 and so on.
- Column B gives the order size (which is demand ÷ column A). This is sometimes referred to as batch quantity.
- Column C gives the total ordering cost, which in this case is £15 * the number of orders made each year (from column A).
- Column D. To calculate holding costs we need to know the average level of stock held. In this stock control model, an order is placed and arrives (order size given in column B) and is gradually depleted to 0 until the next order is placed and arrives. The average holding of stock is therefore order size divided by 2 (column (B ÷ 2).
- Column E gives holding cost, which is calculated by multiplying the average stock level (column D) by the cost of holding one item in stock for 1 year; £3.60 in this scenario.
- Column F is the total variable cost (TVC), which is the sum of ordering costs (column C) and holding costs (column E).
- Column G is the purchase cost, which is price * annual demand; £30 * 4800 in this scenario.
- Column H is the total annual cost, which is the sum of total variable cost (column F) and purchase cost (column G).

TASKS

1. **CONSTRUCT SPREADSHEET 5.1.**
2. **PLOT ORDERING COST, HOLDING COST AND TOTAL ANNUAL COST ON THE SAME GRAPH.**

It can be seen from the spreadsheet model that for the current order size of 400 each month the total annual cost is £144 900. The minimum total annual cost of £144 720 is achieved with an order size of 200. To meet demand, an order for 200 would have to be placed twice a month (fortnightly).

The spreadsheet model does allow us to explore a number of important issues. If for example, we move away slightly from the optimal order size of 200, to say 170 or 240, it does not make much difference to the overall cost. Indeed, the cost difference between the current practice and the optimum practice is only £180 (£144 900 – £144 720), the equivalent of six cases of paper towels. We would agree that £180 is important but we

SPREADSHEET 5.1

	A	B	C	D	E	F	G	H
	Order freq	Order size	Order cost	Av stock	Holding cost	Tot var cost	Purchase cost	Tot annual cost
1	4800.00	15	2400.00	8640.00	8655.00	144000	152655.00	
2	2400.00	30	1200.00	4320.00	4350.00	144000	148350.00	
3	1600.00	45	800.00	2880.00	2925.00	144000	146925.00	
4	1200.00	60	600.00	2160.00	2220.00	144000	146220.00	
5	960.00	75	480.00	1728.00	1803.00	144000	145803.00	
6	800.00	90	400.00	1440.00	1530.00	144000	145530.00	
7	685.71	105	342.86	1234.29	1339.29	144000	145339.29	
8	600.00	120	300.00	1080.00	1200.00	144000	145200.00	
9	533.33	135	266.67	960.00	1095.00	144000	145095.00	
10	480.00	150	240.00	864.00	1014.00	144000	145014.00	
11	436.36	165	218.18	785.45	950.45	144000	144950.45	
12	400.00	180	200.00	720.00	900.00	144000	144900.00	
13	369.23	195	184.62	664.62	859.62	144000	144859.62	
14	342.86	210	171.43	617.14	827.14	144000	144827.14	
15	320.00	225	160.00	576.00	801.00	144000	144801.00	
16	300.00	240	150.00	540.00	780.00	144000	144780.00	
17	282.35	255	141.18	508.24	763.24	144000	144763.24	
18	266.67	270	133.33	480.00	750.00	144000	144750.00	
19	252.63	285	126.32	454.74	739.74	144000	144739.74	
20	240.00	300	120.00	432.00	732.00	144000	144732.00	
21	228.57	315	114.29	411.43	726.43	144000	144726.43	
22	218.8	330	109.09	392.73	722.73	144000	144722.73	
23	208.70	345	104.35	375.65	720.65	144000	144720.65	
24	200.00	360	100.00	360.00	720.00	144000	144720.00	

SPREADSHEET 5.1   contd

A	B	C	D	E	F	G	H
Order freq	Order size	Order cost	Av stock	Holding cost	Tot var cost	Purchase cost	Tot annual cost
25	192.00	375	96.00	345.60	720.60	144000	144720.60
26	184.62	390	92.31	332.31	722.31	144000	144722.31
27	177.78	405	88.89	320.00	725.00	144000	144725.00
28	171.43	420	85.71	308.57	728.57	144000	144728.57

would need to be convinced that all the costs of ordering and holding were adequately represented before shifting away from ordering once a month to twice a month. Would the administrative cost stay at £15 for example? The significant sum of money is the £144 000 purchase cost. Purchasing controls could offer savings, perhaps through the negotiation of a discount, or the use of alternative suppliers or products, or perhaps an organizational effort to cut down any wasteful use. This is another example where a spreadsheet model can help the manager make an informed judgement even though it might not necessarily provide the immediate answer.

The formula has been given for the determination of EOQ. The parameters given are $D = 4800$ cases per annum, $C_O = £15$ per order and $C_H = £3.60$ is the cost of holding one item for one year. It is important that we are consistent in our use of units and both demand and holding costs are per annum. By substitution, we obtain

$$\text{EBQ} = \sqrt{\frac{2 \times 15 \times 4800}{3.60}}$$

$$\text{EBQ} = 200$$

The formula is particular useful in two respects. First, it does give the right answer and allows you to vary the parameters quickly and see the effect. So, for example, if the ordering costs of administration were to increase (increase the £15 in the formula), we would order less frequently and the order size would increase. On the other hand, if the holding costs were to increase (increase the £3.60 in the formula), we would decrease the order size and order more frequently. As we have seen, stock control is about balancing various costs. Secondly, finding the EOQ using the formula gives the relevant order of magnitude (whether 10s, 100s, 1000s) and allows a spreadsheet to be constructed more easily. In this scenario, we could use the formula to know that the spreadsheet would have to include the order size of 200.

TASK

USE THE CHECKLIST GIVEN IN THE SECTION INTRODUCTION TO ASSESS THE EFFECTIVENESS OF THE STOCK CONTROL MODEL DEVELOPED IN SPREADSHEET 5.1.

SCENARIO 14: Bailey Group Hotels – choosing a new hotel location

Your boss has been impressed by your reports on hotel occupancy rates and likely usage of leisure facilities. Your boss now wants you to report on the location of a new hotel given a choice of three possible locations: Sunnyside, Waterside and Bankside. A range of important factors have been identified, such as transport facilities, and these have been given a maximum score to indicate their relative importance. For each of the locations, the management team have considered each factor and assigned an agreed number of points. You are given a summary of this work, shown in Table 5.2.

Your boss would like you to prepare a brief report recommending a location on the basis of this work and suggestions on how this analysis could be improved.

Table 5.2

			Location	
Factor	Maximum score	Sunnyside	Waterside	Bankside
Transport	20	10	18	8
Amenities	15	8	3	8
Workforce	10	6	7	5
Services	15	10	7	6
Expansion	10	2	4	8
Grants	5	1	2	2

The problem you have been presented with has a mix of managerial judgement and descriptive numbers. The numbers are not the result of some rigorous measurement but considered scores. This problem typifies a class of problem, where objective measurement is difficult and scores are allocated. To analyse the scores, we need to develop a **scoring model**.

STATISTICAL BACKGROUND: *measurement*

Qualitative data is concerned with the qualities, characteristics or attributes of interest. Such qualities are most easily described verbally with words like 'good', 'exciting', 'poor value' but are often numerically coded for computational convenience.

Quantitative data is concerned with amounts and can be measured with ruler-type scales. Time, weight and income are examples of such measurement.

Return to Scenario 14

There are many types of scoring model; but we shall only consider the additive model. In this case, it is merely a matter of summing the three columns for location to find a total of 37 for location Sunnyside, 41 for location Waterside and 37 for location for location Bankside. Location Waterside has the highest total score so would be recommended on the basis of this analysis.

In terms of the checklist given in the section introduction:

- The problem presented to you has been only partially solved as suggestions still need to be made on how to improve the analysis.
- The purpose of the analysis was clear in that the best location had to be selected.
- The scoring model is a very simplistic representation of the numerous factors that can lead to the successful location of a hotel. It has assumed that all the significant factors have been included but this is clearly not the case. Population density and the closeness of conference facilities are two excluded factors – we are sure you could list many more. It is assumed that the maximum scores represent the relative importance of each of the factors but there is no objective way to assess this. If a different perspective or different time horizon is used or indeed, different managers, these weightings and scores could change. The exercise is one of quantifying something that is essentially qualitative.
- In this case, scores have been summed but they could have been

ranked or multiplied. The result obtained does depend on the method of analysis.

- The scenario provides little information on how the weightings or scores were derived. For this approach to be effective, you do need genuine group or team activity and a managed consensus.
- The scoring model in this case has a single location (Waterside) with the highest score. However, decisions still need to be made, if two or more locations have the same score and if there are only small differences between locations. What significance could you place on a difference of one point given the level of subjectivity?
- The scoring model does give considerable scope for experimentation and we are able to ask 'what if'. For example, what if transport, workforce and grants were considered equal factors and all given a weight of 10 and the scores were scaled accordingly? Table 5.2 would change to Table 5.3. The totals would now become 33 for location Sunnyside, 34 for location Waterside and 35 for location Bankside. Location Bankside now has the highest score and would be the location recommended by such an analysis.

Table 5.3

Factor	Maximum score	Location		
		Sunnyside	Waterside	Bankside
Transport	10	5	9	4
Amenities	15	8	3	8
Workforce	10	6	7	5
Services	15	10	7	6
Expansion	10	2	4	8
Grants	10	2	4	4

Scoring models can be very useful, particularly if the data is likely to be of poor quality or difficult to quantify. However, you need to be aware of the subjectivity and simplification, and make adequate allowance. The use of a scoring model is a good example of where the problem is qualitative in nature, needs discussion and judgement, and yet the interpretation can be aided by a technique which is essentially quantitative and outcomes are assessed using numbers. You can again evaluate the model against the checklist given in the introduction to this section.

SCENARIO 15: Northbridge District Council – funding for an inner-city farm project

The urban renewal department is now looking at various ways to partially fund an inner-city farm project. There are two main sources of possible funding and you have been asked to evaluate their present worth. It is likely that the project will need both sources to proceed as planned.

One source of funds is a sum of £5000 left in trust for this type of project 3 years ago. The sum was deposited in an account with a guaranteed rate of interest of 10% per annum.

The other possible source of funds is a grant from the European Union. Following preliminary investigations, it is understood that there are three grant options:

Option 1   a lump sum now of £2000, or
Option 2   £1200 now and £1210 at the end of 1 year, or
Option 3   £1000 now, £900 at the end of 1 year and £600 at the end of 2 years

To obtain this grant will incur an immediate administrative overhead of £500 that should be included in any calculations. You have also been advised to work with an interest of 10% as this reflects the current value of money in the market place.

This scenario is going to require a number of mathematical calculations. The current value of a sum of money from the past needs to be determined and the worth now of possible future sums of money also needs to be evaluated. The important concept is the **value of money over time**. The value of money to you, or indeed a business, or any other organization depends on when it is received. £1 now is worth more than £1 next year and worth even more than £1 in 2 years' time. Which would you accept given the choice? £1 now could be saved and interest gained. The time value of money does depend on the rate of interest and the greater the rate of interest, the greater the value placed on money now. To take an extreme example, if the rate of interest were 0 there would be little incentive to save.

BACKGROUND: financial mathematics

Interest

Interest is the gain to be expected from saving a sum of money for an accepted period of time. Interest is usually quoted as a percentage rate per annum. If the interest rate per annum (usually denoted by r) is 10% then that means for each £1 invested for a year, the gain will be 10 pence.

Simple interest

Simple interest describes an arrangement where the interest earned each year is paid out and not added to the invested sum. In this case an investment of £1 will give a return each year of 10 pence but this sum will not grow. The formula for simple interest, I, is

$$I = A_0 * \frac{r}{100}$$

where A_0 is the initial sum invested and r is the rate of interest given in percentage terms (e.g. 10% or 12%).

Compound interest

If interest is compounded, **compound interest**, then the interest is added on at the end of each time period, usually a year, and the invested sum is allowed to grow. If £1 were invested for 2 years, the sum would grow to £1.10 after 1 year and to £1.21 after 2 years (the added 10 pence has also gained 1 pence interest). The formula for the end-of-year sum is

$$A_t = A_0 \left(1 + \frac{r}{100}\right)^t$$

where A_t is the sum after t years.

Present value

Present value is the worth now of a future sum of money. If the rate of interest is 10%, then the value of £1.10 promised in 1 year is now worth £1 and the value of £121 promised for 2 years' time is now worth £100. Think about it! If you are looking at a trade-off between money now and money in the future you must consider what opportunity money now gives you in monetary terms, which must depend on the gains offered by an interest rate. To determine present value you can either use the formula:

$$A_0 = A_t \left(\frac{1}{\left(1 + {r}/{100}\right)^t}\right)$$

or you can use the present value tables given as Appendix F.

Return to Scenario 15

One way to fund the inner-city farm project is to use the £5000 invested for 3 years at 10% per annum. The interest after 1 year would be 10% of £5000 which is £500 (0.10 * £5000) and is also the simple interest. A simple interest of £500 could have been paid out in each of the 3 years. However, most saving schemes retain the money and the sum is compounded, giving compound interest. This could be worked out year by year:

after 1 year:

$$\text{Sum} = £5000 + £500 \text{ (interest)}$$
$$= £5500$$

after 2 years:

$$\text{Sum} = £5500 + £550 \text{ (interest)}$$
$$= £6050$$

after 3 years:

$$\text{Sum} = £6050 + £605$$
$$= £6655$$

or the formula could be used:

$$A_t = A_0\left(1 + \frac{r}{100}\right)^t$$

$$A_3 = 5000\left(1 + \frac{10}{100}\right)^3$$

$$= 5000(1 + 0.10)^3$$

$$= 5000(1.10)^3$$

$$= 5000 * 1.331$$

$$= £6655$$

Given the calculations, we could reasonably expect £6655 for the inner-city farm project funding.

The other source of funds was through the European Union funding options:

Option 1

A lump sum of £2000 now is worth £2000 now. The immediate administrative overhead of £500 is also incurred now which leaves a present value of £1500. Where future sums of money need to be evaluated a common point of comparison is required and that is, what is that sum of money worth now?

Option 2

A sum of £1200 now is worth £1200, a sum of £1210 in 1 year is worth less the £1210 now. It can be shown that a sum of £1100 will grow to £1210 in 1 year if the rate of interest is 10% (£1100 * 1.1). It can be said that £1100 is the present value of £1210 in 1 year's time. To find the present value, we could use the formula

$$A_0 = A_t \frac{1}{\left(1 + \frac{r}{100}\right)^t}$$

$$= 1210 * \frac{1}{\left(1 + \frac{10}{100}\right)^1}$$

$$= 1210 * \frac{1}{(1.10)^1}$$

$$= 1210 * 0.9091$$

$$= £1100$$

where the value 0.9091 is called the **present value factor**, or we could find the present value using the present value tables given in Appendix F.

To use the tables, given the rate of interest of 10% and the time period of 1 year, we would look at the column headed 10% and the row corresponding to 1 year to find the value 0.9091. To find the present value, we would multiply the monetary amount by the present value factor:

$$A_0 = 1210 * 0.9091$$

$$= £1100$$

The present value of option 2 is therefore £1200 (sum now) + £1100 (the present value of the sum available in 1 year) less the immediate administrative overhead of £500 which gives £1800.

Option 3

Given the type of cashflow in option 3, a table or a spreadsheet is constructed using present value factors directly (Table 5.4). The present value or net present value of option 3 is £1814.03. Given that option 3 has the largest net present value, this is the option that would be selected on the basis of this analysis. This approach is referred to as **discounted cashflow**.

Table 5.4

Year	Cash outflow	Cash inflow	Net cash inflow	Present value factor	Present value
Now	500	1000	500		500
1		900	900	0.9091	818.19
2		600	600	0.8264	495.84
					1814.03

You are now in a position to give the advice that the sum of money from the trust is £6655 and that, on the basis of discounted cashflow analysis using an interest rate (or discount rate) of 10%, the best option is option 3 and that is worth £1814.03 now.

You can again refer to the checklist given in the introduction to this section for an evaluation of the model.

SCENARIO 16: Reale Brewery – network modelling

You are working for the marketing department of the Reale Brewery and have recently completed a report on the design of a survey to collect data on the lager market. A market research company was commissioned to produce the questionnaire and has completed this work. You still need to approve the questionnaire and can ask for modifications. The brewery has always used specialist market research companies for surveys of this kind but has decided that in this case, the marketing department should manage the survey as part of a cost reduction exercise. You have been asked to manage this project, outlining the important stages and likely completion date.

You have discussed this survey with your colleagues in the marketing department and agreed that the major tasks are as shown in Table 5.5.

Table 5.5

Activity label	Description	Immediate predecessor	Duration (days)
A	Check and agree questionnaire	–	1
B	Specify sample design	–	1
C	Test (pilot) questionnaires	A	2
D	Print questionnaires	C	4
E	Recruit interviewers	B	7
F	Train interviewers	E, C	3
G	Conduct interviews	F, D	14
H	Evaluate results	G	5

In this scenario, the project to be managed is a survey and we will look at how this can be represented by a **network** diagram. The method can be used for projects of all shapes and sizes. Project management techniques have been effectively used on diverse applications, such as the Winter Olympics, the RAC Rally and the development of new car components. Given that some the activities can be done at the same time, for example the questionnaire can be checked and agreed while the sample design is being specified, the duration of the overall project should be less than the sum of its component parts. In this scenario, the sum of the duration times (activities A to H) is 37 days and we would expect the project duration to be less than this. There is a useful contrast between the relay race and the rugby scrum. If the project is managed like a relay race, then the overall duration is going to take longer as the baton is passed from one runner (or department) to another. In contrast, if the rugby scrum analogy is used, then all the player (departments) should be pushing in the same direction (working on the same problem) at the same time. It is argued that the latter more effectively describes the team-work approach that many companies are seeking.

To use the network technique, the project, in this scenario a survey, is broken down into a series of activities. For the technique to be successfully applied, the activities need to be clearly defined, the relationship between activities clearly understood and reliable time estimates established.

BACKGROUND: networks

Activity

An **activity** is a task or job that takes time and resources, e.g. construct a sampling frame or verify debtors in a sales ledger or write out an agenda. An activity is represented by a line with an arrow (Figure 5.3). It should be noted that the method here is 'activity on the arrow' – it is not the only method.

$$\longrightarrow$$

Figure 5.3

Event

An **event** is a point in time when an activity starts or finishes, e.g. starting the construction of a sampling frame or debtors verified or agenda written. An event or **node** is represented by a circle (Figure 5.4).

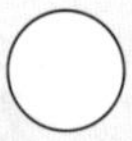

$$\bigcirc$$

Figure 5.4

Dummy activity

A **dummy activity** is used to maintain the logical links within a network but does not consume time or resources. A dummy activity is represented by a broken line with an arrow (Figure 5.5).

Figure 5.5

Network

A **network** is a combination of activities, dummy activities and events which together show how the overall project will proceed (Figure 5.6).

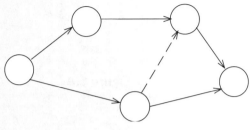

Figure 5.6

Return to Scenario 16

The network for this scenario is shown in Figure 5.7. It can be seen from the network that activity A (check and agree questionnaire) and activity B (specify sample design) can be done at the same time. Working concurrently on activities may have implications for work organization, such as the delegation of work and specialist work groups. The use of the dummy activity should also be noted as

> you can only start activity F (train interviewers) when activity C (test questionnaire) and activity E (recruit interviewers) are completed

but

> you can start activity D (print questionnaires) when activity C (test questionnaire) is complete

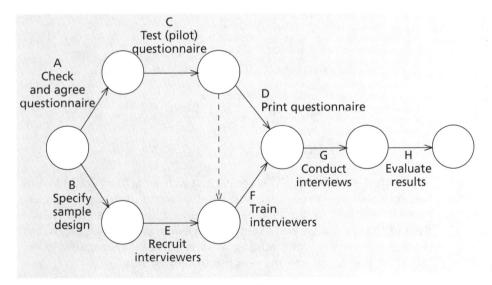

Figure 5.7

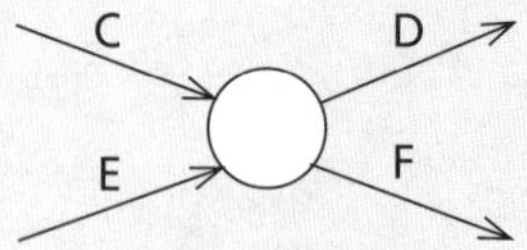

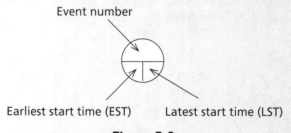

Figure 5.8

It should be noted that the representation in Figure 5.8 would be incorrect.

The network diagram does provide an effective representation of the work that has to be done. To manage the project, we also need to consider the time required by each individual activity and how these activity times amalgamate to give an overall project duration time.

STATISTICAL BACKGROUND: managing time

Notation

An event or node shows the beginning or the end of an activity. The notation in Figure 5.9 is used to identify uniquely the event (event number) and associated times.

Event number

Earliest start time (EST)   Latest start time (LST)

Figure 5.9

Earliest start time

The **earliest start time** (EST) is the earliest time an activity could begin assuming all the preceding activities are completed as soon as possible. The convention is always to begin with 0 at the first event. **Rule of thumb**: the earliest event times are found by moving forward through the network and adding activity times. If there are two or more activities leading to an event use the largest sum.

Latest start time

The **latest start time** (LST) is the latest time an activity can begin without causing a delay in the overall duration of the project. Rule of thumb: the latest start time is found by moving backwards through the network from right to left, and subtracting activity times. If there are two or more activities leading back to an event use the smallest figure.

Critical path

The **critical path** is defined by those activities that must be completed on time for the project to be completed on time. Rule of thumb: generally, the critical path will go through all those activities where the EST is equal to the LST. However, to be sure that an activity is critical, we should check that a measure call 'total float' is equal to 0. In this context, 'float' is a measure of how long an activity can be delayed; clearly there is no scope to delay a critical activity.

Total float

Total float for an activity is the difference between the time available for that activity and the duration of that activity. The total float, sometimes referred as the **slack**, is the amount of time by which the duration or an activity can be extended without that activity becoming critical. The total float for an activity with a start event i and a finish event j can be found as follows:

Total float = LST for j – EST for i – duration time of activity

Return to Scenario 16

The network with EST and LST is shown in Figure 5.10. The critical path is shown by // on the activities B, E, F, G and H.

TASK

CHECK THE FIGURES GIVEN IN THIS NETWORK.

An examination of the last event, in this case event number 8, identifies the duration of the project as 30 days provided the critical activities are kept to time.

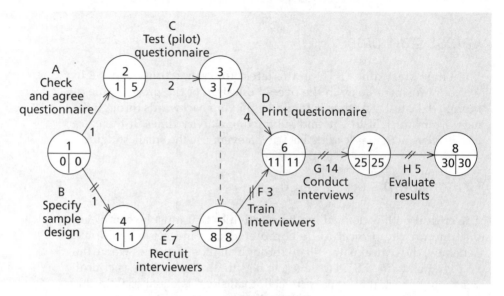

Figure 5.10

The events where the EST and LST are equal provide a good indication of the route followed by the critical path. To determine the critical path, or often, for practical reasons, to check the correctness of the critical path indicated by the equality of the EST and LST, we need to be sure that only those activities with zero total float are considered critical. The determination of the total float for activity C is shown in Figure 5.11 for illustration. The total float available on activity C, test (pilot) questionnaire, is found by considering that part of the network. The total float is therefore $7 - 1 - 2 = 4$ days.

Table 5.6 provides a useful summary of those activities which are critical and therefore cannot be delayed, and also a useful summary of those activities which can be delayed.

The management of any project is likely to involve the allocation of limited resources. It is possible that a non-critical activity is delayed by the total float or less, to release the necessary resources to ensure the critical activities are completed on time.

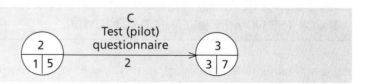

Figure 5.11

Table 5.6

Activity label	Description	LST_i	EST_i	Duration (days)	Total float	Critical path
A	Check and agree questionnaire	5	0	1	4	
B	Specify sample design	1	0	1	0	*
C	Test (pilot) questionnaires	7	1	2	4	
D	Print questionnaires	11	3	4	4	
E	Recruit interviewers	8	1	7	0	*
F	Train interviewers	11	8	3	0	*
G	Conduct interviews	25	11	14	0	*
H	Evaluate results	30	25	5	0	*

* Indicates that the activity is on the critical path.

The checklist given in the introduction can again be used with such a problem-solving technique:

- It is important with any project management activity that the requirements are clearly understood. There is no point in building a Rolls-Royce if the customer want a Mini! Defining the activities is probably the most difficult part of project management and will require a real understanding of the work involved.
- The objectives should clarify the purpose of the project and give a realistic time scale.
- A number of assumptions will need to be made, for example, the weather will allow work to continue without delay on a house-building project. However, an examination of the assumptions will allow the development of contingency plans and any misjudgement to emerge.
- In this scenario, time has been analysed to identify the critical activities (B, E, F, G and H) and determine the overall project duration of 30 days (the sum of duration times is 37 days). It is also possible to include cost considerations and uncertainty but the modelling becomes more complex and you would need to refer to more advanced texts.
- The timing of activities is unlikely to be exact; we do get unseasonally bad weather, for example, which can affect some activities, and we generally have to work with estimates. In some cases, there may be those that can see a benefit in exaggerating the

difficulty of a job and the time it will take. The determination of realistic times can require considerable management judgement.

- A network diagram is an effective management tool that clearly reveals the critical activities and the times required to proceed through the project.
- The time analysis of a network does allow a number of 'what if' type questions. For example, what if activity E, recruit interviewers, took 8 days rather than 7 days? In this case the activity is on the critical path and the project would take one day longer, i.e. become 31 days. Or, what if activity D, print questionnaires, took 6 days rather than 4 days? In this case the activity has a total float of 4 days and a delay of 2 days would make no difference.

Conclusions

Effectively solving problems is likely to be one of the biggest challenges we face. Merely to use descriptive narrative with a few figures will limit the way we can develop our ideas and generate interesting and creative solutions. Using models, whether to plan the layout of a new garden or to manage the stock for a large retailer, will allow us to visualize the problem more effectively, generate solutions and communicate these solutions.

In this section we have only attempted to present a few illustrative models. It is known that modelling does solve business and other problems. You may find it useful when confronted with another problem to consider what parameters and variables describe this problem and what models may apply. Not all models are quantitative. You may be familiar with Maslow's hierarchy of needs, which one could argue is just a model of behaviour.

TASK

1. COPY OUT A SUPPLY AND DEMAND GRAPH FROM AN INTRO-DUCTORY ECONOMICS TEXT.
2. PRESENT THE CASE THAT THIS GRAPH IS ONLY A MODEL.

Questions

1. You are able to hire car engine diagnostic equipment for £6000 a year. To perform the diagnostic test on a typical car takes about 8 minutes at a cost to the business of about £3.00. Market research indicates that you will be able to charge £3.80.

(a) Complete the table (given as spreadsheet 5.2) and identify the break-even point.
(b) Graph the revenue and total cost functions against the annual number of tests on the same graph using spreadsheet 5.2 completed in part (a). Identify the break-even point on this graph and shade and label the areas of loss and profit.
(c) Briefly outline the consequences of the following 'what if' scenarios:
  (i) The fixed cost of hiring the diagnostic equipment increases to £7000 per annum.
  (ii) The charge has to be reduced to £3.60
(d) Given that this equipment is only available for 40 hours each week and there are only 50 working weeks in each year, comment on the feasibility of this project.

SPREADSHEET 5.2

Annual number of tests	Fixed cost £s	Variable cost £s	Total cost £s	Revenue £s	Profit or loss £s
0					
2500					
5000					
7500					
10000					

2. You have been asked to review the purchasing policy for tyres of a public sector transport organization. The tyres cost £50 each and currently 100 are ordered each month to meet the fairly steady demand. It has been estimated that it will cost £10 to hold a tyre in stock for one year and that the cost of placing each order is £15. You are required to:
(a) work out the total annual cost of the current policy of ordering 100 tyres each month;
(b) determine the economic order quantity using the information given and the associated total annual cost;
(c) compare the answers obtained in parts (a) and (b) and comment on the practical implications of any change in policy.

3. A nightclub stocks an expensive champagne which it purchases for £26 per bottle. Demand only averages about 60 bottles a year. The cost of an order (to France) is about £20 when all the elements of cost are allowed for. The cost of holding has two components: a storage cost of £5 per bottle per year and a capital cost of 20% (of purchase price) per annum.
   (a) Determine the economic order quantity and the associated total annual cost.
   (b) What would your advice be if, in the future, the champagne could only be bought in cases of 12?

4. Having just completed a course, using this book, you now find you have three job options A, B and C. The choice is a difficult one and you have decided to use a 'scoring model' to evaluate them. You have identified six factors of particular importance to you and assigned a maximum score (or weight). You have then given each job option a score on each of the factors as shown in Table 5.7. Evaluate the scoring model and clearly identify the preferred outcome (A, B or C).

Table 5.7

Factor	Weight	A	B	C
Conditions	10	6	8	4
Holidays	8	4	7	5
Distance	8	7	4	7
Training	6	5	3	4
Pay	20	16	18	10
Other benefits	6	5	2	3

5. You are now working in the marketing department and have been asked to evaluate the following scoring exercise on two potential products A and B. The results are shown in Table 5.8. You have been asked to evaluate these results using an appropriate method. You will also have to produce a brief report which can make recommendations and can consider the adequacy of the method.

6. An investment of £6000 is being made on your behalf to mature in 3 years' time. You have been given the following options:

   option 1 to invest this money in a simple interest scheme with a rate of interest of 12% per annum;

   option 2 to invest this money in a compound interest scheme with a rate of interest of 10% per annum;

option 3 to invest this money in a compound interest scheme with a rate of interest of 8% on the first £1000, 10% for the next £2000 and 14% for the remainder.

Evaluate these options and argue the case for your preferred option. You can also argue a case for having the money now, but you know that this case has got to be convincing to the trustees to have any chance of success.

Table 5.8

Factor	Level	Product A	Product B	Score
Appeal	Current customers		✓	3
	Mostly current customers	✓		2
	Some current customers			1
	All new customers			0
Stability	Highly stable		✓	3
	Fairly stable			2
	Unstable	✓		1
	Highly unstable			0
Sector	High growth			3
	Some growth	✓		2
	Stationary		✓	1
	Decline			0
Promotion	Little required			3
	Moderate requirement	✓		2
	High requirement		✓	1
	Extensive requirement			0

Table 5.9

Year (end of)	Project 1 (£)	Project 2 (£)
1	−1000	0
2	0	1000
3	1000	1000
4	2000	1000
5	4000	2000

7. You have been asked to evaluate two projects. The first project initially makes a loss and then becomes very profitable by the fifth year, whereas the returns are more steady with the second project. There is some uncertainty as to what discount rate to use and you have been asked to evaluate both projects using a rate of 10% per annum and 15% per annum. Prepare a short report on your findings. The cash flows expected over the next 5 years are given in Table 5.9.

8. You have agreed to co-ordinate an advertising campaign for an environmental group. The main activities and their corresponding duration in days are shown in Table 5.10. The group would like you to draw a network diagram for presentational purposes and to identify the critical activities.

Table 5.10

Activity label	Description	Immediate predecessor	Duration (days)
A	Agree objectives with co-ordinating committee	–	1
B	Prepare media plan	A	3
C	Prepare draft artwork	A	5
D	Book media	B	4
E	Approve artwork	B, C	2
F	Print advertising	E	3
G	Approval by co-ordinating committee	D, F	1

9. You are planning to start a new business and have been given advice on all the activities that have to be completed. To help you launch this new business you have decided to represent this information in the form of a network diagram. The information is summarized in Table 5.11
   (a) Determine the critical path and the overall duration of the project.
   (b) Explain the consequences of the following:
       (i) What if the purchase of office equipment took 4 days?
       (ii) What if the market research took 4 days?
       (iii) What if the identification of suppliers took 7 days?

Table 5.11

Activity label	Description	Immediate predecessor	Duration (days)
A	Market research	–	5
B	Secure finance	A	2
C	Obtain premises	A	10
D	Connect gas	C, B	1
E	Purchase office equipment	C, B	3
F	Connect electricity	C, B	1
G	Identify suppliers	B	5
H	Obtain stock	G	5
I	Test office equipment	E, F	1
J	Safety inspection	D, I	1

Section 6
Uncertainty

Objectives

After studying this section you should be able to:

- understand and explain the concept of probability;

- calculate probabilities for a range of problems;

- know when to add or multiply probabilities;

- understand and apply the concept of conditional probability;

- calculate and explain expected values;

- construct and evaluate a decision tree diagram;

- apply decision criteria;

- distinguish between discrete and continuous probability;

- extract probability for a normal distribution table.

Introduction

This section is concerned with the effective representation of numerical information when events are uncertain. Individuals and organizations have to make decisions on the basis of what they know and what they think might happen. The use of available statistical information, the application of forecasting methods and development of models can all provide a better understanding of the factors that will influence future events, but in many circumstances will not reflect the reality of an organization unless the element of chance is included. The situation faced might be a relatively simple one, such as 'we can only build a wall if the weather is dry' or more complex, like 'we believe there is a good chance that customers will accept a new product in the international market place'. The fact that we can rarely be certain about the weather (in Britain at least!) or about future customer behaviour means we need to develop the language and notation of uncertainty.

Problems that have a certain outcome are referred to as **deterministic**. Given a fixed cost, a unit cost and a price, for example, we can work out the break-even level of output using the approach outlined in Section 5. There is no uncertainty about these parameters as given in the problem (although this is unlikely in the workplace – another probability statement!) and there is generally one correct answer. However, there are a range of problems where the outcomes are uncertain and these are referred to as **probabilistic**. An insurance company knows, for example, that it is taking a risk with each motorist it insures. The company, and the motorist, would like to complete each year without a claim. However, the insurance company takes a calculable risk, knowing that some motorists will make a claim but the majority will not. In this case, it is expected that the profit from the majority will exceed the losses from those that submit successful claims. What the insurance company will never know but would like to know in advance is which motorists will need to make a claim. The insurance company can only assign a measure of chance to each motorist representing historical risk.

SCENARIO 17: Midwest Bank – new business opportunities for a high street bank

You are now working for a well-known 'high street' bank. Your branch has tried to develop its portfolio of work by offering an improved service to those involved in business. The service has already generated a number of new opportunities for the bank and you have been asked to investigate these. The bank is particularly interested in the type of opportunity available, and has kept careful records showing whether a new opportunity comes from the manufacturing sector or non-manufacturing, from a new business or an established one, from a small business or a larger one. All these terms have been clarified by the bank and standard definitions used. The information available on the new opportunities has been presented to you in Table 6.1.

Table 6.1

	Manufacturing		Non-manufacturing	
	Established business	*New business*	*Established business*	*New business*
Small business	90	105	12	18
Larger business	15	30	60	75

The bank is particularly interested in the chances that new business opportunities will come from:

- manufacturing
- small business
- established business
- either a new business or a small business.

There has been an ongoing debate within the bank about the opportunities from established business and your branch manager would answers to the following questions: "What is the chance of a new business opportunity from an established business given the additional information that it is a manufacturing business?' and 'What is the chance of a new business opportunity from an established business given the additional information that it is a larger business?'

The terms **chance** and **probability** tend to be used interchangeably. A dictionary will define chance in terms of 'an unforeseen occurrence', 'risk' or 'likelihood' and we will hear expressions like 'there is a good chance of success' or 'no chance'. Where uncertainty is assessed in a subjective way, often expressed in terms of chance, we do refer to **subjective probability**. Being able to judge the chance of future events is important but what we will attempt to do in this section is to build a rigorous framework which will allow the measurement of probability and will also accommodate the language of chance. In statistics, probability refers to the measurement of chance. In Scenario 17 we are given historical data which will allow the calculation of probability. It is, however, a matter of inference whether these calculated probabilities will be good predictors of the likelihood of future events.

STATISTICAL BACKGROUND: some rules of probability

Measuring probability

The probability of an event, say A, must lie in the range 0 to 1. This can be written as follows:

$$0 \leq P(A) \leq 1$$

where $P(A)$ means the probability of event A. The scale is restricted to the range 0 to 1, with numbers outside this range being meaningless in terms of probability measures. The value 0 means the event cannot happen and the value 1 means the event is certain to happen.

Probabilities can be calculated on the basis of relative frequency. If we are considering sample data then

$$P(A) = \frac{f}{n}$$

where f is the number of times (or frequency) event A happens and n is the size of the sample or total number of trials. As a simple example, if we consider a fair coin being tossed, then we would expect half the outcomes to show a head. In this case the probability of a head would be $\frac{1}{2}$.

Adding probabilities

If events do not overlap (we will illustrate this later) then the sum of all the probabilities must equal 1. If we think about the fair coin again, then the probability of a head plus the probability of a tail must equal 1 because (in theory) no other outcome is possible.

If we are considering alternative outcomes, and it is acceptable that one or the other happens, then we add probabilities. In terms of a general rule, we can write

$$P(A \text{ or } B) = P(A) + P(B)$$

where events A and B are mutually exclusive (statistical language for no overlap). However, if events do overlap then we need to avoid counting twice any outcomes included in both A and B. In this case

$$P(A \text{ or } B) = P(A) + P(B) - P(A \text{ and } B)$$

A simple example will illustrate the use of this formula. We know a fair die has outcomes 1 to 6. The probability of an 'even number' is $\frac{3}{6}$ (outcomes 2, 4 or 6) and the probability of a number '4 or less' is $\frac{4}{6}$ (outcomes 1, 2, 3 or 4), but the probability of an 'even number or a number 4 or less' is not $\frac{7}{6}$ since the outcomes 2 and 4 are counted twice. The outcomes of interest are 1, 2, 3, 4 and 6 giving a probability of $\frac{5}{6}$. In terms of the formula

$$
\begin{aligned}
P(\text{an 'even number' or 'a number 4 or less'}) &= \frac{3}{6} + \frac{4}{6} - \frac{2}{6} \\
&= \frac{5}{6}
\end{aligned}
$$

Return to Scenario 17

Probability has been defined in terms of relative frequency: $P(A) = f/n$. To determine probability then, we need to find this sample size or number of trials (n) and the frequency of event A. Returning to Scenario 17, we can find the sample size by adding all the cell values. This total is 405 and represents the number of new business opportunities considered by the bank. Given that the bank is interested in the chances of new business opportunities from manufacturing, small business and established business we will need to consider each in turn.

The number of new business opportunities coming from manufacturing is

$$90 + 105 + 15 + 30 = 240$$

Check that you agree with these figures extracted from Table 6.1. The probability of new business opportunity coming from manufacturing is therefore

P (new business opportunity from manufacturing)

$$= \frac{240}{405}$$
$$= 0.59 \quad \text{(to 2 decimal places)}$$

The number of new business opportunities coming from small businesses is

$$90 + 105 + 12 + 18 = 225$$

Again check that you agree with these figures. The probability of a new business opportunity coming from a small business is

P (new business opportunity from small business)

$$= \frac{225}{405}$$
$$= 0.59 \quad \text{(to 2 decimal places)}$$

The number of new business opportunities coming from established business is

$$90 + 15 + 12 + 60 = 177$$

The probability of a new business opportunity coming from an established business is

P (new business opportunity from established business)

$$= \frac{177}{405}$$

$$= 0.44 \quad \text{(to 2 decimal places)}$$

The bank is also interested in the joint probability that a new business opportunity comes from either a new business or a small business. The number of new business opportunities coming from new business is

$$105 + 30 + 18 + 75 = 228$$

The number of new opportunities coming from small business is

$$90 + 105 + 12 + 18 = 225$$

If these two figures are added (228 + 225) the total of 453 exceeds even the total number of business opportunities! What has happened? The 105 new, small businesses have been included in both subtotals and have therefore been counted twice. The two categories of business are not mutually exclusive – they do overlap. Using the formula we get

$$P(A \text{ and } B) = P(A) + P(B) - P(A + B)$$

$$= \frac{228}{405} + \frac{225}{405} + \frac{105}{405}$$

$$= \frac{348}{405}$$

$$= 0.86 \quad \text{(to 2 decimal places)}$$

There are a number of useful points that we can note at this stage:

- Probabilities need not be complex or difficult to calculate. In many cases you may be seeking only the proportion (our relative frequency measure of probability) of people or items or things that are described in a particular way, e.g. non-smokers, defective items, small businesses.
- Probabilities are often given as percentages, e.g. the percentage of new business opportunities coming from manufacturing is 59%. It is often convenient and effective to present probabilities as percentages as these are more readily understood, but when using the formula you should always work with the proportion (fraction of 1 form).
- Having found a particular probability, it is easy to find the probability of those not included. The probability of new business opportunities not in manufacturing is

P (new business opportunity from non-manufacturing)

$$= 1 - 0.59$$

$$= 0.41$$

The same result could have been found in a more time-consuming way using the figures from Table 6.1:

$$\frac{12+18+60+75}{4055} = \frac{165}{405} = 0.41 \quad \text{(to 2 decimal places)}$$

- This data comes from one branch and the probabilities only apply to this data set. We could not expect to make inferences about the banking sector as a whole or indeed the economy on the basis of such information. The business of a particular branch will depend very critically on its location. We would also have to justify any assertion that these probabilities will also apply in the future even though we would expect them to be a reasonable guide.

We will need some more statistical background before you can consider the two questions of interest to your branch manager.

STATISTICAL BACKGROUND: *conditional probability*

Additional information

When solving a problem we often have additional information to work with. If, for example, the police know that a get-away car was red, then the number of cars included in any search is reduced and the chances of success increased. **Conditional probability** is written as follows:

$$P(B/A)$$

where this is the probability of B given that A has already happened.

Return to Scenario 17

If we consider the first question, 'What is the chance of a new business opportunity from an established business given the additional information that it is a manufacturing business?' we need now only consider the 240(90 + 105 + 15 + 30) new opportunities from manufacturing business. Of the 240 opportunities only 105(90 + 15) were from established business. The conditional probability is therefore

P(new opportunity from an established business/ manufacturing business)

$$= \frac{105}{240}$$

$$= 0.44 \quad \text{(to 2 decimal places)}$$

In the second question we had to consider 'What is the chance of a new business opportunity from an established business given the additional information that it is a larger business?' The number of larger business is $180(15 + 30 + 60 + 75)$ of which $75(15 + 60)$ are established. The conditional probability is

P(new business opportunity from an established business/larger business)

$$= \frac{75}{180}$$

$$= 0.42 \quad \text{(to 2 decimal places)}$$

As we will see, conditional probability is particularly important when we consider models of decision making where invariably additional information does exist.

SCENARIO 18: Northbridge District Council – funding for an inner-city farm project

You are working for an urban renewal department and have just completed an exercise to evaluate possible ways of partially funding an inner-city farm project. One source of funds is a sum of money that has been left in trust and another source is a grant from the European Union. However, you will still need to wait for confirmation that these sources of funds will be forthcoming. The inner-city farm project will need both sources of funds if it is to go ahead. The director of the project is concerned that any delay in the funding will jeopardize the project and she is now pressing you for a date when these funds will be available. There is some uncertainty about when the confirmation of funding will be given and you have drawn up a table to reflect your state of knowledge and judgement. The table gives the chance (probability) of confirmation being in 1 week, 2 weeks or 3 weeks for each source separately. You believe there is a 10% chance that the grant may be lost. The information is given as Table 6.2.

To be in a position to advise the director of the project you have decided to calculate the chance (the director of the project claims that she cannot understand probability) that the funds from both sources will be confirmed in the first week, both confirmed by the second week and both confirmed by the third week.

Table 6.2

| Number | Probability | |
of weeks	Funds from trust	Funds from grant
1	0.4	0.1
2	0.6	0.3
3		0.5

STATISTICAL BACKGROUND: *some more rules of probability*

Multiplication of probabilities

To calculate the probability that two events will both happen we need to refer to the multiplicative rules of probability. You may be familiar with the example that if the probability of a head from a fair coin is $\frac{1}{2}$, then the probability of two heads is $\frac{1}{2} * \frac{1}{2}$ which is equal to $\frac{1}{4}$.

If events A and B are independent (they do not influence each other) then

$$P(A \text{ and } B) = P(A) * P(B)$$

If the events are not independent, and the probability of event B is influenced by event A then

$$P(A \text{ and } B) = P(A) * P(B/A)$$

where $P(B/A)$ is the conditional probability that event B occurs given that event A has already happened.

Sample space

The sample space refers to a complete listing of all possible outcomes and often provides an effective way of solving probability problems. If we again consider the fair coin example, if the coin were tossed twice the possible outcomes would be

HH, HT, TH, TT

where TH denote tail on the first go and a head on the second go. Given that all the outcomes are equally likely, and there are four outcomes, then the probability of two heads (HH) must be a $\frac{1}{4}$.

In Scenario 18, the sources of funds are independent. The probability of joint events can be found by multiplying corresponding probabilities. The probabilities of getting the funds confirmed from both sources in the first week, second week and third week are calculated below.

Funds from both sources in first week

P(confirmation from trust and from grant in 1 week)

= P(confirmation from trust in 1 week)

* P(confirmation from grant in 1 week)

= 0.4 * 0.1

= 0.04

Funds from both sources confirmed by second week

In this case, before we apply the multiplicative rule of probability, we need to consider how this outcome can be achieved. It is possible that both sums are confirmed in the second week but it could be that one sum is confirmed in the first week and the other sum in the second week. The possible combinations are as follows:

- confirmation of trust in week 1 and confirmation of grant in week 2, or
- confirmation of trust in week 2 and confirmation of grant in week 1, or
- confirmation of trust in week 2 and confirmation of grant in week 2.

There are three possible ways that both sources can be confirmed by week 2 as indicated by the 'or'. What we need to do is calculate the probabilities for the three alternatives and then sum these probabilities. As a rule of thumb, where the operation is AND we multiply probabilities and where the operation is OR we add the probabilities.

P(confirmation from trust and from grant by second week)

= 0.4 * 0.3 or 0.6 * 0.1 or 0.6 * 0.3

= 0.12 + 0.06 + 0.18

= 0.36

Funds from both sources confirmed by third week

The sum from the trust fund should be confirmed in the first or second week; the only source of uncertainty is the grant. We could infer that the probability of funds being confirmed from both sources in the third week is 0.5 (directly from Table 6.2) as only the probability from the grant applies. However, we could consider the possible combinations as follows:

- confirmation of trust in week 1 and confirmation of grant in week 3, or
- confirmation of trust in week 2 and confirmation of grant in week 3.

P (confirmation from trust and from grant by third week)

$$= 0.4 * 0.5 \text{ or } 0.6 * 0.5$$
$$= 0.2 + 0.3$$
$$= 0.5$$

For problems of relatively small scale it is possible to show all the outcomes with associated probabilities and sum appropriately. In Scenario 18, it is possible to show all the probabilities in the form of a table (Table 6.3). It can

Table 6.3

Confirmation of money (in weeks)		
Sum from trust	Sum from grant	Probability
1	1	$0.4 * 0.1 = 0.04$
1	2	$0.4 * 0.3 = 0.12$
1	3	$0.4 * 0.5 = 0.2$
1	Not confirmed	$0.4 * 0.1 = 0.04$
2	1	$0.6 * 0.1 = 0.06$
2	2	$0.6 * 0.3 = 0.18$
2	3	$0.6 * 0.5 = 0.3$
2	Not confirmed	$0.6 * 0.1 = 0.06$

be easily seen from such a table that even if the sum from the trust fund is confirmed in the first or second week there is a 0.1 chance (0.04 + 0.06) that the grant will not be confirmed and the project could not go ahead (although such a decision could still be open to some negotiation).

TASK

USE TABLE 6.3 TO CONFIRM THE RESULTS ALREADY OBTAINED BY USING THE FORMULA DIRECTLY.

SCENARIO 19: Bailey Group Hotels – development of hotel leisure facilities

The hotel group that you are working for are considering the development of leisure facilities in one of their smaller hotels. The existing facilities contribute £12 000 per annum to revenue once direct staff costs are allowed for. Two proposal have been submitted for the development of the facilities:

Proposal 1 that the facilities are substantially improved at a cost of £36 000 per annum. The contribution to revenue after direct staff costs are allowed for is expected to be £60 000 per annum if successful, but only £16 000 if unsuccessful. The chances of success have been judged to be 70%.

Proposal 2 that the facilities are modestly enhanced at a cost of £10 000 per annum. The contribution to revenue after direct staff costs are allowed for is expected to be £25 000 per annum if successful, but only £14 000 if unsuccessful. The chances of success have been judged to be 60%.

You have been asked to evaluate the proposals using suitable decision criteria. You have also been asked to consider what the effect would be if the chances of success for Proposal 1 were increased to 80%.

Choices are rarely as straightforward as they appear in this scenario. The number of alternatives are generally far greater and most problems have a qualitative aspect. However, choices need to be made and we can consider ways of informing this choice.

STATISTICAL BACKGROUND: decision trees

Decision trees

Decision trees refer to a diagrammatic representation of the options and possible outcomes being confronted in a particular problem. Given that there are a number of approaches to a problem and given that an approach can have several outcomes, the representation is by successive branching.

Notation

Within a decision tree, there are points at which a decision needs to be made, denoted by a decision node □ and points that show that the outcome is subject to chance, denoted by a chance node ○.

Expected value

The basis for decisions (the decision criteria), is usually expected value (EV), sometimes referred to as expected monetary value (EMV). Expected value is the return you would get, or expect on average. If you consider, for example, a game of chance with a fair coin where you win £1 if a head is tossed but lose £2 if a tail is tossed, on average you would expect to lose 50 pence per game. To determine expected value, each possible outcome is multiplied by the corresponding probability and the results added. This can be written as:

$$E(x) = \sum(x * P(x))$$

where $\sum$ means 'the sum of', and $E(x)$ is the expected value of x.
 In the case of our simple coin game:

$$E(x) = £1 * \tfrac{1}{2} + (-£2) * \tfrac{1}{2} = -£0.50$$

Other decision criteria

In this section, we will only consider two other decision criteria:

Maximax   In this case, the best possible outcome is identified for each option or alternative. The option with the largest (best) outcome is selected – this is sometimes referred to as the 'best of the best'. This is the criterion of the optimist who is hoping to win and is hoping to win the largest possible amount. This is the criterion of the risk taker.

Maximin   In this case, the worst possible outcome is identified for each option or alternative. Then the option with the largest (or best) worst outcome is selected – this is sometimes referred to as the 'best of the worst'. This is the criterion of the pessimist who expects the worst from each option and makes a choice to give the best return from the worst outcome. This is an example of risk avoidance and does model some business behaviour.

Return to Scenario 19

The decision tree for Scenario 19 is shown below:

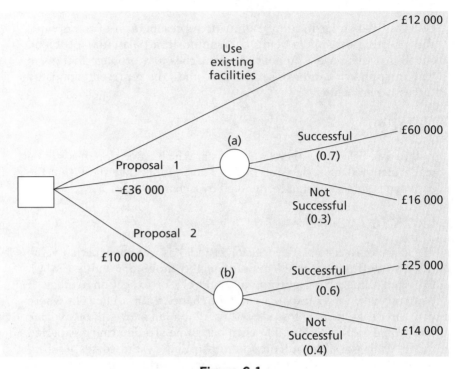

Figure 6.1

It should be noted that three choices actually exist; to continue with existing facilities, to implement proposal 1 and to implement proposal 2. In many case, the option of doing nothing should not be ignored! Where the probability is given for 'success', then by implication the other outcome is 'not successful' with a probability equal to 1 − P(success). For each of these options the expected value can be found:

- **Use existing facilities** The expected return in this case is the actual return of £12 000 as no uncertainty exists about the outcome.
- **Implement proposal 1** The expected value at the chance node (shown as node (a) on the decision tree diagram) is:

£60 000 ∗ 0.7 + £16 000 ∗ 0.3

= £42 000 + £4800

= £46 800

To determine the expected value of the proposal, we need to subtract the cost:

£46 800 − £36 000

= £10 800

The expected return from proposal 1 is £10 800

- **Implement proposal 2** The expected value at the chance node (shown as node (b) on the decision tree diagram) is:

£25 000 * 0.6 + £14 000 * 0.4

= £15 000 + £5600

= £20 600

To determine the expected value of the proposal, we need to subtract the cost:

£20 600 – £10 000

= £10 600

The expected return from proposal 2 is £10 600

On the basis of expected value, the option giving the highest return is to continue to use existing facilities. However, it needs to be understood that the expected value is what will be achieved on average with repeated decisions. If the decision is being made once then you are either successful or not successful. If we consider proposal 1 for example, if it is successful the return will be £24 000 (£60 000 – £36 000) and if it is unsuccessful the loss will be £20 000 (£16 000 – £36 000). The expected value criteria only works well with repeated decisions or trials. In the case of the insurance company, the expected value can be calculated over many policies and the process of averaging is valid. The decision criteria of maximax and maximin are alternatives to expected value. The 'best' and 'worst' outcomes are shown for each of the proposals in the table below:

Option	'best' outcome	'worst' outcome
use existing facilities	£12 000	£12 000
proposal 1	£24 000 (£60 000 – £36 000)	–£20 000 (£16 000 – £36 000)
proposal 2	£15 000 (£25 000 – £10 000)	£4000 (£14 000 – £10 000)

On the basis of the maximax criteria, proposal 1 would be accepted (the best of the best) and on the basis of the maximin criteria the existing facilities would continue to be used (the best of the worst).

The use of decision trees and decision criteria can inform the management of the hotel but essentially there remains a judgement as to which criteria are most appropriate and to what extent the qualitative factors should be weighted. One major advantage of this of this type of modelling is that 'what if' type questions can be considered. In the scenario, there was the question of what would happen if the chances of success for proposal 1 could be increased to 80%. In this case the expected value at the chance node (node (b) on the decision tree diagram) becomes:

£60 000 * 0.8 + £16 000 * 0.2

= £48 000 + £3200

= £51 200

To determine the expected value of the proposal, we again need to subtract the cost:

£51 200 – £36 000

= £15 200

The expected return now from proposal 1 is £15 200

Proposal 2 now has the largest expected value and would become selected on this criterion. The decisions made on the basis of maximax or maximin do not change. As maximax and maximin only consider actual outcomes and not probability they do not take account of increased or decreased chance (or risk). Criteria that cannot take account of probability, whether precisely measured or perceived clearly are very limited in the way they model the decision making process. However, as discussed above, probability effectively describes a long-term average. If you are taking a single decision a measure of chance may be informative but it is a matter of judgement as to the consequences of getting that decision right or wrong.

SCENARIO 19: a supplement

The management group are concerned about the cost implications of proposal 1 and insist that a market research exercise is completed before such a proposal is considered. The market research exercise will cost £2000 and previous experience suggests that on 80% of occasions the report is positive. The accepted view is, that if the market research report is positive then a 90% chance of success could be expected for the proposal whereas if the market research report is received, the management can choose to proceed with proposal 1 or continue to use the existing facilities.

The decision process has become more complex and this is reflected in the new decision tree in Figure 6.2. Decisions now have to be made on the market research report and the options available (in that order). Even though it is natural to work from the left to the right, with the more complex decision tree with decisions at two or more stages, we need to work back from the right to the left. The procedure of working back through a decision tree is called **rollback**. Working back through the decision tree we get:

At chance node (a) expected value $= £60\,000 * 0.9 + £16\,000 * 0.1$

$= £55\,600$

At chance node (b) expected value $= £60\,000 * 0.3 + £16\,000 * 0.7$

$= £29\,200$

At chance node (c) expected value $= £20\,600$ as before

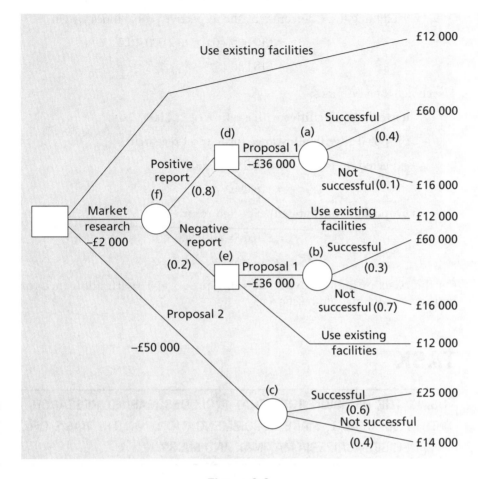

Figure 6.2

At decision node (d) the expected value of proposal 1 is

$$= £55\ 600 - £36\ 000$$

$$= £19\ 600$$

and the (expected) return from existing facilties is £12 000 at decision node (d) the choice would always be proposal 1 with the expected return of £19 600

At decision node (e) the expected value of proposal 1 is

$$= £29\ 200 - £36\ 000$$

$$= -£6800$$

and the (expected) return from existing facilities is £12 000 at decision node (e), the choice would then always be to continue with exisiting facilities. This decision is logical given that a negative market research report would lead us to reject proposal 1.

At chance node (f) we would pursue proposal 1 with an expected return of £119 600 if the report were positive and continue with the existing facilitires with a return of £12 000 if the report were negative.

Weighting these outcomes by the respective probabilities we get

$$= £19\,600 * 0.8 + £12\,000 * 0.2$$

$$= £18\,080$$

The choice then becomes:

use existing facilities with a return of £12 000

proposal 1 (with allowance for market research)

expected return	$= £18\,080 - £2000$
	$= £16\,080$

proposal 2 (unchanged) expected return

$$= £20\,600 - £10\,000$$

$$= £10\,600$$

On the basis of highest expected value proposal 1 (with allowance for market research) would be chosen.

TASK

> **USING THE DECISION TREE THAT INCLUDES MARKET RESEARCH WITH PROPOSAL 1, MAKE RECOMMENDATIONS ON THE BASIS OF THE DECISION CRITERIA MAXIMAX AND MAXIMIN.**

SCENARIO 20: The Stochastic Theatre Group

The Stochastic Theatre Group need to decide the ticket price for their pantomime production. They know that the cost of production will work out at £1000 for each performance and that demand will vary. It is generally accepted by the group that if the price is set at £10 then the numbers for each performance will average 120 with a standard deviation of 15 (they have read Section 2 of this book!). It is also accepted that if the price were increased to £12 then demand for each performance is likely to fall to an average of 100 with a standard deviation of 20. Given your experience with statistical techniques, the group have asked you to work out for each price the probability of breaking even and the expected profit. You have been advised by the authors that demand follows a normal distribution.

In this scenario there is a fixed cost of £1000 for each performance and no unit cost – an additional person in the audience does not add to the cost of production. Therefore at a ticket price of £10, 100 people will be needed to break even and at a ticket price of £12, 83.33 people will needed to break even (we will leave the $\frac{1}{3}$ of a person for now to retain that accuracy within the calculations). To work out the probabilities of breaking even we will need additional statistical background.

STATISTICAL BACKGROUND: the normal distribution

Discrete and continuous measurement

There is important distinction between measurement that is **discrete** and measurement that is **continuous**. Discrete measurement is generally the result of counting, e.g. the number of heads shown by a fair coin or the number shown by a die. The probability assigned to discrete outcomes is referred to as discrete probability and is typically found by using the 'rules' of probability already outlined in this section. Continuous measurement can be represented by the continuum of the ruler scale and can be as precise as the measurement instrument. Typical examples of continuous measurement would be time, weight and height. We could quote the time to complete a job as being 23 seconds or 23.4 seconds or 23.41 seconds or 23.414 9583 seconds depending upon our working accuracy. Probability for continuous measurement is found by using a probability distribution like the normal distribution. When the numbers involved become large, such as monetary values, the normal distribution is often accepted as a reasonable approximation.

The normal distribution

The normal distribution produces a bell-shaped curve as shown in Figure 6.3. It is a probability distribution, so the area under the curve is equal to 1 (you should be able to measure something). The curve is defined by two parameters: the mean and the standard deviation. Given that measurement is continuous you cannot read off a probability of a precise point but need to find the area under the curve corresponding to a range. The range could be described in a variety of ways, such as 'less than 100' or 'between 2.54 and 8.97' or 'greater than 34'. The probabilities are found from the table given in Appendix E.

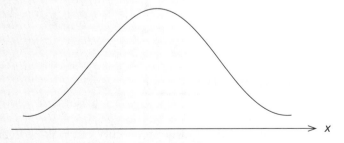

Figure 6.3

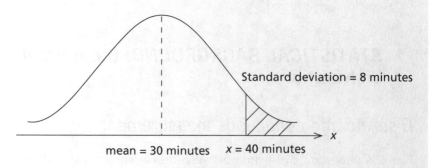

Standard deviation = 8 minutes

mean = 30 minutes   *x* = 40 minutes

Figure 6.4

The table gives the right-hand tail area corresponding to *z*. *z* gives the number of standard deviations the value of interest is away from the mean. This may be written as

$$z = \frac{\text{The value of interest} - \text{the mean}}{\text{Standard deviation}}$$

As an example consider the following. If the average time taken to complete a job was 30 minutes with a standard deviation of 8 minutes, then assuming a normal distribution we could work out the chance that a job would take 40 minutes or more. The situation is represented by Figure 6.4. The value of *z* is as follows:

$$z = \frac{40 - 30}{8}$$
$$= 1.25$$

If we look up the value of *z* = 1.25 in the normal distribution given (the structure of the tables can vary so you will need to check which area under the curve is given) the probability is 0.1056. For communications purpose we may choose to say that there is approximately an 11% chance a job will take 40 minutes or more.

Return to Scenario 20

In this scenario, we are interest in the probability of breaking even which means the probability of 100 or more people when the price is £10 and 83.33 or more people when the price is £12. Let us consider both cases.

Price £10

$$z = \frac{100 - 120}{15}$$
$$= -1.33$$

The negative sign is only directional in this case. We can use the tables to find a tail area corresponding to 1.33 which is 0.0918 but note that this should be the left-hand tail area as the z-value was -1.33. The distribution is shown in Figure 6.5.

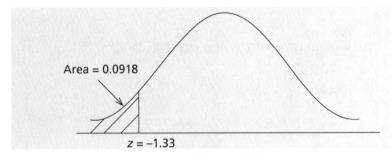

Area = 0.0918

$z = -1.33$

Figure 6.5

What we have now found is the probability of less than 100 people; to find the probability of breaking even or making a profit we need to subtract our answer from 1:

P (break even or profit when price £10)
$$= 1 - 0.0918$$
$$= 0.8164 \quad (\text{or } 82\%)$$

Price £12

$$z = \frac{83.33 - 100}{20}$$
$$= -0.83$$

There is again a negative sign which is only directional. We can use the tables to find a tail area corresponding to 0.83 which is 0.2033 but note that

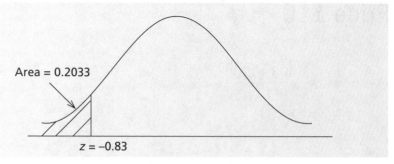

Figure 6.6

this should be the left-hand tail area as the z-value was –0.83. The distribution is shown in Figure 6.6.

We have now found the probability of less than 83.33 people; to find the probability of breaking even or making a profit we need to subtract our answer from 1:

P(break even or profit when price £12)

$$= 1 - 0.2033$$
$$= 0.7967 \quad (\text{or } 80\%)$$

STATISTICAL BACKGROUND: expected value – a note

The average is the expected number. To work out the expected revenue we only need to multiply the price by the average number.

In this scenario, we again need to consider the two possible prices. The expected revenue is the average number * price. Expected profit is found by subtracting cost from revenue.

Price £10

$$\text{Expected profit} = 120 * £10 - £1000$$
$$= £200$$

Price £12

$$\text{Expected profit} = 100 * £12 - £1000$$
$$= £200$$

This may seem an unlikely result, given that the probabilities of breaking even are different. The theatre group can expect the same profits at either price. However, for any one performance they are more likely to break-even by charging £10 for a ticket. By inference, they may be more likely to make a loss at any one performance by charging £12 but they will also be more likely to make a big profit if the performance is profitable.

Conclusions

Many of the problems that we need to consider will have outcomes that are subject to chance. This section has attempted to introduce the ideas of probability and give a number of illustrative examples. In many ways, probability is just a special case of modelling. Probability provides models where answers are given in terms of chance. It is still a matter of judgement how to respond to a level of chance. Clearly it does make a difference whether the chance is 10 to 1, or 100 to 1 or 1000 to 1. How many of us would drive a car if we were not prepared to take a chance? What probability theory does is give a framework to understand chance rather better and make some judgements on the basis of analysis that we can all share.

Questions

1. You have been working on the survey data shown in Table 6.4 where enjoyment of stay is related to length of stay. You now need to work out the following probabilities:
   (a) What is the probability that respondents enjoyed their stay?
   (b) What is the probability that respondents enjoyed their stay, enjoyed their stay a lot or enjoyed their stay very much?
   (c) What is the probability that respondents stayed over 7 nights?
   (d) What is the probability that respondents stayed 7 nights or less?

Table 6.4

	Enjoyed very much	Enjoyed a lot	Enjoyed	Not sure	Did not enjoy	Total
1, 2 or 3 nights	10	13	4	4	3	34
4–7 nights	0	3	6	4	2	15
Over 7 nights	0	1	5	3	6	15
Total	10	17	15	11	11	64

(e) What is the probability that respondents who stayed over 7 nights were not sure whether they enjoyed their stay or did not enjoy their stay?

(f) What is the probability that respondents who stayed 7 nights or less were not sure whether they enjoyed their stay or did not enjoy their stay?

2. The customer complaints department is staffed by a secretary, a clerical assistant and a manager. If the secretary is not able to answer an enquiry directly then it is passed to the clerical assistant. If the clerical assistant is not able to answer the enquiry then it is passed to the manager. It has been observed that the secretary, the clerical assistant and the manager will answer 60%, 60% and 70% respectively of the calls they deal with. What is the probability that a new enquiry will be

(a) answered by the clerical assistant?

(b) answered by the manager?

(c) not answered?

3. A company operates a system with three checking points, A, B and C for the detection of faulty goods. In the present system the three checking points are in series as follows:

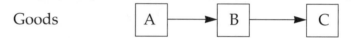

Goods   A → B → C

The chances of detection at the three checking points A, B and C are 50, 40 and 30% respectively. Once faulty goods are detected they are removed from the system.

It has been proposed that the system is changed to allow the checking to be done more quickly and improve the detection rates to 60% on checking point A and 50% on checking point B. In the new system the checking points A and B would operate in parallel as follows:

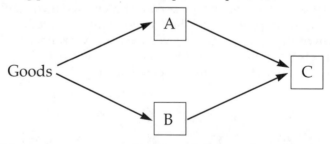

In this new system, 60% of goods would be directed to checking point A and the remaining 40% to checking point B. Thereafter, fault-free goods pass on to checking point C as before.

(a) Determine the probability of not detecting faulty goods in the present system.

(b) Determine the probability of not detecting faulty goods in the proposed new system.

(c) If the cost of detecting faulty goods at checking points A, B and C is £15, £25 and £45 and the cost to the company of non-detection is £200, determine the expected cost of operating each system.

4. You have been offered two possible investments. The first investment gives you an 80% chance of a profit of £10 000 and a 20% chance of a loss of £4000. The second investment gives you a 50% chance of a profit of £20 000 and a 50% chance of a loss of £5000. Represent your choice by a decision tree (remember that you can still choose to do nothing) and evaluate using the criteria of expected value, maximax and maximin. Explain your results.

5. A small company has developed a new road safety product. The company can sell the product design for £25 000 or launch the product itself. If the product is launched without advertising then there is a 50% chance of a return of £36 000 and a 50% chance of a return of £10 000. The company can advertise at a cost of £20 000 in advance of the launch and the effectiveness of the advertising evaluated. We have been told that advertising is effective about 90% of the time with products of this kind. If the advertising is effective, then we believe there is a 80% chance of a return of £70 000 and a 20% chance of a return of £15 000. If the advertising is not effective, then we believe there is a 55% chance of a return of £36 000 and a 45% chance of a return of £10 000. Once the advertising has been evaluated, the company still has the option to sell the design.

   Represent the options for the company by a decision tree and evaluate the criteria of expected value, maximax and maximin. Explain your results.

6. Weekly bonus payments have been found to follow a normal distribution with a mean of £5.67 and a standard deviation £2.30. What proportion of the workforce receive weekly bonus payments of:
   (a) less than £5?
   (b) less than £2?
   (c) more than £10?

7. A company has decided to review the packing process for a breakfast cereal it produces. It is stated on the cereal box that the content weight is 375 grams. However, the weight of the cereal does vary from box to box and is known to follow a normal distribution with a standard deviation of 6 grams. You have been asked to advise the company on the following:
   (a) If the packing process is adjusted so that the average weight packed is 387 grams, what proportion of cereal boxes are underweight?
   (b) If the company wants no more than 1% of cereal boxes to be underweight, what should the average packing weight be adjusted to?

8. One department within a local authority has kept records of how long it is taking those with debts to settle their accounts. The time taken was found to follow a normal distribution with a mean of 46 days and a standard deviation of 8 days. Customers not settling their accounts within 60 days are regarded as 'high risk'.
   (a) What percentage of accounts are regarded as 'high risk'?
   (b) What percentage of accounts are settled within 60 days?
   (c) If only three accounts need further checking what are the chances that they are all 'high risk'?

Section 7
Reflections

We would hope that by the time you come to read this section that you have worked your way through most of the book and been able to understand the content. It is unlikely that you will remember all of the approaches or techniques but that you will have developed an appreciation of what is possible. In many cases reference to a formula is sufficient to identify a useful technique. A formula sheet is included as Appendix G for your reference. In other cases, a problem may be more substantial and complex. We would hope that you have developed a confidence to deal with more difficult problems, even those that are beyond the scope of this book.

All problems need clarification. You could use some variant of the five Ws and H technique (Section 4) to establish who the problem involves, what the problem involves, where the problem is, when the problem exists, why the problem exists and how the problem exists. If you are not absolutely sure what the problem is, how will you know when you have an answer? It is often said that individuals and organizations spend a lot of time solving the wrong problems.

TASK

> **WRITE DOWN EXAMPLES OF WHEN YOU HAVE SPENT TIME SOLVING THE WRONG PROBLEM.**

As an example, you could have spent a lot of time buying a new car battery only to find that your real problem was the alternator. Once a problem has been clarified, it will often involve collecting information from people. The important issue here is, what people? In statistics, the people, or indeed items, of interest define the population. So, depending on the study, the population could be all those eligible to vote in the United Kingdom, all those that smoke within a particular company or all the sports shops in the West Midlands. You must define the population you are working with. If you are using survey information, then the survey must be representative of the population. If your subject of enquiry is sports shops in the West Midlands but you only interview managers of the larger shops then your results cannot be generalized to all sports shops. Your analysis is only ever going to be as good as your data. Quality computer printout may look convincing but the quality of your research will depend more critically on your data collection methods.

There are many techniques given in this book that may or may not be useful. Results can often be easily obtained from available computer packages, such as MICROSTATS. Computers will always tend to give results. The important transferable skill is being able to judge when numerical results are actually useful and how to use them selectively. As with all problem solving, the advice of others can be of great value. If you are preparing for assessment, we would suggest you try the questions given at the end of each section on you own; where appropriate, the answers are given in Appendix H. In the workplace, it is worth checking that the research being done and the statistics being produced do meet the requirements of the end user.

You should now be more confident with numbers. You should be able to recognize when the use of numerical methods can inform judgement and the limitations of these methods. We said in the introductory section that, in our view, the overriding consideration is 'does it make sense?' We hope that you can now make sense of numbers.

Appendix A: A refresher in numeracy skills

Where do we start?

You might want to use this appendix to pick out bits and pieces at times when you need a little extra help. You might want to read it from start to finish. You might be a little concerned that you have to 'do' numeracy as part of your course, and feel that it will be hard work. If you are concerned, your response may be a consequence of previous bad experiences with numbers. This appendix is not just about getting the 'right' answer! – it is about trying to understand how to make sense of numbers and what they can tell you, or, if you prefer, about how not to get conned by other people using numbers incorrectly.

In this section we will cover a few of the basics about using numbers, calculators and computers, just to reassure you that you can actually do things with numbers. You may feel that you can skip this section, and if you can that is perfectly OK.

If you are not sure, try the set of short tests given below.

Objectives

After studying this section you should be able to:

- add numbers together;

- multiply numbers together;

- deal with brackets in numerical expressions;

- write down simple algebraic expressions;

- rearrange algebraic expressions;

- understand equations using two variables;

- use powers of numbers as a shorthand for multiplication;

- sketch simple graphs.

Part 1 Self-check tests

? SELF-CHECK TEST 1: BASIC ARITHMETIC

You should not need to use a calculator to do this test!

1. $4 + 5 \ = $ _____
2. $12 - 8 = $ _____
3. $7 - 26 = $ _____
4. $5 \times 3 \ = $ _____
5. $16 \times 7 = $ _____
6. $3 \times (2) = $ _____

7. $5 \times (-2) \ \ \ = $ _____
8. $(-4) \times (-2) \ = $ _____
9. $4 + 3 \times 2 \ \ \ = $ _____
10. $(4 + 3) \times 2 \ = $ _____
11. $8 \div 2 \ \ \ \ \ = $ _____
12. $-12 \div 3 \ \ \ = $ _____

? SELF-CHECK TEST 2: USE OF POWERS

You should not need to use a calculator to do this test!

1. $2 \times 2 \times 2 \times 2 = $ _____
2. $2^2 = $ _____
3. $3 + 4^2 = $ _____
4. $(3 + 4)^2 = $ _____
5. $3^3 = $ _____

6. $2^3 \times 2^4 = $ _____
7. $3^3 \div 3^2 = $ _____
8. $(4^2 - 1) \div (2^2 + 1) = $ _____
9. $\sqrt{25} = $ _____
10. $\sqrt{(7^2 - 3 \times 4 - 1)} = $ _____

? SELF-CHECK TEST 3: BASIC ALGEBRA

1. If $2a = 6$, then $a = $ _____
2. If $4p = 100$, then $p = $ _____
3. If $6x + 4x = 200$, then $x = $ _____
4. If $x^2 = 49$, then $x = $ _____
5. If $4x + 5y - 4x = 25$, then $y = $ _____
6. Rearrange $6a + 3b = 12$, so that $a = $ _____
7. Rearrange $4x - 5y = 10$ so that $x = $ _____
8. If $5p^2 = 125$, then $p = $ _____
9. If $4a(2a + 3) - 8a^2 = 72$, then $a = $ _____
10. Rearrange $6s^2 + 3s = 12 + 2s^2 + (2s)^2$, so that $s = $ _____

? SELF-CHECK TEST 4: GRAPHS AND MORE ALGEBRA

You will need some graph paper to answer these questions.

1. Draw a graph of $y = 2$ for values of x from 0 to 5.
2. Draw a graph of $y = 2x$ for values of x from –2 to +5.
3. Draw a graph of $s = 2t + 4$ for values of t from 0 to 10.
4. Draw a graph of $y = 3x - 5$ for values of x from –2 to +10. Find the value of y if $x = 4$.
5. Draw a graph of $y = x^2 + 2x + 1$ for values of x from –3 to +3.
6. Draw a graph of $y = -x^2 + 2x + 1$ for values of x from –3 to +3.
7. Find the roots of $x^2 - 5x + 4 = 0$.
8. Find the roots of $x^2 - 5x + 6 = 0$.
9. Find the point where the line $q = 3p + 5$ crosses the line $q = 20 - 2p$.
10. A firm has a fixed cost of £20 and a variable cost of £6 for each unit made. Given a production level of x, write down an expression for the total cost function. If the same firm can sell as many as it can make at a price of £10, and this is the only source of revenue, write down the total revenue function. Determine the production level at which the firm will break even, that is, the value of x where total cost is equal to total revenue.

? SELF-CHECK TEST 5: USE OF YOUR CALCULATOR

This test is simply designed to ensure that you can use the basic functions on your calculator. Since we do not know the exact type of calculator which you have, you may want to refer to your manual if your answers do not match ours. You may also find that your calculator can perform much more complex sums that those below.
   Evaluate each of the following using your calculator:

1. $100 + 527 + 93 + 14 = $ _____
2. $47 - 32 + 5 - 98.5 - 3.1 + 4.03 = $ _____
3. $27 - 4 + 348.3/7 + 4 = $ _____
4. $(27 - 4 + 348.3)/(7 + 4) = $ _____
5. $45 * 6 * 0.34 = $ _____
6. 11% of $327 = $ _____

7. $\dfrac{8 * 453 - 62 * 9}{8 * 724 - (62)^2} = $ _____

8. $\dfrac{89}{7} - 0.3483 * \dfrac{58}{7} = $ ____

9. $\sqrt{(7 * 4 + 3 * 14)} = $ _____

10. $\dfrac{147}{\sqrt{(42 * 729)}}$ = _____

❓ ANSWERS TO SELF-CHECK TEST 1

1.	9	**7.**	−10
2.	4	**8.**	+8
3.	−19	**9.**	10
4.	15	**10.**	14
5.	112	**11.**	4
6.	6	**12.**	−4

How many of them did you get right? We hope that you got more than 4 which means that you got over 40%, which is the sort of calculation that is useful to do and a standard sort of pass mark used by some courses! You may feel that 4 out of 10 is not a lot! We hope that you will, in fact, do rather better than this.

If you want to check on how we got the answers, or remind yourself about doing basic arithmetic, look at Part 2 of this appendix.

❓ ANSWERS TO SELF-CHECK TEST 2

1.	16	**6.**	128
2.	4	**7.**	3
3.	19	**8.**	3
4.	49	**9.**	5
5.	27	**10.**	6

How many of them did you get right? We hope that you got them all right! If you got more than 5 right, give yourself some congratulations, but do check on the other answers.

If you want to check on how we got the answers, or remind yourself about using powers, look at Part 3 of this appendix.

❓ ANSWERS TO SELF-CHECK TEST 3

1.	$a = 3$	**6.**	$a = 2 - 0.5b$
2.	$p = 25$	**7.**	$x = 2.5 + 1.25y$
3.	$x = 20$	**8.**	$p = 5$
4.	$x = 7$	**9.**	$a = 6$
5.	$y = 5$	**10.**	$s = 4$

How many of them did you get right? We hope that you got most of them right! Being able to do some rearrangement of algebraic equations can be very useful and time-saving, so it is worth checking any answers which you did not quite get.

If you want to check on how we got the answers, or remind yourself about doing basic algebra, look at Part 4 of this appendix.

? ANSWERS TO SELF-CHECK TEST 4

1.

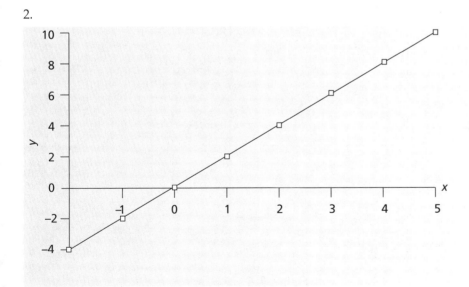

Figure A.1 $y = 2$.

2.

Figure A.2 $y = 2x$.

3.

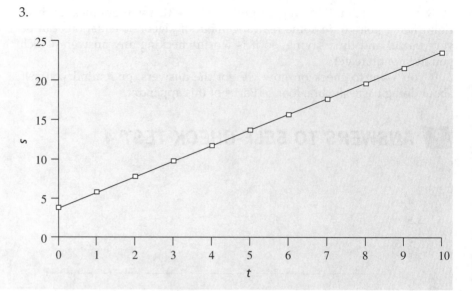

Figure A.3 $s = 2t + 4$.

4.

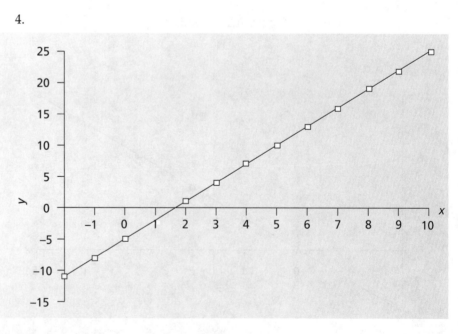

Figure A.4 $y = 3x - 5$.

If $x = 4$, then $y = 7$.

5.

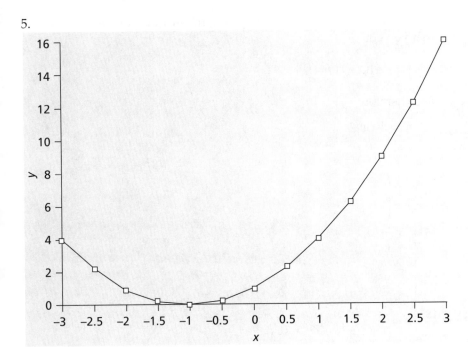

Figure A.5 $y = x^2 + 2x + 1$.

6.

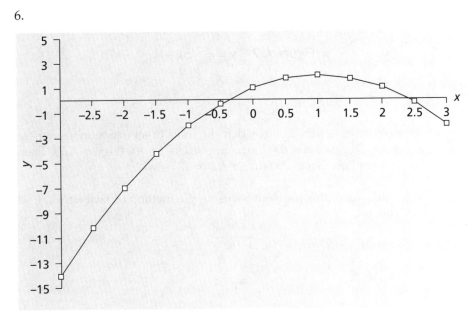

Figure A.6 $y = -x^2 + 2x + 1$.

7. You could solve this problem by using the methods of factorization, so that you get

$$(x - 4)(x - 1) = 0$$

and therefore

$$x = 1 \text{ or } 4$$

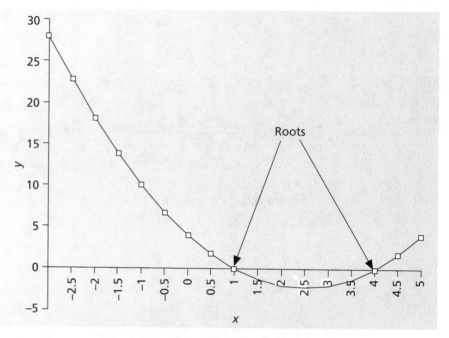

Figure A.7 $y = x^2 - 5x + 4$.

An alternative is to remember that the roots of an equation are where $y = 0$, so you can draw the graph of $y = x^2 - 5x + 4$ (Figure A.7). Then you can read off that $y = 0$ when $x = 1$ or 4.

8. You could solve this problem by using the method of factorization, so that you get

$$(x - 3)(x - 2) = 0$$

and therefore

$$x = 2 \text{ or } 3$$

An alternative is to remember that the roots of an equation are where $y = 0$, so you can draw the graph of $y = x^2 - 5x + 6$ (Figure A.8).

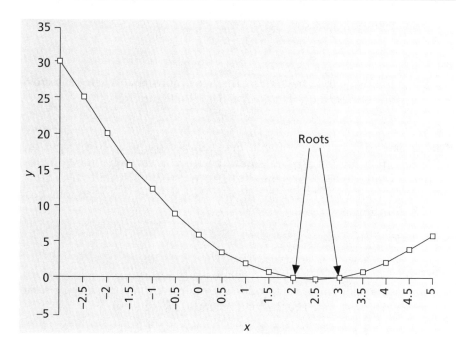

Figure A.8 $y = x^2 - 5x + 6$.

9.   Again there are several ways of doing this question. You might equate the two equations, since q must equal q:

$$3p + 5 = 20 - 2p$$

Rearranging gives

$$p = 3$$

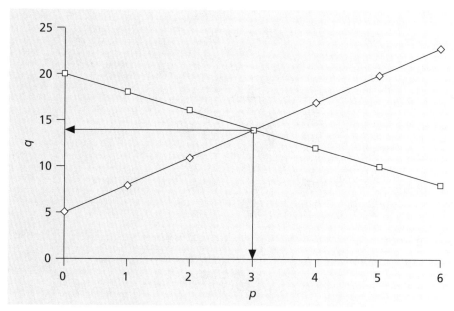

Figure A.9 $q = 3p + 5$ and $q = 20 - 2p$.

and substituting gives

$$q = 14$$

An alternative would be to draw the two graphs, find where they cross each other and read off that $p = 3$ and $q = 14$ (Figure A.9).

10. This is a slightly more difficult question because you have to put the information into an algebraic form before you can solve it. We know that fixed costs (*FC*) are equal to £20 and that each unit costs £6 to make. Given a production level of x, then we can write the total cost (*TC*) function as

$$TC = 20 + 6x$$

Similarly, we know the sales revenue is £10 for each one sold, and if x represents sales (since any production can be sold, we can use the same letter), then we can write the total revenue (*TR*) function as

$$TR = 10x$$

A firm breaks even when its total cost equals its total revenue, so

$$
\begin{aligned}
TR &= TC \\
20 + 6x &= 10x \\
20 &= 4x \\
x &= 5
\end{aligned}
$$

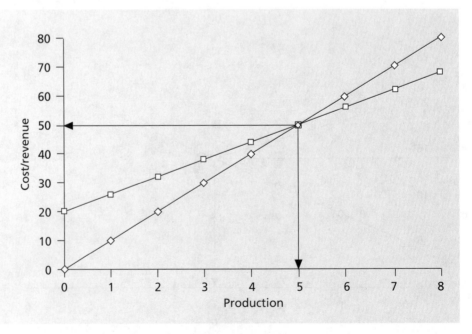

Figure A.10

and by substituting, we can get the actual total cost and total revenue:

$$TR = 10\,(5) = 50$$

$$TC = 20 + 6\,(5) = 50$$

Alternatively, we could have drawn two graphs (Figure A.10) and read off that break-even occurs when $x = 5$ and the totals are 50.

How many of these questions did you get right? We hope that you got most of them right! You may have chosen to find the answers by using algebra, or you may have used the graphs. You may have used a combination of the two.

If you want to check on how we got the answers, or remind yourself about doing graphs, look at Part 5 of this appendix.

? ANSWERS TO SELF-CHECK TEST 5

1. 734
2. −77.57
3. 76.757 142 857 14
4. 33.754 545 454 55
5. 91.8
6. 35.97
7. 1.573 921 971 253
8. 9.828 371 428 571
9. 8.366 600 265 341
10. 0.840 096 016 4603

How many of them did you get right? We hope that you managed to do them all and were able to get most of them right! Remember that your calculator came with an instruction book, and it is worth looking at it to see how it can save you time when doing this sort of calculation.

If you want to check on how we got the answers, or remind yourself about using a calculator, look at Part 6 of this section.

Part 2 Basic arithmetic

We are not concerned with you doing complicated sums using large numbers in your head! We would like you to develop your numeracy skills with small numbers, and to be able to look at a calculation and have a general idea of what the size of the answer should be. If you need to use big numbers, then you can always use a calculator or a computer to take the hard work out of the 'number crunching'.

Addition

Adding numbers together really comes from skills you learned at primary school. So basic sums should be straightforward, for example:

$$4 + 3 = 7$$
$$23 + 35 = 58$$

What you are doing is moving along a line (Figure A.11).

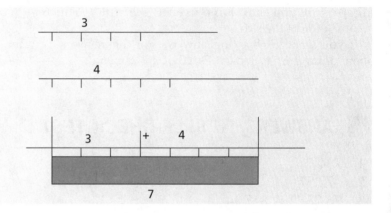

Figure A.11 Addition of line segments.

Subtraction

With subtraction, you are again combining two line sections, but the minus sign means that you are going backwards for one part. For example (see also Figure A.12):

$$6 - 4 = 2$$

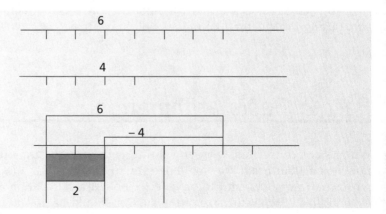

Figure A.12 Subtraction of line segments.

These ideas will work quite well whilst we are dealing with small numbers and when the result we get is positive. If the number that we are subtracting is larger than the other number, then, to understand the process, we need to introduce the idea of zero on the line segment. That is, we have a standard line (like a ruler) with zero marked on it. We can then put the line segments on to this ruler, and read off the result (Figure A.13):

$$4 - 7 = -3$$

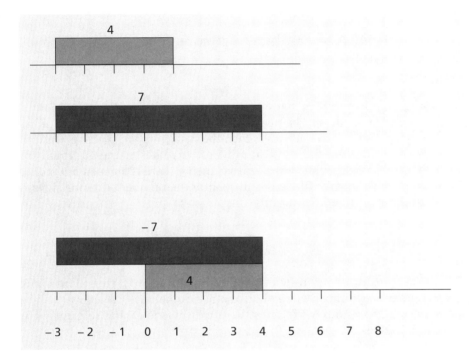

Figure A.13   Subtraction of line segments and ruler.

Multiplication

Multiplication can be thought of as a quick form of addition; if you take 3 times 2, you are taking three line segments of length 2 and adding them together:

$$3 \times 2 = 6$$

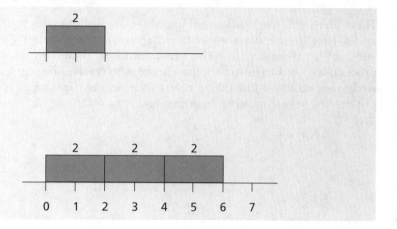

Figure A.14   Multiplication of line segments and ruler.

When one of the numbers that we are multiplying is negative (has a minus sign), then the result will be negative. If both of the numbers that we are multiplying together are negative, then the result will be positive. (In fact, when we are multiplying several numbers together, some of which are positive and some of which are negative, then if there is an even number of minus signs, the result will be positive, but if the number of minus signs is odd, then the result will be negative.)

Division

Division is really the opposite of multiplication. We are trying to find how many times one number will go into another. Sometimes the answer will be a whole number, and sometimes there will be something left over. For example (see also Figure A.15):

$$8 \div 2 = 4$$
$$11 \div 3 = 3 \quad \text{and 2 left over}$$

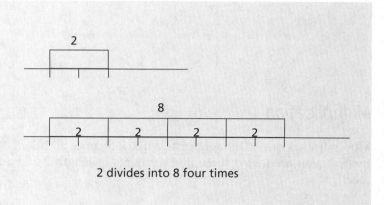

2 divides into 8 four times

3 divides into 11 three times with 2 left over

Figure A.15   Division of line segments.

When either of the numbers is negative, then the result is negative. If both of the numbers are negative, then the result is positive.

Brackets

When the expression that we are trying to evaluate contains brackets, then we need to work out the bit in the brackets first. For example:

$$(3 + 2) \times 6 = 5 \times 6 = 30$$

Note that this is different from $3 + 2 \times 6$, where the answer would be

$$3 + 2 \times 6 = 3 + 12 = 15$$

A rule

There is a rule which we can use when we are faced by complicated looking expressions. You may have come across it before, although it does get presented in slightly different forms from time to time. The rule is often called the **Order of Operations** rule, and can be summarized as:

B	Brackets
E	Exponentiation
D	Divide
M	Multiply
A	Add
S	Subtract

We have dealt with most of these things, except exponentiation which comes in the next part of this section. Following this rule, we can now evaluate (i.e. find the answer for) fairly complicated expressions. For example:

$$(4 + 3) \times 5 - 3 \times (-2 + 7 + 3) \div 4$$

First of all we work out the two brackets:

$$7 \times 5 - 3 \times 8 \div 4$$

Then we divide:

$$7 \times 5 - 3 \times 2$$

Then we do the multiplications:

$$35 - 6$$

and finally, we do the subtraction:

$$\text{Answer} = 29$$

With practice, you may be able to do several steps of such a calculation at once, without having to write down each of the intermediate steps, but, if in doubt, write down each stage.

Below is recheck test 1. Try it now.

1. $10 + 5 = $ _____
2. $6 - 4 = $ _____
3. $8 - 15 = $ _____
4. $4 \times 5 = $ _____
5. $8 \times (-2) = $ _____
6. $15 \div 3 = $ _____
7. $17 \div 4 = $ _____
8. $(3 + 2) \times 5 = $ _____
9. $(4 + 3) \times (9 - 2) = $ _____
10. $(20 + 16) \div (8 - 2) = $ _____

The answers to this recheck are at the end of this appendix. When you check them, if you still have any questions, go back and reread Part 2.

Part 3 Use of powers

Interpreting powers

Powers (or exponentiation) are a shorthand way of writing down a multiplication when we are multiplying a number by itself. So if we are multiplying

$$5 \times 5$$

we could write this as

$$5^2$$

The system will also work if we multiply the same number more than two times:

$$4^6 = 4 \times 4 \times 4 \times 4 \times 4 \times 4$$

For questions like number 3 in self-check test 2, you need to remember the BEDMAS rule and work out the power (or exponent) first, and then do the addition:

$$3 + 4^2 = 3 + 16 = 19$$

Combining powers

Where we have a number raised to a power and that result is multiplied by the same number raised to some power, then you can simplify the expression by adding the powers together. For example:

$$3^4 \times 3^2 = 3^{4+2} = 3^6 = 729$$

The same basic idea works when the two results are to be divided rather than multiplied, but in this case you need to subtract the powers. For example:

$$3^4 \div 3^2 = 3^{4-2} = 3^2 = 9$$

We also need to note the following result:

$$3^4 \div 3^3 = 3^{4-3} = 3^1 = 3$$

and this can be generalized to say that any number raised to the power 1 is the number itself.

Another important result is as follows:

$$3^4 \div 3^4 = 3^{4-4} = 3^0 = 1$$

which means that a number raised to the power zero is equal to 1. This is true for all numbers.

If we take these ideas a little further, we can find another useful result:

$$4^3 \div 4^5 = 4^{3-5} = 4^{-2}$$

but the question remains 'What on earth does this mean?' The meaning of positive powers is fairly obvious if you have read the paragraphs above, but now we need to interpret negative powers. A negative power means that we take 1 divided by the expression (this idea is known as the reciprocal), so the result of the previous answer is

$$4^{-2} = \frac{1}{4^2} = \frac{1}{16}$$

Square roots

The square root of a number is a number that, when multiplied by itself, gives the original answer. For example, the square root of 4 is 2, because

$$2 \times 2 = 4$$

For small numbers, you can often do such calculations in your head, if the result is a whole number. For any other situation you are likely to use the button on your calculator which is marked

$$\boxed{\sqrt{}}$$

There is an alternative way of writing down a square root by using a power. A square root is equivalent to the power of 1/2. We can see that this must be the case since

$$2^{1/2} \times 2^{1/2} = 2^{1/2 + 1/2} = 2^1 = 2$$

By a similar logic, the cube root (i.e. a number which when multiplied by itself three times gives the result) of some number, must be equivalent to a power of 1/3.

Below is recheck test 2. Try it now.

1. $3 \times 3 \times 3 =$ _____
2. $4^2 =$ _____
3. $7 + 2^3 =$ _____
4. $2^3 \times 2^2 =$ _____
5. $4^5 \div 4^3 =$ _____
6. $(2 \times 2 \times 4^3) \div (4^4) =$ _____
7. $\sqrt{49} =$ _____
8. $25^{1/2} =$ _____
9. $3 \times 3^{1/2} \times 3^{1/2} =$ _____
10. $(5 + 2^2)^{1/2} =$ _____

The answers to this recheck are at the end of this appendix. When you check them, if you still have any questions, go back and reread Part 3.

Part 4 Basic algebra

Basic algebra is part of every day life, it is just that we do not always classify it as such! If you see six apples for £0.60p, then you know that they cost 10p each; you have effectively just used algebra, it is just that you did not write it down in any formal sense. If you had written the problem down, you might have said: let a stand for apples, then

$$6a = £0.60p$$

Divide both sides by 6, and you get

$$a = £0.10p$$

Therefore one apple costs £0.10p.

Algebra is often seen as a way of simplifying a problem by using a letter (in this case the letter a) to represent something. Applying some basic rules then allows us to rearrange an expression or equation to obtain a different view of the relationship. We did this in the example above, by going from a position where we knew the price of six apples, to a position where we know the price of a single apple.

This example illustrates the first basic rule that we need: **Whatever you do to one side of an equation, you must do to the other side.** This rule applies, no matter what it is we need to do. For example, if

$$0.5x = 7$$

then multiply both sides by 2, and you get

$$x = 14$$

Similarly, if

$$\sqrt{(2s)} = 6$$

then, if we square both sides, we get

$$2s = 36$$

Divide both sides by 2, to get

$$s = 18$$

As a final example, when we have brackets in the equation, we need to remember the BEDMAS rule from Part 2, and work out the brackets first. For example, if

$$2a\,(4a - 7) - 8a^2 + 70 = 0$$

working out the bracket gives

$$8a^2 - 14a - 8a^2 + 70 = 0$$

Simplifying gives

$$-14a + 70 = 0$$

Adding 14a to both sides gives

$$+14a - 14a + 70 = 14a$$

or $70 = 14a$

and dividing by 14 gives

$$5 = a$$

so we have the answer that a is equal to 5. As you can see, there is no real limit to the number of times you can manipulate the relationship, as long as you do the same thing to both sides.

In many cases, when you are asked to rearrange an equation, you will end up with a numerical value for the letter, but sometimes, all you need to find out is the value of one of the letters expressed as a **function** of the other one. This is the way in which people have developed formulae, some of which you are going to use during this course. If we start off with an expression like this:

$$4x - 12y = 60$$

and we want to express x as a function of y, the first step is to get just the bit with x in it on one side, and all of the rest on the other side. We can do this by adding 12y to both sides:

$$4x - 12y + 12y = 60 + 12y$$

This now simplifies to

$$4x = 60 + 12y$$

and, if we divide by 4, we get

$$x = 15 + 3y$$

This answer does not give us a specific numerical value for x, but it does tell us how x is related to y. It also allows us to find the specific value for x, if we are given a specific value for y; for example, if we are told that $y = 2$, then we can substitute this specific value into the relationship which we have found:

$$x = 15 + 3 (2)$$

therefore

$$x = 15 + 6 = 21$$

What we have just done is the basis for using various formulae that you might need when you try to apply numeracy to various situations. It is also the way in which we can use algebra to represent relationships, and these can also be used to show the same situations graphically. We will do more on this in the next part.

Below is recheck test 3. Try it now.

1. If $4d = 24$, then $d = $ _____
2. If $2x + 3x = 37$, then $x = $ _____
3. If $3y^2 = 192$, then $y = $ _____
4. If $a + 3b + 4a - b + 5a - 2b = 5$, then $a = $ _____
5. Rearrange $7c + 2h = 4$ so that $h = $ _____
6. Rearrange $5x - 2y + 6 = 3x + 4y + 10$ so that $x = $ _____
7. If $\sqrt{(3f)} = 18$, then $f = $ _____
8. If $6p(2p + 4) - 12p^2 = 24$, then $p = $ _____
9. Rearrange $3z + 2y - 30 = 0$ so that $z = $ _____. If we are told that $y = 6$, find the specific value for z
10. If $4a(a - 3) + 6 - 2a(2a - 4) = 10$, then $a = $ _____

The answers to this recheck are at the end of this section. When you check them, if you still have any questions, go back and reread Part 4.

Part 5 Graphs and more algebra

Being able to draw graphs can be very useful when trying to see what is happening in a particular situation. In this part we will remind you about some of the basic techniques for drawing graphs, and show how you can take an algebraic expressions and create a picture of it. You will find that if you have access to a computer spreadsheet package, it will be able to draw the pictures for you, but remember that we need to understand the basics so that we (and you) do not make silly mistakes.

The axes

To draw a graph, we need a pair of axes; these are two lines drawn at right angles to each other, and usually with a scale attached to them. An example is shown in Figure A.16. You also need to label the axes; here we have labelled the horizontal axis as x and the vertical axis as y. (This is fairly conventional!)

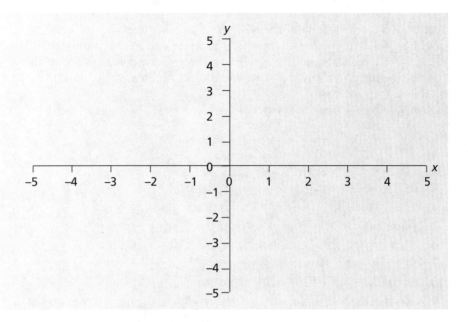

Figure A.16   Graph axes.

Once we have these axes, we can identify any point by quoting the **horizontal position** (x-value) and the **vertical position** (y-value), always in that order. So if we want to show the point $x = 3$ and $y = 5$, we can go along the x-axis to the point marked 3, and then up until we are level with $y = 5$. It is a convention that such a point is referred to as (3, 5) and it is shown in Figure A.17 as the point A.

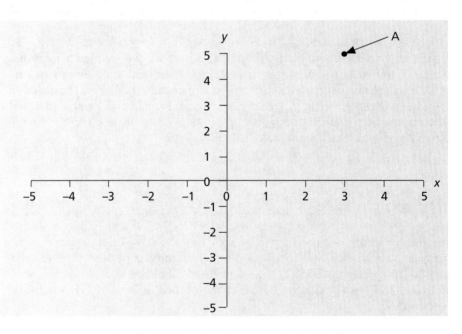

Figure A.17   Graph axes and point (3, 5).

Straight line graphs

When we want to draw the graph of a straight line (also known as linear graphs or functions), we can do this by finding two (or more) of the points on the line, and then joining them up with a ruler. You know from the last part that if you have a relationship between x and y, you can work out the specific value of y for a specific value of x. We need to use this idea to draw these graphs. For example, if you want to draw the graph of $y = 5$ for values of x from 0 to 5, then we can see that no matter what the value of x, the value of y is always equal to 5! This would mean that the graph will just be a straight line where $y = 5$. It is shown in Figure A.18.

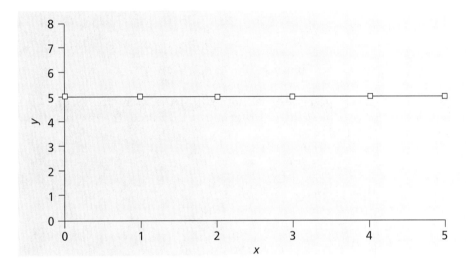

Figure A.18 $y = 5$.

Even where the function is not quite so simple, drawing a graph is relatively easy. If we start with the equation $y = 10 + 4x$ for which we want to draw the graph for values of x from -1 to $+5$, then we can find two points on the graph and join them with a ruler. You could take any two points, but since we are given two points in the question, we might as well use these.

If $x = -1$, then

$$y = 10 + 4(-1) = 6 \quad \text{(Point A)}$$

If $x = 5$, then

$$y = 10 + 4(5) = 30 \quad \text{(Point B)}$$

Marking these two points on a set of axes, and joining them up gives the graph shown in Figure A.19.

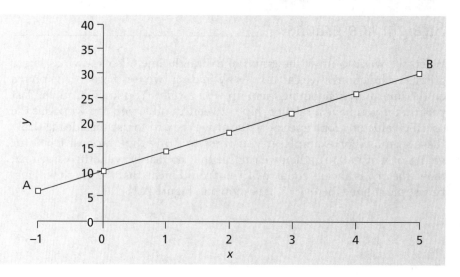

Figure A.19 $y = 10 + 4x$.

Just to reinforce the point, here is another example. Draw the graph of the function $y = 20 - 2x$ for values of x from 0 to 10. Taking the two points we were given: if $x = 0$, then

$$y = 20 - 2(0) = 20$$

and if $x = 10$, then we have

$$y = 20 - 2(10) = 0$$

Plotting these on to a pair of axes, gives the graph shown in Figure A.20.

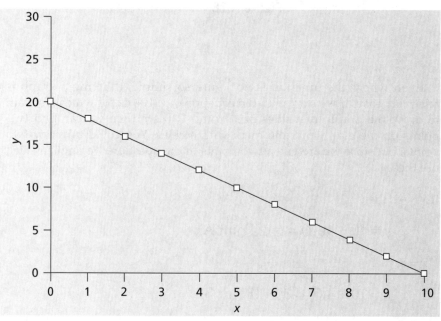

Figure A.20 $y = 20 - 2x$.

We are not, of course, restricted to putting just one graph on a pair of axes. If you want to find out where two graphs cross (or are equal to each other) then you can draw both graphs on the same axes and read off the point of intersection. For example, if we have two functions

$$y = 20 - 2x$$

and

$$y = 2 + 2x$$

we can draw both graphs and find that they cross each other at $x = 4.5$ and $y = 11$. This is shown in Figure A.21.

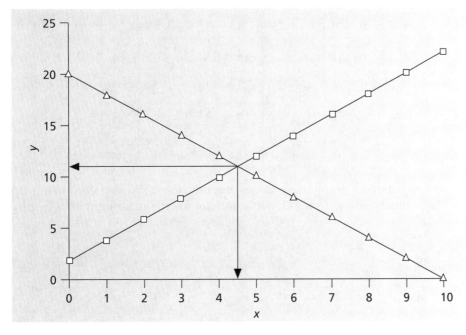

Figure A.21 $y = 20 - 2x$ and $y = 2 + 2x$.

Non-linear graphs

When we come to non-linear graphs we have a bit more of a problem! We cannot use straight lines and a ruler to join up the points, and we need to work out a lot more points before we can draw the graph. We can do this by hand for fairly easy functions, or, if you have access to one, you could do it on a spreadsheet.

Using a function with an x^2 in it (known as a **quadratic function**), we will try to evaluate it at various points and then draw its graph. Starting with $y = x^2 - 8x + 12$, we can draw up a table to work out the values of each part of the function, and then add the various bits together. Taking values of x from 0 to 10, we can work out the values of x^2 as follows:

x	0	1	2	3	4	5	6	7	8	9	10
x^2	0	1	4	9	16	25	36	49	64	81	100

In a similar way, we can work out $-8x$ for the same range of x-values:

x	0	1	2	3	4	5	6	7	8	9	10
$-8x$	0	-8	-16	-24	-32	-40	-48	-56	-64	-72	-80

and, of course, we know that the last bit of the function is always equal to $+12$. If we now put all of these bits together, we can find the value of y:

x	0	1	2	3	4	5	6	7	8	9	10
x^2	0	1	4	9	16	25	36	49	64	81	100
$-8x$	0	-8	-16	-24	-32	-40	-48	-56	-64	-72	-80
$+12$	$+12$	$+12$	$+12$	$+12$	$+12$	$+12$	$+12$	$+12$	$+12$	$+12$	$+12$
y	$+12$	$+5$	0	-3	-4	-3	0	$+5$	$+12$	$+21$	$+32$

and we can now graph these values, but remember that you need to join up the points by using a smooth curve and not a series of straight lines (Figure A.22).

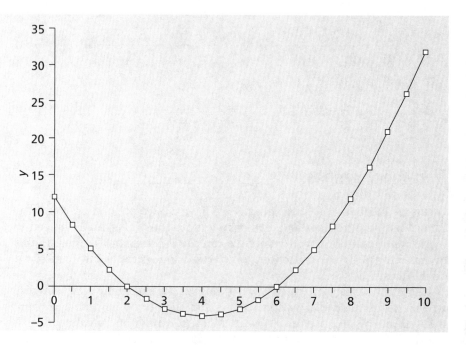

Figure A.22 $y = x^2 - 8x + 12$.

Roots

The roots of an equation are the points where the graph of the function crosses the x-axis, i.e. where $y = 0$. You can just read them from the graph. If you look back at Figure A.22, you can see that $y = 0$ when $x = 2$ and when $x = 6$, so we can say that the roots of the function $y = x^2 - 8x + 12$ are equal to 2 and 6.

There are alternative ways of finding the roots of an equation, and we will briefly look at two of them. (You may find that this section is not relevant for some courses.)

Roots by factorizing

To do this, the first step is to put $y = 0$, so for our example above, we have

$$x^2 - 8x + 12 = 0$$

We want to split the function up into two brackets multiplied together, so that

$$(x + a)(x + b) = x^2 - 8x + 12$$

The question is 'How do we find the values of a and b?' First of all, let us multiply out the brackets. To do this we multiply each bit of the second bracket by the x in the first bracket and then add on the $+ a$ multiplied by each bit of the second bracket – sounds complicated, but is quite easy! Doing it in stages: multiplying each bit of the second bracket by the x in the first bracket gives

$$x^2 + bx$$

the $+ a$ from the first bracket multiplied by each bit of the second bracket gives

$$ax + ab$$

and putting them together gives

$$x^2 + bx + ax + ab = x^2 - 8x + 12$$

$$x^2 + (a + b)x + ab = x^2 - 8x + 12$$

Looking at the result we have obtained, we can see that ab must be equal to 12 and that $(a + b)$ must be equal to -8. So we need to find two numbers which when we multiply them together give an answer of 12 and when we add them together, give an answer of -8. If you think for a moment, you should get these two numbers to be -2 and -6. So we can rewrite the function as

$$x^2 - 8x + 12 = (x - 2)(x - 6) = 0$$

Now, for the answer to be equal to 0, either the first bracket is equal to 0, so

$$(x - 2) = 0$$
$$x = 2$$

or the second bracket is equal to 0, so

$$(x - 6) = 0$$
$$x = 6$$

So the roots of the quadratic function are $x = 2$ and $x = 6$.

Roots by formula

The alternative to using the factorizing method is to use a formula, and many people prefer this because it gives the answer without having to puzzle out the values that fit into the brackets. The formula works with a standard equation:

$$ax^2 + bx + c = 0$$

and the roots are found by using

$$\text{Roots} = \frac{-b \pm \sqrt{(b^2 - 4ac)}}{2a}$$

Here is an example of using the formula. Given that $x^2 - 5x + 4 = 0$, find the roots. Compare the given equation with the standard equation to get the values of a, b, and c.
Here we have

$$a = +1 \qquad b = -5 \qquad c = +4$$
$$\text{(Remember that } x^2 \text{ means } +1 \text{ times } x^2)$$

Substituting into the formula gives

$$\text{Roots} = \frac{-(-5) \pm \sqrt{[(5)^2 - (4)(+1)(+4)]}}{2(+1)}$$
$$= \frac{(+5) \pm \sqrt{(25 - 16)}}{2}$$
$$= \frac{(+5) \pm \sqrt{9}}{2}$$
$$= \frac{(+5) \pm 3}{2}$$

Now the ± means + and − so we get

$$\text{Roots} = \frac{+8}{2} \quad \text{and} \quad \frac{+2}{2}$$

$$= +4 \quad \text{and} \quad +1$$

The advantage of the formula is that it works even when the roots are not whole numbers, as you can see from the next example. Given that $y = 2x^2 + 5x - 6$, find the roots of the equation. Comparing this with the standard equation gives $a = 2$, $b = 5$ and $c = -6$, and using the formula gives

$$\text{Roots} = \frac{-(5) \pm \sqrt{[(5)^2 - 4(2)(-6)]}}{2(2)}$$

$$= \frac{-5 \pm \sqrt{(25 + 48)}}{4}$$

$$= \frac{-5 \pm \sqrt{73}}{4}$$

$$= \frac{-5 \pm 8.544}{4}$$

$$= \frac{3.544}{4} \quad \text{or} \quad \frac{-13.544}{4}$$

$$= 0.886 \quad \text{or} \quad -3.386$$

So we can see that the roots of this equation are not whole numbers.
   Below is recheck test 4. Try it now.

1.   Draw a graph of $y = 4$ for values of x from −2 to +5.
2.   Draw a graph of $y = -3$ for values of x from 0 to +10.
3.   Draw a graph of $a = 20 - 4b$ for values of b from 0 to 5.
4.   Draw a graph of $y = 3x - 6$ for values of x from −2 to +10.
5.   Draw a graph of $y = x^2 + 2x + 4$ for values of x from −3 to +3.
6.   Draw a graph of $y = -x^2 + 2x + 4$ for values of x from −3 to +3.
7.   Find the roots of $y = x^2 - 7x + 12$. Draw the graph for $x = 0$ to 6.
8.   Find the roots of $y = x^2 - 4x - 12$. Draw the graph for $x = -2$ to +6.
9.   Find the point where the lines, $y = 8 + 7x$ and $y = 30 - 4x$ cross.
10.   A firm has a fixed cost of 100 with a variable cost of 10 per unit of production. Its only source of revenue is from sales, and the selling price is 20. It can sell as many as it makes. Find the break-even point for the firm.

The answers to this recheck are at the end of this appendix. When you check them, if you still have any questions, go back and reread Part 5.

Part 6 Use of calculators

Calculators vary tremendously in what they can do, but all calculators will carry out the basic functions of addition, subtraction, multiplication and division. Yours will probably also be able to find square roots. You should find that if you completely master the use of your calculator, it will save you a large amount of work and time. However, you do need to look at what you are doing, since it is very easy just to put numbers blindly into the calculator and accept the result (even if it does not make sense). In this part we are concerned with just the basic functions that are available on most calculators. You may need to remind yourself of the BEDMAS rule from Part 2.

One aim you should have in using your calculator is to avoid writing down intermediate answers. To do this you need to plan the way in which you enter the problem into the machine, and then all you need to write down is the final answer. The reason for doing this, apart from it saving you work (!), is to ensure that the intermediate results use as many decimal places as possible, as this will affect the accuracy of final result.

Basic functions

The four basic arithmetic functions are controlled by the usual four buttons:

| + | Addition |

| − | Subtraction |

| × | or | * | Multiplication |

| ÷ | or | / | Division |

and we would anticipate you having little difficulty in actually pressing the appropriate one when required. For example, if you need to work out 23 * 4 * 0.875 you would switch the calculator on, then

Type 23   Press | × |

Type in 4   Press | × |

Type in .875   Press | = |

and the result of 80.5 will be shown on the display.

Percentages

To work out a percentage of a number you need to remember that the decimal equivalent of a percentage is obtained by dividing the percentage by 100. So 10% becomes 0.10, 13.5% becomes 0.135, and so on. You can then use the decimal equivalent to carry out a multiplication and hence obtain the result. For example; to find 16.5% of 356 785, you would

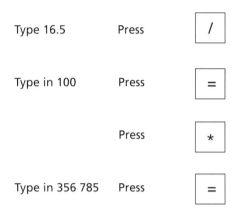

Type 16.5	Press	/
Type in 100	Press	=
	Press	*
Type in 356 785	Press	=

and the result of 58 869.525 would be displayed.

Powers

The next two keys you will need are

$\sqrt{}$ Square root

x^2 Square

their meaning is fairly obvious, as long as you remember the BEDMAS rule. For example, evaluate (a) $\sqrt{4} \times 9$ and (b) $\sqrt{(4 \times 9)}$. For (a) you would

Type 4	Press	$\sqrt{}$
	Press	$\times$
Type in 9	Press	=

and the result of 18 would be displayed.

For (b) you would

Type 4	Press	$\times$
Type in 9	Press	$=$
	Press	$\sqrt{}$

and the result of 6 would be displayed.

Note that we have used the BEDMAS rule here to evaluate the brackets first, and then work out the square root of the answer.

Sign change

The next key we need is

$+/-$ Sign change

This key will change the sign of whatever is shown on the display, and is useful when you are working out a fairly complicated sum. For example, evaluate $345 - 4 \times 23.986$:

Type 4	Press	$\times$
Type in 23.986	Press	$=$
	Press	$+/-$
	Press	$+$
Type in 345	Press	$=$

and the result of 249.056 would be displayed.

Reciprocal

The last of the standard keys which will be of use to you is

This will work out 1 divided by whatever is shown on the display and is useful when you are working out division problems. For example, evaluate $7534/(4.987 \times 58.9)$:

Type 4.987	Press	$\times$
Type in 58.9	Press	$=$
	Press	$1/x$
	Press	$\times$
Type in 7534	Press	$=$

and the result of 25.649 030 433 29 would be displayed.

Note that we have shown the answer to 11 decimal places. You would not normally quote an answer to this many decimal places; you would probably quote the answer as 25.649.

Memory

Finally, if your calculator has a memory, then you can store an intermediate result there whilst you work out something else, and then recall the value in the memory to complete the sum. The buttons you will find on your calculator are probably marked as

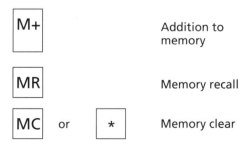

For example, evaluate

$$\frac{42.47 * 85.38}{347.8 * 1.3047}$$

Type 42.47	Press	$\times$	
Type in 85.38	Press	$=$	
		M+	
	Press	CE	
Type in 347.8	Press	$\times$	for clear display
Type in 1.3047	Press	$=$	
	Press	1/x	
	Press	$\times$	
	Press	MR	
	Press	$=$	

and the result of 7.990 945 549 934 would be displayed.

Below is the recheck test 5. Try it now. Evaluate each of the following using your calculator:

1. $42.3 + 7.9 + 2.1 = $ _____
2. $3.57 - 4.2 + 4.852 + 7.631 - 2.4785 - 3.8421 = $ _____
3. $32.483 - 7.85/3.1 + 6 = $ _____
4. $(32.483 - 7.85)/(3.1 + 6) = $ _____
5. $12.47 * 8.39 * 2.47 = $ _____
6. 13% of $62 = $ _____
7. $\dfrac{12 * 7521 - 32 * 451}{12 * 475 - (32)^2} = $

8. $\dfrac{77}{12} - 1.246 * \dfrac{48}{12} =$

9. $\sqrt{(17 * 3 + 45 * 2)} =$

10. $\dfrac{356.48}{\sqrt{(4592.1 * 3.876.483)}} =$

The answers to this recheck are at the end of this appendix. When you check them, if you still have any questions, go back and reread Part 6.

Part 7 Answers to recheck tests

? ANSWERS TO RECHECK TEST 1

1.	15	6.	5
2.	2	7.	4 and 1 left over, or 4.25
3.	−7	8.	25
4.	20	9.	49
5.	−16	10.	6

When you check these answers, if you still have any questions, go back and reread Part 2.

? ANSWERS TO RECHECK TEST 2

1.	27	6.	1
2.	16	7.	7
3.	15	8.	5
4.	32	9.	9
5.	16	10.	3

When you check these answers, if you still have any questions, go back and reread Part 3.

? ANSWERS TO RECHECK TEST 3

1.	$d = 6$	6.	$x = 3y + 2$
2.	$x = 7.4$	7.	$f = 108$
3.	$y = 8$	8.	$p = 1$
4.	$a = 0.5$	9.	$z = \ \ 10 - 2y/3$
5.	$h = 1/2\,(4 - 7c)$		$z = 6$
	or $h = 2 - 3.5c$	10.	$a = -1$

When you check these answers, if you still have any questions, go back and reread Part 4.

? ANSWERS TO RECHECK TEST 4

1.

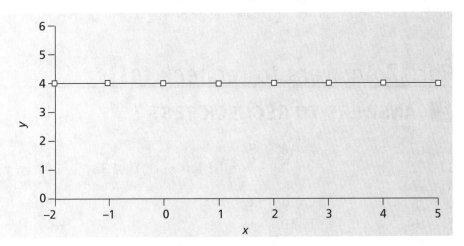

Figure A.23 $y = 4$.

2.

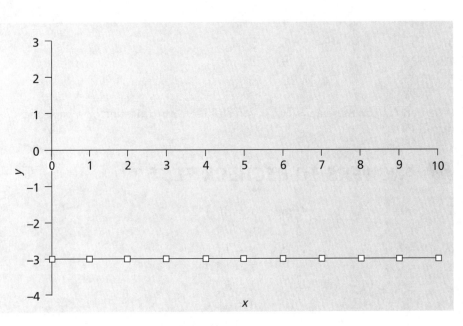

Figure A.24 $y = -3$.

3.

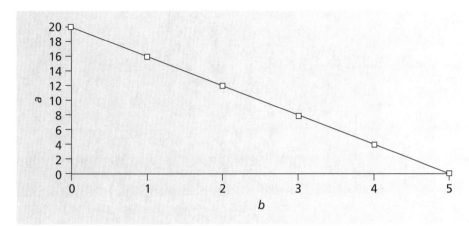

Figure A.25 $a = 20 - 4b$.

4.

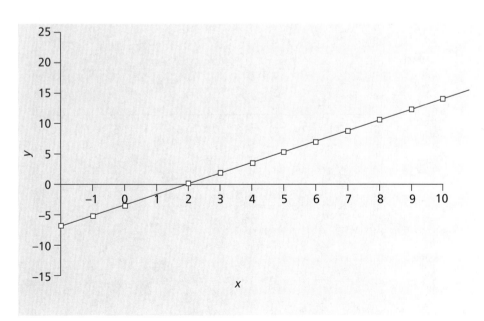

Figure A.26 $y = 3x - 6$.

5.

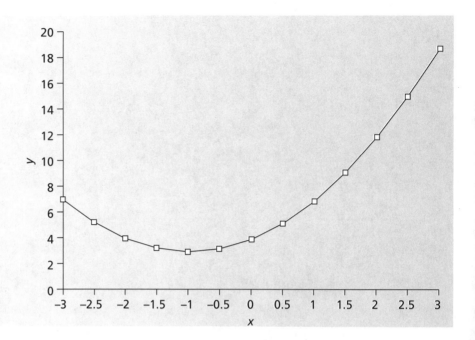

Figure A.27 $y = x^2 + 2x + 4$.

6.

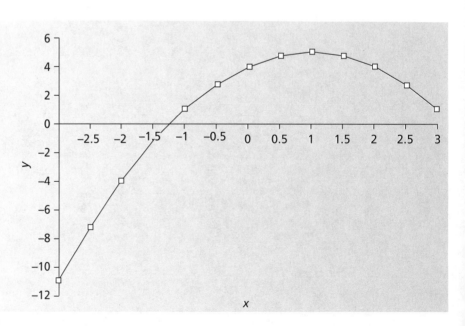

Figure A.28 $y = -x^2 + 2x + 4$.

7. $y = x^2 - 7x + 12 = 0$
    $= (x - 3)(x - 4) = 0$

Therefore roots at $x = 3$ and 4.

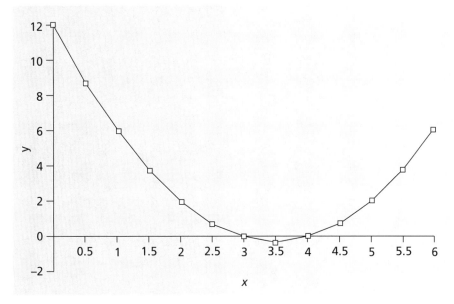

Figure A.29 $y = x^2 - 7x + 12$.

8. $y = x^2 - 4x - 12 = 0$
    $= (x - 6)(x + 2) = 0$

Therefore roots at $x = -2$ and $+6$.

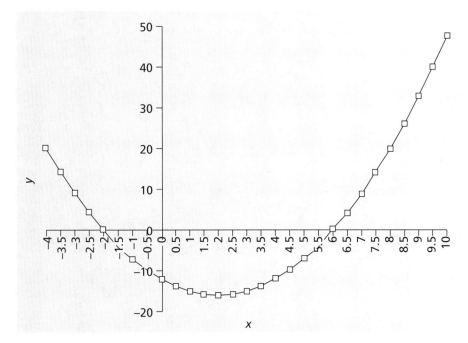

Figure A.30 $y = x^2 - 4x - 12$

9. To find where the two lines cross, we can put them equal to each other.

$$
\begin{aligned}
y &= 8 + 7x = 30 - 4x \\
11x &= 22 \\
x &= 2 \\
y &= 22
\end{aligned}
$$

Alternatively, we can draw the graphs (Figure A.31).

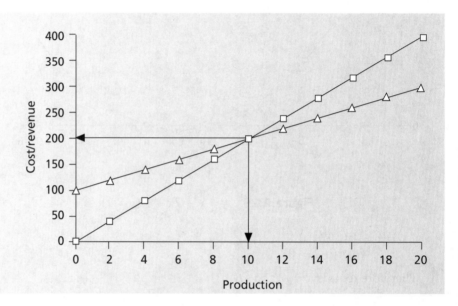

Figure A.31 $y = 8 + 7x$ and $y = 30 - 4x$.

10.
$$
\begin{aligned}
\text{Total cost } (TC) &= 100 + 10x \\
\text{Total revenue } (TR) &= 20x \\
\text{Break-even at } TR &= TC \\
100 + 10x &= 20x \\
100 &= 10x \\
x &= 10 \\
TR &= TC = 200
\end{aligned}
$$

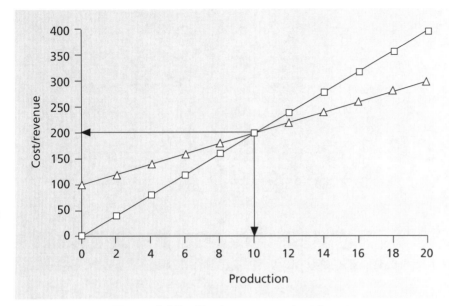

Figure A.32   Total revenue and total cost.

When you check these answers, if you still have any questions, go back and reread Part 5.

❓ ANSWERS TO RECHECK TEST 5

1. 52.3
2. 5.5324
3. 35.950742
4. 2.706 923 076 923
5. 258.419 551
6. 8.06
7. 16.214 713 430 28
8. 1.432 666 666 667
9. 11.874 342 087 04
10. 0.084 491 021 119 21

When you check these answers, if you still have any questions, go back and reread Part 6.

Appendix B: MICROSTATS manual

Introduction and tutorial

What is MICROSTATS?

MICROSTATS has been designed as a general purpose, easy-to-use statistics package for use on IBM and IBM-compatible machines with at least 256K of memory. It closely resembles the MINITAB statistical package written by the University of Pennsylvania which is to be found in many academic institutions. However, although the overall design and philosophy are consistent with those of MINITAB, there are significant differences between the two packages, not least in size, functions and price. MICROSTATS may be seen as an integrated program which fulfils the function of an introduction to more specialized statistical software such as MINITAB or SPSS (Statistical Package for the Social Sciences).

Capacities of MICROSTATS

MICROSTATS is written in Turbo Pascal which makes it both compact and fast in operation. The program consists of the principal MICROSTATS module which is kept in memory at all times and a series of overlay files which are switched in and out of memory automatically when required. On a floppy disk system, this process rarely takes more than a second or so and provides no noticeable delay whilst on a hard-disk system, it appears almost instantaneous. It is obvious, therefore, that all of the MICROSTATS modules must be kept together on the same disk or subdirectory for the correct operation of the program.

   The MICROSTATS worksheet allows for 200 rows of some 45 columns of data which constitute 9000 elements of data. (MINITAB, <Version 8>, by contrast, allows a storage capacity of 16 184 elements of data which is practically double.) If memory constraints are a real problem then it is probably time to graduate on to a more powerful package in any case.

   To install MICROSTATS, follow the instructions in the small text file named READ.ME! (At the MS-DOS prompt, type READ.ME!) The installation process is simple but illicit or uninstalled programs will not run.

If you need a statistical package in order to analyse a social survey, then a better application program may well be TURBOSTATS contained in the text *Survey Design and Analysis using TURBOSTATS* by M. C. Hart (Chapman & Hall, 1993). TURBOSTATS allows for the naming and labelling of both variables and values in a manner similar to SPSS and the output is, in fact, modelled upon the FREQUENCIES and the CROSSTABS facilities of that particular package.

How does MICROSTATS work?

MICROSTATS assumes that the user has several columns of data organized in a worksheet and is organized to reproduce (and eventually manipulate) that worksheet. The fundamental concept, which it is important to appreciate early on, is that MICROSTATS primarily manipulates columns of data and expects that data will be numerical, and not textual. In this, it differs from a spreadsheet which typically handles text and formulae in addition to numbers.

Columns of data, which are the basic unit of analysis used in the MICROSTATS system, may be called by a number which must be preceded by the letter C (or c) and no intervening space, e.g. C1. Columns of data may also be allocated a name up to eight characters long and this name may also be used to refer to data provided that the name is always enclosed in (the same!) single quotation marks, e.g. 'MARKS'. (On some IBM keyboards, this is the quotation mark found on the same key as the @ symbol or the shifted 7.)

MICROSTATS works by scanning a line which is input to the computer after the user has responded to the MICROSTATS prompt (Command ?) with a command and then pressed ENTER. It picks out the keyword that it needs (or more specifically, the first four letters of a keyword) and then checks it against an internal dictionary of some 110 words. If the keyword is found, then MICROSTATS will activate the subroutine which performs the analysis suggested by the user. Notice that MICROSTATS **does not necessarily display anything on the screen after certain commands** – if you get the Command ? prompt back and no error message, you can generally assume that the system has obeyed your request! If you want to see the results of your commands, you can generally PRINT out the relevant columns to satisfy yourself that your command has worked!

If you use a command that MICROSTATS does not recognize (e.g. you may have mistyped it) then you will get a warning beep and a 'Word not found' message.

MICROSTATS will take the whole of an input line and 'parse' it, which means that the relevant information will be extracted and the rest of the line will be ignored. Generally, everything that is not a keyword, a column number (preceded by C) or a value will be ignored. This means that you can address MICROSTATS with English-type commands, provided that your first word is always a keyword. Later on, as your familiarity with the system increases, you can progress to the shortened form of the command if you prefer. For example, assume that we have a column of data in C1 and we wish to multiply this column by 10 and put the results into C2. We can use the 'long form' of the command:

MULTiply data in C1 by 10 and put the result into C2

Or we could use the 'short' form of the command (which is what MICROSTATS actually acts upon):

MULT C1 10 C2

Notice in the long form of the command that only the first four letters are significant. If we made a mistake in any of the letters from the fifth onwards then MICROSTATS would ignore this.

If you forget any of the words in the MICROSTATS dictionary, then you can either press ? or type the keyword HELP which will give you access to one of eight HELP screens where the commands are displayed in logical groups.

Getting started

Assuming that you have the computer 'booted up' under MS-DOS, then merely insert the MICROSTATS disk and type MS-RUN. This runs the MS-RUN batch file which runs the MICROSTATS system. MICROSTATS should load, give a title page and invite you to press RETURN to start. You will be presented with information of the size of your worksheet and the Command ? prompt. Try the following, not forgetting to press RETURN (or ENTER) at the end of each line:

SET data into C1

At this stage, a new prompt will appear as follows:

DATA >

and you should then type in some data with at least one space as a separator before each number:

DATA > 3 4 5 6 7 8 9

As soon as you press RETURN, the DATA > prompt will reappear and you could enter as many more lines of data as you wish.

You should not attempt to enter more than one full line of data (i.e. 80 characters of data) at a time – it is always possible to enter additional data on subsequent lines.

To finish entering your data, make sure that you have pressed ENTER at the end of the previous line and the DATA > prompt is still in front of you. Now type END to signify that you have finished and the data you have just entered will be displayed to you on the screen with an indication of the number of items that you have input. The whole transaction will look like this:

Command ? SET data into C1

DATA > 3 4 5 6 7
DATA > END

1. 3.000
2. 4.000
3. 5.000
4. 6.000
5. 7.000

5 data items entered in C1

Command ?

When the Command ? prompt reappears, you may now issue another command. Print out the data that you have just entered with the following command:

Command ? PRINT data in C1

C1
(n=5)

1.   3.000
2.   4.000
3.   5.000
4.   6.000
5.   7.000

and the data that you have just entered will appear on the screen.

Now that you have some data in the computer, try the following command:

Command ? DESCribe C1

and you should see the following output:

Count of	C1 =	5
Minimum of	C1 =	3.000
Maximum of	C1 =	7.000
Sum of	C1 =	25.000
Sum of squares of	C1 =	135.000
Mean of	C1 =	5.000
Median of	C1 =	5.000
Mode of	C1 = (No mode)	

```
--------------------------------------------------
Standard  dev-n  [pop'n]     of    C1  =  1.414
Standard  dev-n  [sample]    of    C1  =  1.581
--------------------------------------------------
Skew                         of    C1  =  0.000
Standard error of mean       of    C1  =  0.707
Quartiles   [Q1]   [Q3]      of    C1  =  3.500 and 6.500
Percentiles [10]   [90]      of    C1  =  3.000 and 7.000
--------------------------------------------------
```

(The meaning of these statistical terms are explained in Section 2.)

You may now like to try some of the other commands that will perform statistics upon a single column of data. For example, try giving the command

Command ? SUM data in C1

and then try extending the command even further by trying

Command ? SUM data in C1 – put data into C2

In this case, the sum of the data in C1 will be put into as many rows of C2 as there are rows in C1. However, note that

SUM C1 put into 1 row of C2
    (will only use row 1 of C2)

To give names to your two data columns, then use the NAME command as follows:

Command ? NAME C1 'DATA' and C2 'SUM'

Now type INFO or the full command INFOrmation and you will see the status of your worksheet displayed as follows:

C1   'DATA' n=5
C2   'SUM'   n=5

43 columns of length 200 still available for use

You should get used to using the following two commands frequently as they help you to keep track of your worksheet:

INFO   (checks on the number and length of your columns)

PRINT Cx   (where x is a column number e.g. C1 or a range e.g. PRINT C1–C5)

Going further

Let us assume that you still have the numbers

3 4 5 6 7

contained in C1. You can PRINt C1 to check whether this is still the case. Now we are going to create a second column of data to explore some of the other possibilities offered by MICROSTATS. Try the following:

Command ? MULTiply C1 by C1 – put result into C2

If you prefer, you may use the short form of the command which merely gives MICROSTATS the bare minimum that it requires, i.e. the first four letters of the keyword and the columns that it must use to operate upon. The short form of the command is

Command ? MULT C1 C1 C2

MICROSTATS will respond equally well to either the short or the long form of the command – feel free to use whichever seems more natural to you.

If the Command ? prompt returns and there has been no error message, we can assume that the command has been successfully performed. To check this out, we can ask MICROSTATS to perform the following:

Command ? PRINt C1 and C2

and we should find that C2 contains the square of C1, i.e. each number in C1 has been multiplied by itself and then put into C2.

In the printout on the screen, you will notice that MICROSTATS has printed out each number to three places of decimals. It does this 'by default' but it is possible to alter this by using a command such as

Command ? DISPlay C1 to 2 dp

If you then PRINt C1 and C2 once again, you will see that you have output to two places of decimals in C1. You can experiment with this if you like.

Now we are going to do some more serious work. If a statistician wishes to see how much of one variable is associated with another, (s)he generally wishes to generate a statistical measure known as a **correlation coefficient** (see page 154). If you have ever done this longhand, you will know what a lot of effort is involved. MICROSTATS will do this for you quickly and easily by using the command

Command ? CORRelate C1 and C2

You should obtain a result that informs you that the correlation of C1 and C2 is equal to 0.9931, as well as other statistical information giving you the probability that you could have obtained this result by chance alone (in this case, about 3 in every 10 000 cases!).

This indicates a very high positive correlation. The correlation coefficient can take a value of +1 for a perfect positive correlation, –1 for a perfect negative correlation or any value in between. A value of very close to +1 indicates a very high degree of association between the two sets of values, which is not surprising considering that one is the square of the other.

If we wish to derive a mathematical equation to link together the two sets of observations, we use what statisticians call a **regression equation** (see page 143). This is an equation that informs you on the basis of the data that the computer has what would be a predicted value for one variable once we are given a specific value for the other. Try the command

Command ? REGRESS C2 upon C1

and your output should inform you that the regression equation of C2 upon C1 is equal to

$$y= -23.0000 + 10.0000 * X$$

The asterisk is a standard method in computing of saying 'multiplied by' and this regression equation is telling us that 'y' will take a value of 10.000 times a particular value of 'X' minus 23.0.

Now give names to the two variables created by using the commands

Command ? NAME C1 'Number' and C2 'Square'

Command ? INFO

Finally, we are going to do something which is visually more exciting and also shows that you can use names in commands as well as column numbers. Once we have allocated names to columns we are quite free to use them instead of column numbers. We must ensure that the names are exactly those which have been allocated. For example, the names 'NUMBER' and 'NUMBER ' look exactly alike to a human reader but are regarded as quite different names by the computer, where the space would be regarded as an additional character.

If we now use the PLOT command as follows:

Command ? PLOT 'Number' v 'Square'

then we will see a plot of the two variables in which the maximum and minimum of each variable are displayed, as well as the names of the variables and the correlation coefficient. If you perform the plot in reverse order, i.e. PLOT 'Square' v 'Number', you will find the axes are now reversed.

To clear the system of data, we can now type

Command ? ERASE C1 C2

and the two columns of data will be 'rubbed out'. You may check that this is so by using INFO which will inform you that all of the columns are empty and unnamed and give you the total available on the system.

This concludes the tutorial on the use of the MICROSTATS system. The following sections will describe how to use the more sophisticated features contained in the package. This also assumes that you have a certain degree of statistical knowledge so that you can understand what type of analysis is being performed, and also that you are aware of the underlying assumptions.

You can also try to use some of the other simple commands that are contained in the complete list of MICROSTATS commands and experiment to discover what they do.

Library of MICROSTATS commands

Entering data

SET data into C1

    DATA > 3 4 5 6 7 8 9
    DATA > 10 11 12 13 14
    DATA > END

Use for entering data one column at a time. A long column of data may be split over several MICROSTATS input lines but your input line should not exceed about 100 characters. As a rule of thumb, whenever the cursor goes on to the second 'screen line' then you should press ENTER to register that line of data.

The SET command will overwrite any data already contained in that column. If you wish to append data to a column, then use the APPEnd command which has the same format as SET.

To exit, type END, or X (or nothing at all) on a blank data line and not at the end of a series of numbers.

    READ data into C1-C3
       DATA Row 1 > 1 4 7
       DATA Row 2 > 2 5 8 3

    Too many data items – re-enter line
       Data Row 2 > 2 5

    Too few data items – re-enter line
       Data Row 2 > 2 5 8
       Data Row 3 > 3 6 9
       Data Row 4 > END

       3 rows of data entered into C1-C3

Use for entering data into several columns simultaneously. This is best used when you are more experienced in data entry. Note that the number of columns indicated and the number of data items per line must tally exactly. Do not leave spaces on either side of the hyphen.

In the example, exactly three data items per line are expected. If you supply more or less then the system will warn you and prompt you to re-enter the correct number of data items.

APPEnd the data to C1

This works in exactly the same way as SET but appends data.

NAME data in C1 'name1' and C2 'name2'

This names the data – check that you use the correct apostrophe!

Column statistics

SUM data in C1
SUM data in C1 put into C2
SUM data in C1, put into 1 row in C2

If a second column is specified but with no other value, then the sum of C1 will be put into as many rows of C2 as there are rows in C1. If you specify a value, e.g. 1, then this value will indicate how many rows of C2 should be filled. Commands which work in an identical fashion are as follows:

COUNt	Number of data items in the column.
MAXImum	The maximum value in a column.
MINImum	The minimum value in a column.
AVERage or MEAN	Both commands give the arithmetic mean.
MEDIan	The median measure of central tendency, i.e. the value which occupies the central position once the data has been sorted into ascending order.
MODE	The mode or the most frequently occurring value. If there are multiple modes, then only the first identified will be shown.
STANdard dev-n	Standard deviation calculated with a divisor of N (population).
STDE	Standard deviation calculated with a divisor of $N-1$ (sample).
SSQ (sum of squares)	The sum of x-squared, i.e. each value is squared and then the x-squareds are summed.

SEMEan	Standard error of the mean.
SKEW	The skew of the distribution. A positive skew indicates that the median is to the left (i.e. smaller) than the mean whilst a negative skew indicates that median is to the right (i.e. larger) than the mean.
QUARtiles	Similar to the median except the data is divided into four quarters and the first and third quartile are shown.
PERCentiles	Similar to quartiles except the nth (and 100-nth) percentiles are shown. If n is not specified the 10th and 90th percentiles are shown.
DESCribe	This command will give summary statistics of any one column:

Count	Sum
Minimum	Mean
Maximum	Median
Sum of squares	Mode
Standard deviation	(population)
Standard deviation	(sample)
Standard error of the mean	
Quartiles	Percentiles (10th) and (90th)
Skew	

(NB one column of data only!)

PRINT C1

PRINT C1–C7

You may print out any one column or up to seven adjacent columns of data. Any columns in excess of seven will be ignored. Do not leave a space on either side of the hyphen.

After a screenful of data (20 items) you will be prompted whether to view more data or exit the printing of the data.

Arithmetic on columns

You may perform simple arithmetic on your columns using either another column or a number. The results may be put into another column or even stored straight back into the original column, in which case they overwrite the previous contents. Examples include:

ADD C1 to C2 put into C3

SUBT C2 from C1 put into C3

MULTiply C1 by 10 put into C3

DIVIde C4 by 10 put into C4

RAISe C1 to the power of 3 put into C5

RECIprocal of C1 put into C11

NB. Once you have performed these manipulations, the MICROSTATS Command ? prompt will return. Print out the relevant columns if you want to satisfy yourself that the results are as you intended them to be.

Manipulations upon columns

These manipulations allow you to transform the data in some way (e.g. by taking a log or square root) – you may then put the transformed data into another or even back into the same column. The manipulations include the following:

SQRT of C1 put into C2	(SQRT = SQUARE ROOT)
ABSolute of C1 put into C2	(ABS = ABSOLUTE)
ROUNd C1 to x decimal places	(ROUND to specified no. of decimal places)
INT eger C1 put into C2	(INT = integer)
LOGE C1 put into C2	(LOGE = Natural LOG)
EXPOnent C2 put into C3	(EXPO = EXPONENT)
LOGTen C1 put into C2	(LOGTen = Log to base 10)
ANTIlog C1 put into C2	(ANTIlog = antilogarithm)
SORT C1 put into C2	(SORT into ascending order)

(To sort data in C1 into a descending order, put –1 at the end of the command line thus: SORT C1 C2 –1.)

RANK data in C1, put into C2 (–1 for descending order)

(RANK gives a ranking number, i.e. when the numbers are arranged in order from lowest to highest, the lowest is awarded a rank of 1, the next lowest a rank of 2 and so on. When values are equal, the relevant ranking numbers are 'shared out'. If –1 is specified, the rank order will be from the highest to lowest.)

> COPY data in C1 to C3   (copies data from C1 into C3)

> COPY data from C1–C5 to block starting at C11

(Copies the BLOCK of data from C1–C5 into a new block starting at C10. NB No spaces on either side of the hypen.)

Plots

MICROSTATS will perform a **scatter plot** or **scattergram** of data on two matching variables. The typical plotting command is

> PLOT C1 C2

but before you issue the command, you should take some elementary precautions. For example, try printing out the data to ensure that the columns are different, i.e. that one column is not a copy of the other, or that one column does not contain identical values.

If you observe numbers rather than asterisks (*) in your plot, this is because MICROSTATS is informing you that two data points are 'mapped' on to the same data coordinates. Notice that the plots will be scaled and the minimum, mid-point and maximum of each given as well as the column names (if any).

The first column that you specify will be the vertical axis and this is usually called the 'dependent' variable (as it 'depends' in causal terms upon the second variable). The second column specified will be the horizontal axis and this is usually called the 'independent' variable (which you might think of, loosely, as the 'cause'). The dependent variable is usually designated by the letter 'y' and independent variable by the letter 'x'. For example, if we had two variables in which one was student grant ('GRANT') whilst the other was level of parental income ('INCOME'), then 'GRANT' would be the dependent variable (i.e. 'y') and would be entered first whilst 'INCOME' would be the independent variable (i.e. 'x') and would be entered second:

> PLOT 'GRANT' v 'INCOME'

Notice also that the correlation coefficient is calculated and displayed in the top right-hand corner of the graph.

Plots are useful to see if there is a tendency for the data to cluster and form one of the following patterns:

- A 'line' sloping upwards from bottom left to top right. The more closely the data clusters around such a line, the more it suggests a 'positive correlation' in which as one variable increases, so does the other.
- A 'line' sloping downwards from bottom right to top left. The more closely the data clusters around such a line, the more it suggests a 'negative correlation', i.e. one variable increases as the other decreases.
- No apparent pattern at all. This suggests the absence of association which would be no correlation (or only a very small one).

Histograms, tally

The HISTogram command requests a plot of a single variable so that you can examine its shape. A typical histogram of random numbers from 1 to 100 would show the following:

Command ? HISTogram of data in C1

Choose first midpoint, interval   (y/n?)   y

First mid-point ? 5.5   Interval ? 10

Middle of Interval	Number of Observations	
5.5	10	**********
15.5	8	********
25.5	13	*************
35.5	8	********
45.5	8	********
55.5	12	************
65.5	6	******
75.5	9	*********
85.5	9	*********
95.5	17	*****************

There are several things to note about the HISTogram command:

- You are given the option to choose the first mid-point and the interval. If you press 'n' or just RETURN then the command will choose what appear to be sensible defaults depending upon the shape of the data but which may appear strange to you. If you choose to select the mid-point and the interval, then you should have at least a rough idea of what the data 'looks like' before you start.
- Notice that statistically the mid-points may not be just where you expect them to be. For instance, in the example given above,

then all of the data lying in the range 0.5 upwards to 10.49999 downwards would be regarded as lying within the first block. The mid position of a range which extends from 0.5 to 10.4999 is $(10.4999 - 0.5)/2$ (i.e. 5) + 0.5 which is 5.5 (to the nearest one place of decimals) and not 5.0!

- The HISTogram command cannot deal very sensibly with very small or very large numbers. Under such circumstances, it is probably sensible to scale them up (or down) yourself and put the data into a new column and then try the effects of HIST on the scaled column. For example, a range of 100 numbers in the range 0–1 are best scaled up to 0–10 or even 0–100. After all, the HISTogram analysis is only intended to give you a visual representation of the actual 'shape' of the data rather than a precise mathematical result and therefore such scaling up or down is quite legitimate.

Tally

If you have 'discrete' data, i.e. data which can take one of a range of values (e.g. numbers such as 1, 2, 3 which may be answers in a questionnaire) then TALLY will be superior to a histogram. Up to 20 consecutive integers will be accepted and the columns displayed are as follows:

VALUE	(i.e. the number itself)
N	(the number of occurrences)
CUM_N	(cumulative total of Ns)
PERCENT	(the percentage)
CUMPCT	(the cumulative percentage)

Label

You can construct a 'universal' set of up to 20 labels (maximum width of eight characters) that will explain the output of both TALLY and CHISQUARE commands as follows:

LABEL 'Male' 'Female'

LABEL 10 'Yes' 'No'

This will start labelling from the tenth value onwards.

LABEL with no parameters will give you a list of all allocated labels. To clear the labels, use a null string e.g.

LABEL " " "

Remember that labels are not 'bound' to any particular column and need redefining for each new analysis.

Bivariate statistics

Bivariate statistics is the name given to the statistical analysis of pairs of data, such as that dealt with already in the PLOT command. The following bivariate statistics are provided:

> CORRelate C1 and C2

In this case, the 'Pearson product-moment correlation coefficient' between the two stated variables will be performed. Before you issue the command, check the following two points:

- Via INFO make sure that you have equal numbers of data in each column.
- Via PRINT make sure that all of the values of one or other column are not identical. If they are, the command will fail and computer may well abort.

In order to intepret the value of the correlation coefficient, read the entry under PLOT on pp. 278–9. It is particularly important to remember the following three points and see page 154:

- A high positive (or negative) correlation coefficient cannot be taken to imply causation.
- A high (or low) correlation may be significant in purely statistical terms but not be significant in social scientific terms. For example, a high correlation between heights and weights of a general sample of the population is not surprising, as taller people are generally heavier.
- Conversely, the absence of a correlation may not achieve statistical significance but may be highly significant in terms of a social scientific model. The absence of a relationship where we might be led to expect one (for example between unemployment and mental illness) might prove to be highly significant in terms of social scientific theory, even though the result does not achieve a degree of statistical significance.

> REGRess C1 upon C2
>
> REGRess C1 upon C2 with intercept in C3, slope in C4,
>   value of x, put predicted y in C5
>   e.g. REGR C1 C2 C3 C4 10 C5

A regression line, sometimes known also as a 'least squares' line, is a line that best fits a series of data pairs and which can be used to predict one variable once we know:

- the regression equation itself
- the value of the independent variable.

The general form of a regression equation is

$$y = a + b * (x)$$

where y = dependent variable (that we wish to discover), x = independent variable (which may be given), a = intercept and b = slope (see page 143).

MICROSTATs will also calculate R-sq (i.e. R^2) which is the 'coefficient of determination'. The correlation coefficient 'r' is the square root of the coefficient of determination.

Worked example

Put the following data pairs into C1 and C2 where C1 = salary and C2 = years of education since age 15:

C1	C2
5000	2
3000	4
6000	5
4000	6
7000	7
6000	8
9000	9

Then get the regression equation, as follows:

Command ? REGRess C1 upon C2

Regression of C1 upon C2 =

y = 2401.6393+ 565.5738 * X   (R-sq = 0.47591)

Now try the longer form of the command, but this time we wish to know what salary can be expected from an individual with 3 years of 15+ education.

Command ? REGRess C1 on C2,a in C3,b in C4,x=3, result in C5

y = 2401.6393+ 565.5738 * X   (R-sq= =0.47591)

Command ? PRINt C3–C5

	C3	C4	C5
	(n= 1)	(n= 1)	(n= 1)
1.	2401.6393	565.574	4098.361

Here the critical result is in C5 that tells us that with 3 years of post 15+ education (x=3) the predicted level of salary will be

$$y = 2401.6393 + (565.574 * 3)$$
$$= 4098.361$$

Whereas in correlation the result does not depend upon which variable is C1 and C2, the same is not true of regression. In regression, the dependent variable is regressed on to the independent variable. In terms of our example, salary (the dependent variable) will be regressed upon education (the independent variable). If you experiment by trying to regress C2 on C1 then you will see a very different result, so it is important that the order of variables is understood before you use this command.

If you suspect that the data is curvilinear (e.g. the kind of relationship that is met when one number is the square or higher power of the other number) then try a logarithmic transformation of the data before you start to perform the regression command.

CONTingency table of data in C1 and C2

The CONTingency table command is designed to 'table' those cases where we have integer numbers in two columns which represent 'coding' numbers, e.g. in C1 we might have the numbers 1–2 which represent female and male whilst in C2 we might have numbers 1–5 representing five categories of political identification. Such data is often known as 'categorical' data. If we wish to see how many of one category are represented in the other (e.g. how many female Conservatives) then we would use the CONTingency table command.

Worked example

Use the following commands which put 100 random cases of either 1, 2 in C1 and either 1, 2, 3, 4, 5 in C2.

Command ? IRAN 100 cases from 1 to 2 put into C1

Command ? IRAN 100 cases from 1 to 5 put into C2

Now table the result:

Command ? CONTingency C1 with C2

You should get a result similar in appearance to the following – it will probably not be identical because the random number generator may well have produced a different pattern of data to fill C1 and C2:

```
        C2 > 1     2     3     4     5
            -----------------------------
C1    1     | 8 | 12 |  5 | 13 | 13 |   51
            -----------------------------
      2     |11 |  9 | 10 |  9 | 10 |   49
            -----------------------------
            19    21    15    22    23   100
```

There are two points to note about this command:

- Only try to table consecutive integers up to a maximum of 10 in each direction of the table.
- If you wish to put the cell results into another column for later analysis by chi-square then specify a third column as the starting point:

e.g. CONT C1 with C2, results from C10 onwards.

In this case, MICROSTATS responds with a message:

Data fed into C10–C14

and you can confirm this result by PRINTing out the relevant columns of data.

Note that you can put five or less cell contents into the new block. If you attempt to put more than five, then the command will be ignored. (This is because the CHI-Square command which uses these results will only accept a table 5 cells wide by 5 cells deep.)

You may also produce a CONTingency analysis of one column of data but in this case the command TALLY (p. 280) is probably superior.

CHISquare of data in C3–C5

The CHISquare command will accept a block of up to five rows/columns and perform a chi-square test upon the data. The underlying statistical assumption is that data is measured at the nominal level (e.g. code numbers representing a sex or a political party). To demontrate CHISquare, put in the following data using the random number generator. We are going to generate a sex coding (1, 2) in C1 and a political party coding in C2 (1, 2 or 3):

Command ? IRAN 100 nos from 1 to 2 put into C1

Command ? IRAN 100 nos from 1 to 3 put into C2

Command ? CONTingency C1 and C2 put cells into C3

```
      C2 >      1    2    3
              -------------------
C1      1  |  18 |  14 |  14 |    46
              -------------------
C2      2  |  19 |  19 |  16 |    54
              -------------------
                37   33   30      100
```

Data fed into C3-C5

A 'one-sample' CHISquare is also allowed, i.e. specification of one column of data (in which case, the number of 'expected' cells is inferred by splitting the total number of cases equally between the number of cells in the column). Up to 10 rows are allowed in a one-sample test.
    See LABEL (p. 280) for instructions how to label the rows of output.

CHISquare of data in C3–C5

Expected frequencies are printed below observed frequencies:

	C3	C4	C5	Totals
1	18	14	14	46
	17.02	15.18	13.80	
2	19	19	16	54
	19.98	17.82	16.20	
Totals	37	33	30	100

```
                0.06   +   0.09   +   0.00   +
                0.05   +   0.08   +   0.00   +
```

Total chi-square = 0.280   df = 2   p = 0.8695

(You will not get exactly these results because the random number generator will have generated a different pattern of initial data but it should not be too dissimilar.)
    CHISquare takes the initial sets of data in each cell (the 'observed') data and then works out the 'expected' data in each cell on the assumption that one variable is exactly proportionately represented within the other. In this case, we are trying to see if there are sex differences in the way in which people vote. For each cell, the 'expected' differences are worked out according to the formula

$$\frac{(\text{Observed–Expected})^2}{\text{Expected}}$$

and this is the chi-square for that cell. Finally all of the chi-squares are summed, the degrees of freedom (df) calculated according to the rule

$$(\text{Number of rows} - 1) * (\text{number of columns} - 1)$$

and the probability is worked out. The probability means the likelihood that we could have achieved a chi-square value as large as this by chance (where 1 = certainty or 100% whilst 0 = impossible or 0%). Any probability which is greater than 0.05 (or 5%) means that there is not a statistically significant difference in the proportions of C2 represented in C1 (in terms of this example, a sex difference in voting behaviour). The level of 5% is only a convention in statistics – we could choose 1% to be even more sure of our results should we so wish.

Points to note about chi-square are:

- The data should be measured at the nominal level, i.e. categories such as male/female.
- Cells with an expected frequency of less than 5 can generate chi-squares that give a misleading result. If this is the case, then a warning message will be given. It is generally best to combine categories to make the numbers in each cell so much larger.
- Zero cells may abort the analysis, with a division by zero error! Make sure that you have no zero cells in the analysis before you start by combining categories if necessary.

(See page 93)

Data generation

There are times when it is useful to generate displays of data for demonstration purposes. The following commands are provided in MICROSTATS:

GENErate values from 1 to 100 in C1

This will generate data from the first value to the second value stated in the relevant number range, and can be used to provide an index number for a series of data.

DEFIne the value of 10 into the first 5 rows of C1

This allows a constant to be put in as many rows of the column as you desire.

IRANdom 100 random integers from 1 to 100, put into C1–C5

IRANdom 100 random nos from 1 to 100, put into C1 seed = 625

This is an integer random number generator. You should remember to state the numbers of integers required, followed by the lower limit, the upper limit and the destination column. If a seed is specified, you can repeat the same series of random numbers (seed=3125 by default).

URANdom 100 random numbers and put into C2 (seed = integer)

URANdom 100 random numbers and put into C2–C5

The URANdom random number generator generates floating point numbers in the range 0 to 1 and puts the required number in the destination column. You can multiply them up if required, to give numbers in the required range. The 'seed' number allows you to generate identical data if desired.

Edit commands

It is often necessary to edit data because it may have to be manipulated or sifted to meet particular needs. The following editing commands are supplied:

PICK the rows from 1 to 2 in C1 and put into C2

This command enables the user to 'top' or 'tail' a column to ensure it is generally correct. If you had entered one too many items in a column in error, then the PICK command could be used to put the correct number of items back into the same or a different column.

RECOde the values from 3 to 5 in C1 to 1 and put into C2

This command enables the user to 'degrade' the data. For example, if there were several political parties coded 1 to 6 then they could be reduced to 2 groups by recoding all the values from 1 to 3 to a 1 and all the values from 4 to 6 to a 2.

CHOOse values 1 to 5 in C1 (and corresponding C2) and put into C3 and C4

This is one of the most powerful editing commands, as it enables us to make subgroups for further analysis. For example, if males/females were coded as 1, 2 in C1 then the 'male' data could be separated from the 'female' data.

Worked example

SET C1
    DATA > 1 2 1 2 1 2 1 2 1 2
    DATA > END

```
SET C2
DATA > 3 2 7 4 2 6 4 2 1 4
DATA > END
```

CHOOSE 1 in C1 (corr C2) and put into C3 and C4

PRINT C3 C4

	C3	C4
	(n= 5)	(n= 5)
1.	1.000	3.000
2.	1.000	7.000
3.	1.000	2.000
4.	1.000	4.000
5.	1.000	1.000

As you can see, the coding number in C1, i.e. 1, and the corresponding data from C2 have been sifted out and put into C3 and C4.

OMIT data from 5 to 7 in C3 put into C4

This data is the obverse of the CHOOse command. Whereas CHOOse will select the data that you request and transfer that data over to the destination columns, the OMIT command will transfer over all of the data except that which you wish to omit.

JOIN the data in C2 to the end of C1 and put back into C1

Notice here that the data you wish to join to the end of the other column is specified first – you have the opportunity to put the newly augmented column in a new column or back into one of the original ones.

SUBStitute (or PUT) the value of 10 into row 9 of C2

This command would be used if you had made an error (e.g. in data input) that you wish to correct after having entered the data. Remember that the value that you wish to substitute is specified first, and the row of the column for which it is destined is specified second.

LET Cx(y) = Value

This performs the same function as SUBStitute but in a somewhat more intuitive manner. For example, if you had entered the series of numbers 10 20 3 40 50 in C1 and you had intended the third number to be 30 and not 3, you may correct your error at the end of data entry by

LET C1(3) = 30 (i.e. put 30 into the 3rd row of C1)

DELETE row 2 from C1
DELETE row 2 from C1–C5

This command will delete a row of data from a column (or a block of columns). Be careful with any DELETE or ERASE command as, once deleted, the data cannot be recovered.

INSErt the value n1 after row n2 of Cx
INSErt the value Cx after n rows of Cy

The INSErt command allows the user to place either a single value OR another column after a specified row number of a column. This command is most useful if DELEte has removed a row in error, or if a number has been skipped during input with SET.

ERASE data in COLUMNS C3–C5

This command erases single columns or blocks of columns.

COPY C1 into C2
COPY the block from C3–C6 into a new block starting at C13

The simple version of copy performs a straight copy of one column into another. The more advance version will copy a block of data but the user should specify the source columns using a hyphen (no spaces!) and the start of the new block.

DISPlay the data in C3 to 1 decimal place
DISPlay the data in unchanged cols to 2 decimal places

This command alters the displayed value to the required number of decimal places but not the value which MICROSTATS holds internally which will be about 10 places of decimals.

You may either change one column specifically or the rest of the unchanged columns by specifying no column number. To display no decimal places use the command DISPlay 0 (rather than the command DISPlay with no parameters).

ROW Commands

The ROW commands exactly parallel the column statistics on p. 275–6 except that they operate upon rows across columns rather than individual columns which is the usual method of analysis. When any of the ROW commands are issued, a table is given from which users may select the value(s) in which they are interested. The ROW commands are as follows:

RDEScribe	the data in row 1 of C1–C5
RSUM	of data in row 1 of C1–C5, put results into C6
RSSQ	(Sum of Squares) row 1 of C1–C5, put into C6
RMEAn	of data in row 1 of C1–C5, put results into C6
RMEDian	of data in row 1 of C1–C5, put results into C6
RMODe	of data in row 1 of C1–C5, put results into C6
RMINimum	of data in row 1 of C1–C5, put results into C6
RMAXimum	of data in row 1 of C1–C5, put results into C6
RSTAndard	dev-n [pop'n] data in row 1 of C1–C5, results in C6
RSTD	dev-n [sample] data in row 1 of C1–C5, results in C6
RSEMean	stand. error of mean of row 1 of C1–C5 results in C6
RSKEw	(skew) of data in row 1 of C1–C5, results in C6
RQUArtiles	of data in row 1 of C1–C5, results in C6
RPERcentiles	of data in row 1 of C1–C5, results in C6

You may specify one row only for the relevant statistics.

If you do not specify a row but instead specify an extra column, then the results of each row will be put into the relevant row of the 'extra' column. For example,

RMEAN C1–C5 C6

will put the mean of each row of C1–C5 into C6.

Statistical testing

To perform a statistical test of data which has been measured with a ratio or interval level of measurement, we can use either of the TWOSample or the POOLed commands. The TWOSample command assumes that we wish to test the hypothesis that the means of two samples differ statistically from each other. The underlying assumption is that the population variances need not be approximately equal.

Worked example

IRAN 100 values from 1 to 100, put into C1 and C2

TWOS C1 and C2

Twosample t C1 vs. C2

	n	mean	stdev	se mean
C1	100	52.9200	29.9504	2.9950
C2	100	48.4400	27.2528	2.7253

95.00 PCT C.I. for mu C1 – C2 : (–3.508, 12.468)
ttest mu C1   = mu C2   (vs. n.e.) :

T= 1.106   p = 0.2699 approx. d.f. = 196

The output requires some interpretation. For information, the means, standard deviations, standard errors and 95% confidence intervals (= C.I.) of the mean are displayed. The critical results come on the last line of the display where the critical values are those for T and p. The letter T indicates the number of standard errors by which the two means differ and p, the probability of getting results like this by chance factors (where p varies from 0 to 1). As a rough rule of thumb, we would expect a significant result for T to be anything in excess of the value of 2.00. The value of p gives us the probability that the means differ by an amount that they do under the influence of chance factors alone. A significant result is achieved when p is equal to or less than the value of 0.05 (i.e. there is a 5% chance or less that the observed differences could have occurred by chance alone). The inference is, therefore, that non-chance factors are operating in which case we reject the null hypothesis that the population means (mu) are equal and accept the alternative hypothesis that the populations means (mu) are not, in fact, equal.

The d.f. (degrees of freedom) figure is used by MICROSTATS internally to calculate the values for T and p. Usually it is a figure approximately equal to (n1 + n2 – 2) where n1 is the number of rows of data in the first column and n2 is the number of rows in the second column.

POOLed test for C1 vs. C2

The output and interpretation of the POOLed test are almost identical to that of the TWOSample command. However, this command may be used if the user is confident that the two populations have approximately equal variances. If in doubt, the user should generally use the TWOSample test.

MANN-Whitney test

This is a non-parametric test which is generally regarded as almost as powerful as its parametric analogue (TWOSample test or 't' test). The data may be measured at the ordinal level (as internally, the calculations are performed upon ranked data). For a full interpretation of 'u', the user should consult a statistical source. The Mann–Whitney test is regarded as closely related to the Wilcoxon rank-sum test. Strictly speaking, the test is used to evaluate the difference between population distributions, not population means, but when the distributions of the groups are similar the test does in fact measure differences in central tendency. Column lengths are limited to 100 in this command, as the test requires the columns to be joined together.

As with the TWOSample and POOLed test, the critical values are those for T and the probability. As a rule of thumb, one is looking for a T value of approximately 2.00 or greater and a probability equal to or less than 0.05 (2-tailed test) in order to achieve evidence that the distributions differ from each other significantly. (Small samples (i.e. < 11) will require reference to Mann–Whitney tables to ascertain the significance level.)

KOLMogorov-Smirnov tests (one sample and two sample)

The Kolmogorov–Smirnov (or K–S) test is a non-parametric test which is much less cumbersome than the traditional chi-square test. It tests the cumulative frequency distributions (observed against expected) and reports a figure which needs to be interpreted by reference to K–S tables. It is most suited to the analysis, for example, of questionnaire items and is used in the following way. If there are four potential answers to a question and any answer is as likely as any other then the 'expected' cumulative frequencies will be 25, 50, 75 and 100%. The test will take the actual distribution of answers, test them against 'expected' and report the result.

If there are prior expectations of the results (e.g. testing against previous data) then these may be placed in the second column for a two-sample test. For example, out of 80 answers to a question such as 'Should the death penalty be retained?' scaled as (1) strongly opposed (2) opposed (3) in favour and (4) strongly in favour, we collect the following data:

1   (7 people)   2   (15 people)

3   (20 people)   4   (38 people)

and then analyse the data as follows:
(First set the data 7, 15, 20, 38 in C1)

KOLM C1

Kolmogorov-Smirnov [D] = 0.225
    (Consult tables for significance)

If we have the proportions from a previous questionnaire, then we can put these into C2 and perform the analysis:

KOLM C1 C2

(In this case, the 'expected' frequencies are those taken from C2 instead of the assumption of an equal spread which would be the case in a one-sample test.)

TTEST data in C1 against a value of 50

This test is used to test a sample mean against a known value or population mean. The critical value is to observe whether or not the value is equal to or less than $p = 0.05$ in which case we conclude that there is a statistically significant difference between the sample mean and the value.

TDIST 1.9603 at 2500 df

This calculation will give the user the proportion of a distribution (one- and two-tailed) that corresponds to the value for the degrees of freedom specified. It may be thought of as an alternative to look-up tables.

TINT for data in C1 at 95%

This command gives the user the confidence intervals for the data at the confidence level requested.

CHID for value 3.84 at 1 df

This command is another alternative to a look-up table. It provides the user with the probability of achieving the specified value at specific degrees of freedom. In the above example, we would get the response.

Probability = 0.0500

which informs us that with a normal chi-square table of 2×2, i.e. two rows and two columns which is 1 d.f. then a value of 3.84 would be achieved only 0.05 (5% of the time) by chance factors alone.

Normal distribution

To generate a sample that has the shape of a 'normal', i.e. bell-shaped distribution, use the following command:

NORMal 200 values into C1

By default, the mean will be 0.00 and the standard deviation (sigma) will be 0.15. To specify your own mean and standard deviation, specify them as the second and third values on the command line, e.g.

1st value   2nd value   3rd value

v   v   v

> NORMal 200 values, mean 100, sigma 15 in C1

To specify a seed (to help generate identical distributions) then make the seed (= 3125 by default) an odd integer between 0 and 32 767, thus:

> NORMal 200 values, mean 100, sigma 15 in C1, seed = 625

To draw a sample (from any column of data) then use:

> SAMPle 20 values from C1, put into C2-C3

A seed may be specified to draw the same sample, if needed:

> SAMPle 10 values from C1 put into C2, seed = 625

The seed may be any odd integer from 0 to 32 767 (6125 by default). You can also set the default random number generator seed thus:

> SEED x (where x is the integer seed value)

Time series analysis

> LTREnd C1 C2 (Linear TREnd of data in C1, put into C2)

This performs a linear trend (i.e. regression) of the data (assumed to be 'y' in C1) against an imaginary column of data (assumed to be 'x' with values from 1 . . . n). The results are then placed in C2.

> MAVE C1 C2 (Moving AVErage of data in C1, put into C2)

This performs a four-quarter moving average for the data in C1, putting the results in C2. The user should ensure that the number of rows is exactly divisible by 4 to give accurate results. Note that the first two rows and last two rows of a moving average column are 0 (representing no data).

> ADDM (ADDitive Model of data in C1)

The form of the command is:

> ADDM C1 C2 C3 C4   (where all four columns are essential! NB Hyphens are not allowed here)

C1 contains the [A]ctual date
C2 contains the [T]rend line
C3 contains the [S]easonal data
C4 contains the [R]esidual data

A table of quarterly deviations is printed together with the average quarterly deviation. The average of the residual data is also computed and this should take a value close to zero.

MULM (MULtiplicative Model of data in C1)

The form of this command, and the output from it, are almost identical to ADDM (above). The syntax is the same and the only difference is that the average of the residual data should approximate to a value of 1.0 and not zero.

Retrieve and save files

RETRieve (and then follow instructions)

RETRieve a:myfile

This command retrieves files that have been previously saved under MICROSTATS. It will not retrieve other files which might be accessed with FREAd.

SAVE (and then follow instructions)

SAVE a:myfile

This command will save the workfile for the user. No extension should be used as MICROSTATS actually saves two files, one of which is in specially coded numerical format (for fast access and compact disk storage) and the other of which is a text file in which names, if allocated, are stored. The user does need to be concerned with such details but it does explain why two files will appear on the disk for every worksheet saved, one with a .MCS extension and the other with a .NAM extension.

FREAd

FREAd a:datafile

The FREAd command will read, or attempt to read, any file in which data has been saved in a straight ASCII format. As FREAd can only read in completely 'rectangular' blocks of data, it is important that any data that is exported by another package should be absolutely rectangular. For example, to export a spreadsheet of 2×10 columns and 2×5 columns, then pad the last columns to 10 with zeros to make a 'rectangle' that is 2×10. Adjustments could be made once the data is successfully imported into MICROSTATS.

Remember that MICROSTATS will only read numerical and not textual data. The user will be prompted for the start column of the data, which will then be read into consecutive columns.

If data is prepared using a text or word processor for input into MICROSTATS as well as other packages, then any legitimate data separator (; or , or <space>) may be used.

FWRIte

FWRIte will write out data as a straight ASCII file with a choice of delimiters allowed. Before using this command, remind yourself of the start and end columns by using INFO as FWRIte will request your start and end columns.

FERAse
FERAse myfile

FERAse will erase any type of file whether saved under MICROSTATS or not. If there are non-MICROSTATS files that the user wishes to erase, then the full file name with drive letter, name and extension should be given.

Directory management

DIREctory [A:] (or DIR)

DIREctory will list all of files on the logged drive (by default), or the files on the specified drive.

Note that DIR does not change the logged disk drive. In addition to the normal directory display, a separate list of MICROSTATS files is given. Wildcard characters such as * or ? are not implemented in this command.

LOGD
LOGD A:

LOGD with no parameter will remind you of the drive upon which you are currently logged, and at the same time issue a directory of files.

LOGD with a legitimate file disk-drive parameter will both log the user on to the specified drive and also issue a directory.

CHDIR [Dr:] Subdirectory

This changes the logged subdirectory (and also gives a list of files). If a drive is specified, then the user is logged on to that drive also.

DISK [Dr:]

This gives system information on the drive including percentage used as a percentage of total disk space, and the free bytes available.

General commands

HELP (or ?) (The F1 key may also be used)

HELP gives access to eight help screens and an index page. At the bottom of each page the user may access the [N]ext Page, [L]ast Page, [E]xit or specify a page number to access directly.

STOP

STOP completes the work session. The user is prompted to save the worksheet and also asked to confirm the exit in order to ensure that an accidental exit does not occur.

NAME

This names columns of data, e.g.

NAME C1 'Heights' C2 'Weights'

Take care that the same, single, apostrophe is used.

INFOrmation

This command informs the user of the numbers of columns (and their length) still available for use. The column numbers, names allocated (if any) and number of data items in each column will be notified.

MICROSTATS users should use this command frequently to check on the status of their worksheet and to confirm that the data that they have in their worksheet conforms with their expectations. Similarly, PRINT should be used in conjunction with INFO to check on the data in columns.

PRINT C1
PRINT C1–C5
PRINT C10 C2 C5 C8

PRINT is a command which always requires information as to which columns of data to print. If a range of columns is requested, then it should be specified with a hyphen but with no spaces on either side of the hyphen. Only seven consecutive columns may be printed if the hyphen form of the command is used and it is not generally sensible to attempt to print out more than seven columns if the user wishes to preserve a 'clean' screen display.

Long columns will stop after 20 items (a screenful) and prompt the user to view the next screenful or to exit to the next command. Names are displayed together with column contents.

PRON

The PRON command stands for PRinter ON. Output normally directed to the screen will now appear on the printer. In some cases, this may mean performing 'blind' so the user should have rehearsed a particular sequence of commands first to verify their effect, taken a note of the same and then repeated the same with the PRON switch toggled on.

PROF

The PROF command stands for PRinter OFf. Output will be redirected back to the screen for a normal 'dialogue'.

NOTE

NOTE displays a comment for documentation purposes. MICROSTATS will ignore any data on a note line and in this respect it resembles REM in a BASIC program.

FKEY

This gives two diagrams of the distribution of commands on the function keys. It may also be activated with SHIFT-F1. The diagrams may be dumped to a printer to provide templates if desired.

PRTSC

This command enables the user to obtain a screen-dump (as the normal PrtSc key is often used to 'SNAP' screens). This function may also be activated by either CTRL-PRTSC or CTRL-Pg Dn (one or other will almost certainly work on your computer).

CLEAR

This command clears the screen (before a screen-snap for example, or a screen-dump to the printer). If the printer is engaged with PRON then a form-feed will also be sent to the printer.

Avoiding crashes!

Despite the warnings built in at various points, MICROSTATS will occasionally crash or 'abort' when it cannot cope with certain error conditions, e.g. a calculation which involves a division by zero.

Here are some tips and hints to minimize the occasions upon which MICROSTATS will abort, or at least to make sure that the consequences are not too dire!

- Do make sure that you do not enter more than a lineful (or a little over) of data in the SET command.
- Do save your precious data after a fair amount of typing or column manipulation. A SAVE every 15–20 minutes only takes a few seconds and ensures that the potential loss of time is limited to this amount.
- Do make use of INFO, PRINT and the HELP screens in order to keep a check on the status of the worksheet.
- Do keep a note of events that caused the system to crash and avoid them in the future!

Saving output with SNAP

Although not technically a part of the MICROSTATS package, SNAP is a specialized 'Terminate-and-Stay-Resident' program that allows you to take up to 30 'snapshots' of your screen. When you conclude running MICROSTATS within the batch file MS.BAT, then the 'snapshots' you have taken will be 'developed' under the names SNAPSHOT.01 . . . SNAPSHOT.30. They will be written on to the drive you have specified when the main program exits. A supplementary program, DEVELOP, is run automatically from the MS-RUN batch file and will 'develop' your snapshots on to your floppy. These files may then be incorporated into a word processor or text editor of your choice for incorporation into other documents. If you wish to collate several snapshot files together into one working file, then this is easily accomplished by typing the following command from DOS:

COPY SNAPSHOT .* OUTPUT.DOC

with the result that all of the 'snapshot' files will be stitched together into one output file, named OUTPUT.DOC.

The following five files are essential for the 'clean' operation of SNAP. These are:

MARK.COM	which marks the position of SNAP.EXE in memory
SNAP.EXE	the 'snapshot' Terminate-and-Stay-Resident program
DEVELOP.EXE	the 'developer' program

TSR.COM
RELEASE.COM $\left.\right\}$ two files that between them release the memory used by SNAP back to DOS.

The Commands PRON and PROF may still be used to retain a measure of compatibility with MINITAB. However, the SNAP system may still be preferred on the grounds that the output files produced allow for a degree of editing (e.g. to eliminate error messages) that the PRON/PROF routines do not.

Alphabetical index of commands

? (= HELP)
ABS
ADD
ADDModel
ANTIlog
APPEnd
AVERage

CHID
CHDIrectory
CHISquare
CHOOse
CLEAR
CONTingency
COPY
CORRelate
COUNt

DEFIne
DELEte
DESCribe
DIREctory (or DIR)
DISK
DISPlay
DIVIde

NAME

NORMal distribution

NOTE

OMIT

PERCentile

PICK

PLOT

POOL

PRINt

PROF

PRON

PRTScreen

PUT

QUARtiles

RAISe

RANK

RDEScribe

READ

RECIprocal

RECOde

REGRess

RETRieve

RMAXimum

RMEAn

RMEDian

RMINimum

RMODe

ROUNd

RPERcentiles

RQUArtiles

RSKEw

RSSQ (row sum of squares)

Appendix C: Introduction to spreadsheets using Lotus 1-2-3™

Objectives

After reading and working through the examples in this appendix you should be able to:

- enter data into a spreadsheet;
- use formulae to perform calculations;
- build a simple model using Lotus 1-2-3;
- create and print graphs of your data.

Getting started

Switch on the computer.(!)

 Put in your own floppy disk, which must be formatted.

If you are now in Windows open the Applications window. Point to and click on Lotus 1-2-3 icon. When the next screen appears you will see that 123 is highlighted at the top left of the screen; this is what we want, so just press RETURN and wait a few seconds. If your system does not use Windows, change to the subdirectory for Lotus, and type in Lotus. You should now get into the package, and when the first screen appears, you will see that 123 is highlighted at the top left of the screen, this is what we want, so just press RETURN and wait a few seconds.

Looking around

There are three bits to the keyboard that you are sitting at! Although keyboards differ, there are 10 or 12 keys called the **function keys**, the many keys in the middle are the **main keyboard**, and usually there are 16 keys on the right known as the **number pad**; you may also have **movement keys** with arrows printed on them. It is quite possible to use Lotus via the mouse, but the advantage is small. This will depend in part on the version of Lotus that you are using – if you have a version with a number below 4, then using the keyboard directly is probably the best approach; if you have Version 4, then the mouse will prove quicker. These notes assume that you are using a version with a number less than 4, but the basic principles apply to all spreadsheets, although the detailed instructions may differ slightly from version to version.

What you can see on the screen are the letters A, B, C, etc. across the top, and the numbers 1, 2, 3, 4, etc. down the left-hand side. These letters and numbers tell us where we are in the spreadsheet. Any letter and number combination defines a **cell**, so if you were in cell G45, you would be in column G and row 45. You are currently in cell A1, provided that you have not touched any other keys in the meantime!

Before you start to move around inside the spreadsheet, notice that the word READY is at the top right-hand corner of the screen, as we do different things with the spreadsheet, different words will appear here, such as WAIT.

At the top left you will see A1 since we are currently in cell A1. Using the movement keys, press the arrow pointing to the right twice (it is the number 6 key on some keyboards). You will see the cursor move to the right, and if you look at the top left you will see that the reference has changed to C1.

Keep pressing the right arrow key until you cannot go any further. Which letters represent the column which is furthest to the right?

Now press the HOME key and you will be taken back to cell A1. In fact, wherever you are in a Lotus spreadsheet, the HOME key will always take you back to cell A1.

Press the downward-facing arrow key until you can go no further. Which number represents the last row of your spreadsheet? (As a short cut, use the PgDn key several times).

Press the HOME key. You should now be back at cell A1.

What you have just done is to find out how big the spreadsheet can be. For most purposes to do with this book, you will only be using a fraction of this size!

Putting something into the spreadsheet

There are three different things that you can put into the cell of a spreadsheet:

- Words
- Numbers
- Formulae.

The first two are very easy, the third one just takes a little thought!

Words

To put a word into a cell, just move the cursor to the cell where you want the word to appear (using the movement keys, or the mouse) and simply type in the word(s). When you have typed in the word, press the RETURN key. Try it. Put the word Wood into cell A3 and press the down arrow. Now put the words Window frames into cell A4. Everything looks OK, but if you move the cursor to cell B4 you will see that it covers up ames of the word frames which you have just put into cell A4. This is because the cells are only nine characters wide when you create a spreadsheet. Do not panic!

To make the cells in column A wider, put the cursor back into column A (it does not matter where), and then press the / (slash) key on the bottom right-hand side of the main keyboard. You will see a series of words appear at the top of the screen. These are the menus which allow you to control various aspects of your spreadsheet.

To make the column wider, make sure that the word Worksheet is highlighted, and press RETURN. You will see another menu appear. Use the movement keys to highlight the word Column (because we want to do something to a column), and press RETURN. There is yet another menu. With the words Set Width highlighted, press RETURN, and you will see (at the top of the screen) that the current width of the column is 9. Type in the number 15 (the new width required) and press RETURN again. The menus have now disappeared and column A is 15 spaces wide.

Now SAVE your spreadsheet, again using the menus. Get to the menus by pressing the slash key (/) and select the word File. (You can either use the movement keys to highlight the word and then press RETURN, or, for more speed, just press the first letter of the word, in this case F). From the subsequent menu select Save and you will see a proposed name appear. Use the backspace key (at the top right of the main keyboard) to delete the suggested name, and type in A:MATILDA. Then press RETURN. The A: tells the machine to save the spreadsheet on to the floppy disk (so that you can take it away with you!) and MATILDA is the name of the file, so that you can find it next time you want to use it.

N.B. It is good practice to save your spreadsheet (or any other work you do on a computer) about every 10 minutes (just in case ...).

Numbers

Putting numbers into cells is exactly the same as putting words in. Take the cursor to the cell where you want the number to appear, and type in the number; when you have done this, press the RETURN key. Go to cell B3 and put in the number 30. Then go to cell B4 and put in the number 5. Now go to cell C3 and put in the number 1.45, and put the number 45.98 into cell C4.

Now SAVE your spreadsheet again. This time, after / File Save the name suggested is correct (MATILDA), so just press RETURN and then R for Replace.

Formulae

Now we come to the clever bit. What you need to do is to multiply the numbers in the B column by the numbers in the C column and put the results in the D column. **But the golden rule of spreadsheets is never do any calculations by hand or by calculator – always make the machine do the work.**

To put a formula into the spreadsheet, take the cursor to the cell where you want the answer to appear. In this case it is cell D3. Now type in

$$+B3*C3$$

You will see that this appears at the top left-hand side of the screen. Now press the RETURN key. N.B. If you miss out the + sign, the machine assumes you are putting in words. The initial + is essential. The number 43.50 will appear in cell D3, and if you look at the top left-hand corner of the screen, you will see the formula which you have just typed in. So the answer is where you wanted it to be, but the memory stores the formula which gave the answer. Go to cell D4 and put in a formula to multiply B4 by C4. (You should get the answer 229.90.)

Now SAVE your spreadsheet again. (/ F S RETURN)

Making it all presentable

As it stands, your spreadsheet does the calculations, but it would not necessarily be very clear to anyone else what the various numbers represent. (If you were to leave this spreadsheet and come back to it in a month, you would probably have forgotten what the columns represent). Therefore we need to put labels on to the columns and rows.

Go to cell A2 and type in the word Item, and press RETURN. Now put the word Amount in cell B2, the word Cost in cell C2, and the word Total in the cell D2. This now makes a little more sense to anyone else looking at your spreadsheet, but it still looks untidy since the numbers do not appear below the words! To correct this, go to cell B2 and press the F2 key (on the left-hand side of the keyboard) to Edit a cell, and you will see

'Amount

at the top left of the screen. Use the arrow keys to get the cursor to the A of Amount, and press the backspace key to delete the '. Now type in " and press RETURN. The word will now move to the right-hand side of the column, to match the positioning of the numbers. Do the same to the words Cost and Total. Your spreadsheet now looks fairly tidy.

 Now SAVE your spreadsheet again.

Doing a bit more

You are now going to add a few extra rows to your spreadsheet, so that you can then perform some extra operations. Starting at row 5, add the lines shown in Table C.1. Now we want to do the calculations for the new items which we have added into the spreadsheet – but you do not need to put in any more formulae!

Table C.1

Row	A	Column B	C
5	Doors	3	36.78
6	Glass	24.1	0.55
7	Sand	12.3	2.50
8	Cement	37	9.63
9	Bricks	2400	0.37

Take the cursor to cell D4 – you should see the formula which you put into the cell appear at the top left of the screen (+B4*C4). We want to copy the formula, so we need the menus. Press the slash key (/) followed by the letter C (for Copy) and you will see a message appear suggesting where to copy from (in this case D4). Since this is correct, press RETURN. A new message appears suggesting where to copy to (again suggesting D4). This is not correct, so press the down arrow, to get to cell D5 – you will see the reference at the top of the screen change to D5 – this is now correct, so press RETURN. You will see the number 110.34 appear in cell D5. You have just succeeded in copying a formula from one cell to another. Notice that the machine copies the basic idea of multiplication down to the next row, and updates from B4 and C4 to B5 and C5.

If you need to copy a formula to more than one other cell, it is almost as quick. Get the cursor to cell D5 (if it is not already there) and then press the slash key, the C for Copy and RETURN to copy from cell D5. Now move the cursor to D6, but instead of pressing RETURN immediately, press the full stop. You will see two full stops appear at the top of the screen after the D6. Now press the down arrow key three times, until the reference D9 is shown at the top of the screen and the cells D6 to D9 are highlighted. Now press RETURN and you will see that the formula has been copied to all of the cells. You can copy from a range of cells too.

 Now SAVE your spreadsheet again.

Additions

If all you want to do is add the contents of two cells together, then you can just put in a formula, such as +B23+F56; even three numbers could easily be dealt with in this way. However, if there is a whole column or row of figures that need to be added together, then we can use a special formula which is considerably quicker. To add up a column, say, you first need to identify the first cell and the last cell that are going to be added together. In the case of the MATILDA spreadsheet that you are creating, we want to add up the Total column, column D. The first cell is D3 and the last cell is D9. Take your cursor to cell D11, where we want to put the answer. Because you are using a special formula, you need to start with a special symbol (@). What you should type in is

@SUM(D3..D9)

and the answer you will get is 1672.06. Put the word Sub-Total into the cell A11.

 Now SAVE your spreadsheet again.

Now go to cell A13 and put in the word Labour, to cell A15 and put in Total Cost, to A17 and put in VAT, and to A19 and put in the word Bill. In cell B13 put 55 and in cell C13 the number 18.95. In cell B17 we want to put

17.5%, but if you type this you may get .18 or.175 in the cell, depending on the exact way in which the package has been set up. Complete the spreadsheet by multiplying cell B13 by cell C13 and putting the result in cell D13. Add the labour cost to the sub-total and put the result in cell D15. Work out the VAT by multiplying the figure in cell D15 by 0.175, and then add the VAT to the total cost and put the result in cell D19.

 Now SAVE your spreadsheet again.

Further tidying

To make your spreadsheet look even clearer to others, you can now add a few finishing touches.

Go to cell D18 and press the ' key to con the machine into thinking that you are putting in a word, rather than a number, and then press the – on the main keyboard about eight times, and then press RETURN. Now take the cursor to cell D19. To get the amount shown as pounds go to the menus, press

/	for the menus
R	for Range
F	for Format
C	for Currency
RETURN	for 2 decimal places
and RETURN	to confirm that it is for cell D19

You may just see the answer, but you may see ********. If this is the case, do not panic. All this means is that the contents of the cell are too wide to fit into the current width. With the cursor somewhere in the D column, use

/

W

C

S

10

RETURN

to widen the column. You probably now know enough to tidy up other bits of the spreadsheet so that it looks like Table C.2

Table C.2

Item	Amount	Cost	Total
Wood	30.00	1.45	£43.50
Window frames	5.00	45.98	£229.90
Doors	3.00	36.78	£110.34
Glass	24.10	0.55	£13.26
Sand	12.30	2.50	£30.75
Cement	37.00	9.63	£356.31
Bricks	2400.00	0.37	£888.00
Sub-total			£1672.06
Labour	55.00	18.95	£1042.25
Total cost			£2714.31
VAT		0.175	£475.00
Bill			£3189.31

 Make sure you have saved your spreadsheet.

Better quality presentation can be achieved if a package such as Wysiwyg is on the machine. There are also many other add-in packages which can be used, or you can import your data into a DTP package.

Doing more – graphs

Spreadsheets can also be linked into the graphing facility in Lotus 1-2-3. To illustrate this we will create a second spreadsheet called HERBERT. (Make sure that you have saved MATILDA), and then clear the spreadsheet by typing

/ W E Y

Do this now!

Pie charts

Put the following information into the first two columns of your spreadsheet:

Type	Amount
Alpha	50
Beta	20
Gamma	30
Delta	10

The first graph which you will create will be a pie chart. This is suitable for showing the relationship between a small group of items, say the sources of finance for a local authority, or where the money raised is actually spent.

Take the cursor to cell B2 and press the slash key. Type

G	for Graph
T	for Type
P	for Pie
A	for which data set to use

Press the full stop (.) and use the down arrow key to highlight the other figures in the column. Press RETURN. This is to tell the machine which numbers are to go into the pie. Now type V for View to look at your pie chart. Press any key to go back to the spreadsheet.

To improve the presentation of the graph, we need to do a little more work. First of all we need to put a title on to it. Type O for Options. Type the letter T for Title, and F for First Line and put in Product Sales, then press RETURN. Then type Q for Quit. Now view your pie chart again.

 You can now save the pie chart to disk by typing S for Save and making sure that the machine saves to A:PIE. Once it is saved, type Q for Quit. NB In Lotus it is necessary to save each graph if you want to print it out at a later stage.

Line graphs

The other most commonly used graph is a line graph to show the level of some measure over time, such as income level, percentage paying a tax, or number of people using a service.

Table C.3

Year	Visitors	Income
1	350	200
2	400	250
3	450	320
4	600	420
5	590	400
6	490	380
7	530	410
8	580	560
9	620	580
10	735	678

Create a new spreadsheet and call it MAURICE and put the information in Table C.3 into columns A, B and C. Now take the cursor to cell A2 and press the slash key, then

G   for Graph

T   for Type

L   for Line

X   for the X axis

then type a full stop and use the down arrow to highlight all of the numbers in the column. Press RETURN. Now type A for the first data set, take the cursor to B2, press the full stop, and use the arrow keys to highlight all of the numbers in the column. Press RETURN. Now view your graph.

Now get back to the graph menu by pressing the space bar. You are going to add a graph of income to the graph of visitors. Press B for the second data set, now take the cursor to cell C2, press the full stop and use the arrow keys to highlight all of the numbers in the column. Press RETURN again. Now view your graph again.

 Save your graph now, calling it LINE.

As you will have seen, there are several other types of graph that you can draw – you should try these out for yourself.

Printing spreadsheets and graphs

To print a spreadsheet, we again use the menus. Press the HOME key to get back to cell A1. Use

/	for the menus
P	for Print
P	for Printer
RETURN	
.	full stop

and use the arrow keys to highlight all of the information that you want to print. Press RETURN. Type G for Go and you should get a printed copy of your spreadsheet at the local printer.

If you have built a fairly big spreadsheet, you may not be able to get it to fit onto a single page of paper. One way out of this is to change the size of type used.

To print a graph, you need to get out of Lotus 1-2-3 spreadsheet and into a different part of the package. Having saved your spreadsheet, type

/	for menus
Q	for Quit
Y	for Yes

and you will get back to the first screen that you saw some time ago. If you have had enough, type E for Exit, but if you want to carry on, type P for Printgraph. You will now see a new screen which contains various references on where to find the graph you want to print, where to find the various fonts and which hardware you are using. Type I for Image-Select and you should get a list of graphs which are on your floppy disk. Select the Pie Chart. Type G for Go, and provided that the printer is correctly set up, you should now get a graph. Once it is printed, you can either print more graphs, or type E for Exit and Y for Yes.

End bit

If you have followed all this appendix, you know enough to build basic spreadsheets and to draw a few graphs.

Reminders

Function keys – on the left of the keyboard

F1 – help
F2 – edit a cell

Exercises

1. Build the following spreadsheets and draw the appropriate graphs:
   (a) Find the salary bill for an organization which has the groups of workers shown in Table C.4

Table C.4		
Group	*Number*	*Average salary*
Manual	2 500	8 750
Office	247	10 034
Junior managers	116	15 327
Middle managers	31	21 673
Top managers	17	43 668

   (b) Create a pie chart for the number of workers in each group.
   (c) Create a pie chart for the salary bill for each group.

2. Put the data in Table C.5 into a spreadsheet.

Table C.5

Year	Income	Expenditure
1	500	470
2	650	600
3	640	650
4	720	780
5	890	850
6	1001	890
7	990	950
8	960	990

(a) Create a line graph of income.
(b) Create a line graph of expenditure and put it on to the same axes.
(c) Calculate the difference between income and expenditure in a new column. Create a graph of this new column.

Appendix D: EZESTATS

EZESTATS is a program designed to teach you elementary statistics. If you already know some statistics but need a quick refresher course, then EZESTATS wil prove especially useful.

In EZESTATS, you are usually given some screens of information and are then asked a question to test your understanding. This 'interactive' mode of learning helps to ensure that you have understood the material at one stage before you move on to the next.

To run EZESTATS, all you have to do is to type

      EZE

at the MS-DOS prompt of your distribution disk. After the opening screens, you will enter the INFO interpreter and you are then given the following choice:

- Start
- Menu options and short cut keys

If you would like more information on how to use the INFO interpreter, then choose the second option. If you choose the first option, you will enter the first EZESTATS screen.

EZESTATS uses 'highlighted' buttons to go forward, back or to choose an option. You may need to adjust the contrast controls on your monitor (particularly if you are using a monochrome screen or a laptop computer) in order to see more clearly which buttons are highlighted. Pressing ESC at any time will give a menu which allows you to 'navigate' your way to any page in the lesson.

EZESTATS comes divided into two parts for convenience. Each lesson will take from 40 to 60 minutes to complete depending upon your progress, so you should be able to undertake the whole of the course in about 2 hours.

Appendix E: Normal distribution tables

Areas in the right-hand tail of the normal distribution

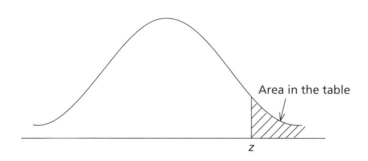

Area in the table

z

Table E.1

z	.00	.01	.02	.03	.04	.05	.06	.07	.08	.09
0.0	.5000	.4960	.4920	.4880	.4840	.4801	.4761	.4721	.4681	.4641
0.1	.4602	.4562	.4522	.4483	.4443	.4404	.4364	.4325	.4286	.4247
0.2	.4207	.4168	.4129	.4090	.4052	.4013	.3974	.3936	.3897	.3859
0.3	.3821	.3783	.3745	.3707	.3669	.3632	.3594	.3557	.3520	.3483
0.4	.3446	.3409	.3372	.3336	.3300	.3264	.3228	.3192	.3156	.3121
0.5	.3085	.3050	.3015	.2981	.2946	.2912	.2877	.2843	.2810	.2776
0.6	.2743	.2709	.2676	.2643	.2611	.2578	.2546	.2514	.2483	.2451
0.7	.2420	.2389	.2358	.2327	.2296	.2266	.2236	.2206	.2177	.2148
0.8	.2119	.2090	.2061	.2033	.2005	.1977	.1949	.1922	.1894	.1867

Table E.1 *contd*

z	.00	.01	.02	.03	.04	.05	.06	.07	.08	.09
0.9	.1841	.1814	.1788	.1762	.1736	.1711	.1685	.1660	.1635	.1611
1.0	.1587	.1562	.1539	.1515	.1492	.1496	.1446	.1423	.1401	.1379
1.1	.1357	.1335	.1314	.1292	.1271	.1251	.1230	.1210	.1190	.1170
1.2	.1151	.1131	.1112	.1093	.1075	.1056	.1038	.1020	.1003	.0985
1.3	.0968	.0951	.0934	.0918	.0901	.0885	.0869	.0853	.0838	.0823
1.4	.0808	.0793	.0778	.0764	.0749	.0735	.0721	.0708	.0694	.0681
1.5	.0668	.0655	.0643	.0630	.0618	.0606	.0594	.0582	.0571	.0559
1.6	.0548	.0537	.0526	.0516	.0505	.0495	.0485	.0475	.0465	.0455
1.7	.0446	.0436	.0427	.0418	.0409	.0401	.0392	.0384	.0375	.0367
1.8	.0359	.0351	.0344	.0336	.0329	.0322	.0314	.0307	.0301	.0294
1.9	.0287	.0281	.0274	.0268	.0262	.0256	.0250	.0244	.0239	.0233
2.0	.02275	.02222	.02169	.02118	.02068	.02018	.01970	.01923	.01876	.01831
2.1	.01786	.01743	.01700	.01659	.01618	.01578	.01539	.01500	.01463	.01426
2.2	.01390	.01355	.01321	.01287	.01255	.01222	.01191	.01160	.01130	.01101
2.3	.01072	.01044	.01017	.00990	.00964	.00939	.00914	.00889	.00866	.00842
2.4	.00820	.00798	.00776	.00755	.00734	.00714	.00695	.00676	.00657	.00639
2.5	.00621	.00604	.00587	.00570	.00554	.00539	.00523	.00508	.00494	.00480
2.6	.00466	.00453	.00440	.00427	.00415	.00402	.00391	.00379	.00368	.00357
2.7	.00347	.00336	.00326	.00317	.00307	.00298	.00289	.00280	.00272	.00264
2.8	.00256	.00248	.00240	.00233	.00226	.00219	.00212	.00205	.00199	.00193
2.9	.00187	.00181	.00175	.00169	.00164	.00159	.00154	.00149	.00144	.00139
3.0	.00135									
3.1	.00097									
3.2	.00069									
3.3	.00048									
3.4	.00034									

Table E.1 *contd*

zz	.00	.01	.02	.03	.04	.05	.06	.07	.08	.09
3.5	.00023									
3.6	.00016									
3.7	.00011									
3.8	.00007									
3.9	.00005									
4.0	.00003									

Appendix F: Present value tables

Table F.1

Years	1%	2%	3%	4%	5%	6%	7%	8%	9%	10%
1	.9901	.9804	.9709	.9615	.9524	.9434	.9346	.9259	.9174	.9091
2	.9803	.9612	.9426	.9426	.9070	.8900	.8734	.8573	.8417	.8264
3	.9706	.9423	.9151	.8890	.8638	.8396	.8163	.7938	.7722	.7513
4	.9610	.9238	.8885	.8548	.8227	.7921	.7629	.7350	.7084	.6830
5	.9515	.9057	.8626	.8219	.7835	.7473	.7130	.6806	.6499	.6209
6	.9420	.8880	.8375	.7903	.7462	.7050	.6663	.6302	.5963	.5645
7	.9327	.8706	.8131	.7599	.7107	.6651	.6227	.5835	.5470	.5132
8	.9235	.8535	.7894	.7307	.6768	.6274	.5820	.5403	.5019	.4665
9	.9143	.8368	.7664	.7026	.6446	.5919	.5439	.5002	.4604	.4241
10	.9053	.8203	.7441	.6756	.6139	.5584	.5083	.4632	.4224	.3855
11	.8963	.8043	.7224	.6496	.5847	.5268	.4751	.4289	.3875	.3505
12	.8874	.7885	.7014	.6246	.5568	.4970	.4440	.3971	.3555	.3186
13	.8787	.7730	.6810	.6006	.5303	.4688	.4150	.3677	.3262	.2897
14	.8700	.7579	.6611	.5775	.5051	.4423	.3878	.3405	.2992	.2633
15	.8613	.7430	.6419	.5553	.4810	.4173	.3624	.3152	.2745	.2394
16	.8528	.7284	.6232	.5339	.4581	.3936	.3387	.2919	.2519	.2176
17	.8444	.7142	.6050	.5134	.4363	.3714	.3166	.2703	.2311	.1978
18	.8360	.7002	.5874	.4936	.4155	.3503	.2959	.2502	.2120	.1799
19	.8277	.6864	.5703	.4746	.3957	.3305	.2765	.2317	.1945	.1635
20	.8195	.6730	.5537	.4564	.3769	.3118	.2584	.2145	.1784	.1486
21	.8114	.6598	.5375	.4388	.3589	.2942	.2415	.1987	.1637	.1351
22	.8034	.6468	.5219	.4220	.3418	.2775	.2257	.1839	.1502	.1228
23	.7954	.6342	.5067	.4057	.3256	.2618	.2109	.1703	.1378	.1117
24	.7876	.6217	.4919	.3901	.3101	.2470	.1971	.1577	.1264	.1015
25	.7798	.6095	.4776	.3751	.2953	.2330	.1842	.1460	.1160	.0923

Table F.1   *contd*

Years	11%	12%	13%	14%	15%	16%	17%	18%	19%	20%
1	.9009	.8929	.8850	.8772	.8696	.8621	.8547	.8475	.8403	.8333
2	.8116	.7972	.7831	.7695	.7561	.7432	.7305	.7182	.7062	.6944
3	.7312	.7118	.6931	.6750	.6575	.6407	.6244	.6086	.5934	.5787
4	.6587	.6355	.6133	.5921	.5718	.5523	.5337	.5158	.4987	.4823
5	.5935	.5674	.5428	.5194	.4972	.4761	.4561	.4371	.4190	.4019
6	.5346	.5066	.4803	.4556	.4323	.4104	.3898	.3704	.3521	.3349
7	.4817	.4523	.4251	.3996	.3759	.3538	.3332	.3139	.2959	.2791
8	.4339	.4039	.3762	.3506	.3269	.3050	.2848	.2660	.2487	.2326
9	.3909	.3606	.3329	.3075	.2843	.2630	.2434	.2255	.2090	.1938
10	.3522	.3220	.2946	.2697	.2472	.2267	.2080	.1911	.1756	.1615
11	.3173	.2875	.2607	.2366	.2149	.1954	.1778	.1619	.1476	.1346
12	.2858	.2567	.2307	.2076	.1869	.1685	.1520	.1372	.1240	.1122
13	.2575	.2292	.2042	.1821	.1625	.1452	.1299	.1163	.1042	.0935
14	.2320	.2046	.1807	.1597	.1413	.1252	.1110	.0985	.0876	.0779
15	.2090	.1827	.1599	.1401	.1229	.1079	.0949	.0835	.0736	.0649
16	.1883	.1631	.1415	.1229	.1069	.0930	.0811	.0708	.0618	.0541
17	.1696	.1456	.1252	.1078	.0929	.0802	.0693	.0600	.0520	.0451
18	.1528	.1300	.1108	.0946	.0808	.0691	.0592	.0508	.0437	.0376
19	.1377	.1161	.0981	.0826	.0703	.0596	.0506	.0431	.0367	.0313
20	.1240	.1037	.0868	.0728	.0611	.0514	.0433	.0365	.0308	.0261
21	.1117	.0926	.0768	.0638	.0531	.0443	.0370	.0309	.0259	.0217
22	.1007	.0826	.0680	.0560	.0462	.0382	.0316	.0262	.0218	.0181
23	.0907	.0738	.0601	.0491	.0402	.0329	.0270	.0222	.0183	.0151
24	.0817	.0659	.0532	.0431	.0349	.0284	.0231	.0188	.0154	.0126
25	.0736	.0588	.0471	.0378	.0304	.0245	.0197	.0160	.0129	.0105

Appendix G: Formula sheet

Arithmetic mean:

$$\overline{X} = \frac{\Sigma X}{n}$$

$$\overline{X} = \frac{\Sigma fX}{\Sigma f}$$

Range: Highest value – Lowest value

Standard deviation:

$$s = \sqrt{\left[\frac{\Sigma X^2}{n} - \left(\frac{\Sigma X}{n}\right)^2\right]}$$

$$s = \sqrt{\left[\frac{\Sigma fX^2}{\Sigma f} - \left(\frac{\Sigma fX}{\Sigma f}\right)^2\right]}$$

Quartile deviation:

$$QD = \frac{Q_3 - Q_1}{2}$$

Coefficient of variation

$$= \frac{\text{St. deviation}}{\text{Mean}} \times 100$$

Simple index: $\text{Index} = \dfrac{P_n}{P_0} \times 100$

Rebased index

$$= \frac{P_n}{P_*} \times 100$$

Laspeyres price

$$= \frac{\Sigma(P_n Q_0)}{\Sigma(P_0 Q_0)} \times 100$$

Laspeyres quantity $= \dfrac{\Sigma(P_0 Q_n)}{\Sigma(P_0 Q_0)} \times 100$

Paasche price $= \dfrac{\Sigma(P_n Q_n)}{\Sigma(P_0 Q_n)} \times 100$

Paasche quantity $= \dfrac{\Sigma(P_n Q_n)}{\Sigma(P_n Q_0)} \times 100$

Value index $= \dfrac{\Sigma(P_n Q_n)}{\Sigma(P_0 Q_0)} \times 100$

Sample size: $\text{Size} = \dfrac{z^2}{e^2} \times p \times (100 - p)$

Additive time series modes:

$$A = T + S + R$$

where A is the actual observation, T the trend, S the seasonal factor and R the random factor.

Linear regression to estimate the equation $y = a + bx$:

$$b = \frac{n\Sigma xy - \Sigma x \Sigma y}{n\Sigma x^2 - (\Sigma x)^2}$$

$$a = \frac{\Sigma y}{n} - b\frac{\Sigma x}{n}$$

The coefficient of correlation:

$$r = \frac{n\Sigma xy - \Sigma x \Sigma y}{\sqrt{\{(n\Sigma x^2 - (\Sigma x)^2)(n\Sigma y^2 - (\Sigma y)^2)\}}}$$

The economic order quantity formula:

$$\text{EOQ} = \sqrt{\left(\frac{2x C_O \times D}{C_H}\right)}$$

where EOQ is the economic order quantity, C_O the ordering cost, C_H is the cost of holding one unit for one year and D is annual demand.

Financial mathematics:

$$\text{Simple interest } (I) = A_0 \times \frac{r}{100}$$

where A_0 is the initial sum invested and r is the rate of interest given in percentage terms.

Compound interest:

$$A_t = A_0\left(1 + \frac{r}{100}\right)^t$$

where A_t is the sum after t years.

Present value:

$$A_0 = A_t \times \frac{1}{\left(1 + \frac{r}{100}\right)^t}$$

Expected value:

$$E(x) = \Sigma(x \times p(x))$$

Probability
Adding probability:

$$P(A \text{ or } B) = P(A) + P(B) - P(A \text{ or } B)$$

if events are **mutually exclusive**

$$P(A \text{ or } B) = P(A) + P(B)$$

Multiplying probability:

$$P(A \text{ and } B) = P(A) \times P(B/A)$$

where $P(B/A)$ is the conditional probability that event B occurs given that event A has already happened.

if events A and B are **independent**

$$P(A \text{ and } B) = P(A) \times P(B)$$

Normal distribution:

Z gives the number of standard deviations the value of interest is away from the mean:

$$Z = \frac{\text{the value of interest } - \text{ the mean}}{\text{the standard deviation}}$$

Appendix H: Answers to problems

Section 2

SPREADSHEET H.1   QUESTION 1

Age Group	MID-PT	Men (f1)	Women (f2)	f1X	f2X	f1XX	f2XX	CF1	CF2
under 20	18	20	35	360	630	6480	11340	20	35
20 but under 25	22.5	40	44	900	990	20250	22275	60	79
25 but under 30	27.5	37	21	1017.5	577.5	27981.25	15881	97	100
30 but under 35	32.5	35	18	1137.5	585	36968.75	19013	132	118
35 but under 40	37.5	20	33	750	1237.5	28125	46406	152	151
40 but under 45	42.5	9	34	382.5	1445	16256.25	61413	161	185
45 but under 50	47.5	7	33	332.5	1567.5	15793.75	74456	168	218
50 but under 55	52.5	12	18	630	945	33075	49613	180	236
55 but under 60	57.5	40	32	2300	1840	132250	105800	220	268
60 but under 65	62.5	36	0	2250	0	140625	0	256	268
TOTALS		256	268	10060	9817.5	457805	406196		

SPREADSHEET H.1 QUESTION 1

Age Group	MID-PT	Men (f1)	Women (f2)	f1X	f2X	f1XX	f2XX	CF1	CF2
128	MEAN	39.30	36.63						
134									
	ST DEV	15.62	13.18						
	MEDIAN	29.19	34.44						
64	QUART1	25.54	23.64						
67									
192	QUART3	56.50	47.42						
201									

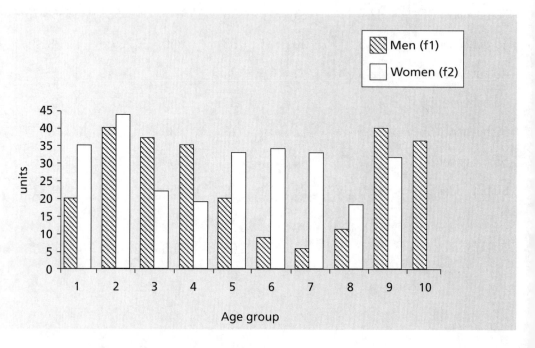

Figure H.1 Bar chart of age profile.

MICROSTATS WORKSHEET   QUESTION 2

	C1	C2	C3	C4	C5	C6
	'Receptio'	'Porters'	'Cleaners'	'Waiters'	'Cooks'	'Managers'
	(n= 9)	(n= 17)	(n= 25)	(n= 24)	(n= 3)	(n= 4)
1.	2.000	1.000	6.000	3.000	24.000	6.000
2.	3.000	2.000	12.000	6.000	39.000	27.000
3.	27.000	2.000	9.000	4.000	2.000	4.000
4.	4.000	1.000	4.000	9.000		90.000
5.	1.000	3.000	13.000	7.000		
6.	2.000	12.000	27.000	2.000		
7.	3.000	14.000	6.000	1.000		
8.	1.000	1.000	36.000	10.000		
9.	2.000	7.000	8.000	12.000		
10.		2.000	10.000	9.000		
11.		1.000	17.000	4.000		
12.		1.000	19.000	17.000		
13.		2.000	25.000	28.000		
14.		2.000	1.000	14.000		
15.		2.000	39.000	7.000		
16.		1.000	6.000	2.000		
17.		1.000	50.000	12.000		
18.			24.000	10.000		
19.			17.000	9.000		
20.			23.000	8.000		
21.			27.000	2.000		
22.			19.000	6.000		
23.			1.000	12.000		
24.			2.000	1.000		
25.			1.000			

MICROSTATS WORKSHEET   QUESTION 2 contd

Command ? DESC C1			
Count of	C1	=	9
Minimum of	C1	=	1.000
Maximum of	C1	=	27.000
Sum of	C1	=	45.000
Mean of	C1	=	5.000
Median of	C1	=	2.000
Standard dev-n [pop] of C1	=		7.832
Standard dev-n [samp] of C1	=		8.307
Command ? desc c2			
Count of	C2	=	17
Minimum of	C2	=	1.000
Maximum of	C2	=	14.000
Sum of	C2	=	55.000
Mean of	C2	=	3.235
Median of	C2	=	2.000
Standard dev-n [pop] of C2	=		3.843
Standard dev-n [samp] of C2	=		3.961
Command ? desc c3			
Count of	C3	=	25
Minimum of	C3	=	1.000
Maximum of	C3	=	50.000
Sum of	C3	=	402.000
Mean of	C3	=	16.080
Median of	C3	=	13.000
Standard dev-n [pop] of C3	=		12.696
Standard dev-n [samp] of C3	=		12.958

MICROSTATS WORKSHEET   QUESTION 2 *contd*

Command ? desc c4

Count of   C4   =   24

Minimum of   C4   =   1.000

Maximum of   C4   =   28.000

Sum of   C4   =   195.000

Mean of   C4   =   8.125

Median of   C4   =   7.500

Standard dev-n [pop] of C4   =   5.946

Standard dev-n [samp] of C4 =   6.074

Command ? desc c5

Count of   C5   =   3

Minimum of   C5   =   2.000

Maximum of   C5   =   39.000

Sum of   C5   =   65.000

Mean of   C5   =   21.667

Median of   C5   =   24.000

Standard dev-n [pop] of C5   =   15.195

Standard dev-n [samp] of C5 =   18.610

Command ? desc c6

Count of   C6   =   4

Minimum of   C6   =   4.000

Maximum of   C6   =   90.000

Sum of   C6   =   127.000

Mean of   C6   =   31.750

Median of   C6   =   16.500

Standard dev-n [pop] of C6   =   34.816

Standard dev-n [samp] of C6 =   40.203

prof

SPREADSHEET H.2   QUESTION 3

| Month | Library | Facility | |
		Leisure Comp	Sundown Park
January	252	665	401
February	268	851	305
March	304	843	359
April	245	735	453
May	220	648	518
June	194	504	678
July	164	778	944
August	208	1045	937
September	199	834	834
October	216	842	601
November	275	851	3054
December	299	734	372
TOTAL	2844	9330	9456
Average	237	777.5	788
Income	£0	£55,980	£67,824
Total Income		£123,804	

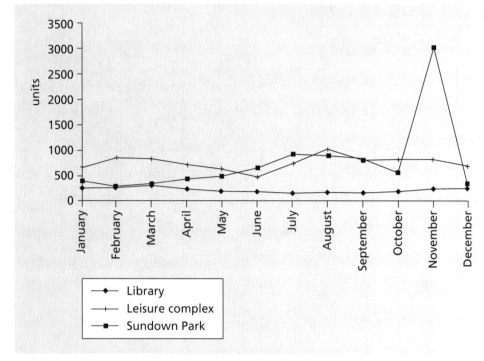

Figure H.2   Average weekly users.

SPREADSHEET H.3   QUESTION 4

Year	Company Price	Company Unit Sales(m)	Company COGS (£m)	Company Expenses (£m)	Industry Price Index (1980=100)	Retail Prices Index (1990=100) RPI	Indust (90=100) IND PR	CO Prices CO PR	CO Sales CO SALES
1985	15	14	145	35	159	69.3	82.383	71.43	87.5
1986	16	15.2	170	38	169	75.6	87.565	76.19	95
1987	18	15.1	185	45	174	83.7	90.155	85.71	94.4
1988	20	16.2	205	60	180	90.2	93.264	95.24	101
1989	21	16.1	220	72	186	95.4	96.373	100	101
1990	21	16	225	80	193	100	100	100	100
1991	23	15.4	235	94	200	105.3	103.63	109.5	96.3
1992	24	14.9	235	101	205	107.2	106.22	114.3	93.1
1993	25	14.8	240	111	209	109.1	108.29	119	92.5
1994	25	15.2	249	120	211	111.3	109.33	119	95

SPREADSHEET H.3   QUESTION 4   contd

	Revenue	Gross Profit	Net Profit	Profit Ratio					
1985	210	65	30	14.29					
1986	243.2	73.2	35.2	14.47					
1987	271.8	86.8	41.8	15.38					
1988	324	119	59	18.21					
1989	338.1	118.1	46.1	13.64					
1990	336	111	31	9.23					
1991	354.2	119.2	25.2	7.11					
1992	357.6	122.6	21.6	6.04					
1993	370	130	19	5.14					
1994	380	131	11	2.89					

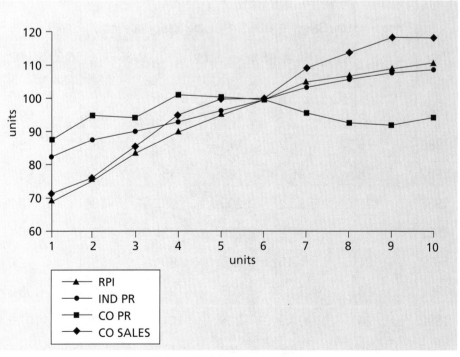

Figure H.3   Indices over time.

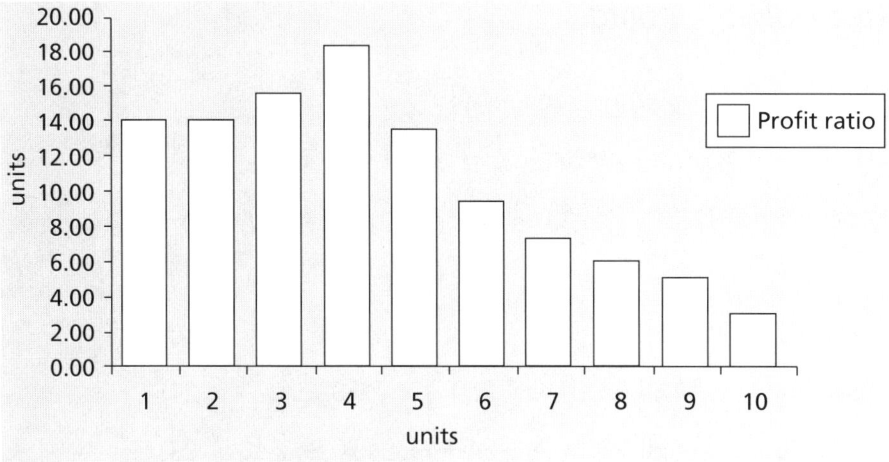

Figure H.4   Profit ratio.

SPREADSHEET H.4   QUESTION 5

		19X1		19X2		19X3	
Hotel Food Bill							
Item	Price	Quantity	Price	Quantity	Price	Quantity	
Vegetables-							
Potatoes	£0.12	500	£0.15	520	£0.15	525	
Broccoli	£0.85	300	£0.80	320	£0.90	310	
Courgettes	£0.56	290	£0.68	310	£0.64	320	
Swede	£0.20	150	£0.18	120	£0.19	110	
Cauliflower	£0.88	250	£0.94	280	£0.98	290	
Salad-							
Tomatoes	£0.40	305	£0.45	325	£0.48	315	
Water Cress	£0.75	60	£0.95	65	£1.05	66	
Lettuce	£0.50	288	£0.60	312	£0.60	355	
Cucumber	£0.49	604	£0.55	582	£0.60	577	
Peppers	£0.88	602	£0.94	642	£0.93	665	

SPREADSHEET H.4   QUESTION 5   contd

	19X1		19X2		19X3		
Hotel Food Bill							
Item	Price	Quantity	Price	Quantity	Price	Quantity	
Fruit-							
Apples	£0.45	155	£0.48	165	£0.49	165	
Oranges	£0.66	194	£0.68	250	£0.72	246	
Bananas	£0.99	205	£0.92	241	£0.86	231	
Meat-							
Beef-prime	£4.50	110	£4.60	130	£4.55	140	
Beef-other	£2.55	185	£2.58	180	£2.61	160	
Lamb	£2.86	241	£2.95	234	£2.99	230	
Pork	£2.46	253	£2.48	231	£2.58	224	
Fish-							
Salmon	£5.99	50	£6.24	70	£6.99	90	
Squid	£2.15	20	£2.81	60	£2.76	110	
Cod	£1.88	105	£1.96	96	£2.55	90	
Plaice	£2.55	64	£2.64	85	£2.88	103	
Basics-							
Bread	£0.50	250	£0.55	260	£0.61	265	
Butter	£1.22	200	£1.25	250	£1.26	230	
Margarine	£0.89	300	£0.91	240	£0.91	210	
Lard	£0.75	60	£0.78	65	£0.81	50	
Herbs	£0.75	300	£0.78	320	£0.99	350	
Spices	£0.65	200	£0.85	240	£0.80	260	
Milk	£0.29	1050	£0.31	1160	£0.31	1240	
Cream	£1.25	640	£1.35	680	£1.40	710	

SPREADSHEET H.4   QUESTION 5 contd

Item	P0Q0	P1Q0	P2Q0	P1Q1	P2Q2	P0Q1	P0Q2
Vegetables-							
Potatoes	60	75	75	78	78.75	62.4	63
Broccoli	255	240	270	256	279	272	263.5
Courgettes	162.4	197.2	185.6	210.8	204.8	173.6	179.2
Swede	30	27	28.5	21.6	20.9	24	22
Cauliflower	220	235	245	263.2	284.2	246.4	255.2
Totals	727.4	774.2	804.1	829.6	867.65	778.4	782.9
Salad-							
Tomatoes	122	137.25	146.4	146.25	151.2	130	126
Water Cress	45	57	63	61.75	69.3	48.75	49.5
Lettuce	144	172.8	172.8	187.2	213	156	177.5
Cucumber	295.96	332.2	362.4	320.1	346.2	285.18	282.73
Peppers	529.76	565.88	559.86	603.48	618.45	564.96	585.2
Totals	1136.72	1265.13	1304.46	1318.78	1398.15	1184.89	1220.9
Fruit-							
Apples	69.75	74.4	75.95	79.2	80.85	74.25	74.25
Oranges	128.04	131.92	139.68	170	177.12	165	162.36
Bananas	202.95	188.6	176.3	221.72	198.66	238.59	228.69
Totals	400.74	394.92	391.93	470.92	456.63	477.84	465.3
Meet-							
Beef-prime	495	506	500.5	598	637	585	630
Beef-other	471.75	477.3	482.85	464.4	417.6	459	408
Lamb	689.26	710.95	720.59	690.3	687.7	669.24	657.8
Pork	622.38	627.44	652.74	572.88	577.92	568.26	551.04
Totals	2278.39	2321.69	2356.68	2325.58	2320.22	2281.5	2246.8

SPREADSHEET H.4   QUESTION 5 contd

Item	P0Q0	P1Q0	P2Q0	P1Q1	P2Q2	P0Q1	P0Q2
Fish-							
Salmon	299.5	312	349.5	436.8	629.1	419.3	539.1
Squid	43	56.2	55.2	168.6	303.6	129	236.5
Cod	197.4	205.8	267.75	188.16	229.5	180.48	169.2
Plaice	163.2	168.96	184.32	224.4	296.64	216.75	262.65
Totals	703.1	742.96	856.77	1017.96	1458.84	945.53	1207.5
Basics-							
Bread	125	137.5	152.5	143	161.65	130	132.5
Butter	244	250	252	312.5	289.8	305	280.6
Margarine	267	273	273	218.4	191.1	213.6	186.9
Lard	45	46.8	48.6	50.7	40.5	48.75	37.5
Herbs	225	234	297	249.6	346.5	240	262.5
Spices	130	170	160	204	208	156	169
Milk	304.5	325.5	325.5	359.6	384.4	336.4	359.6
Cream	800	864	896	918	994	850	887.5
Totals	2140.5	2300.8	2404.6	2455.8	2615.95	2279.75	2316.1
Overall Totals	7386.85	7799.7	8118.54	8.64	9117.44	7947.91	8239.5

SPREADSHEET H.4   QUESTION 5 contd

Index Numbers	Year	Laspeyres Price	Lespeyres Quantity	Paasche Price	Paasche Quantity	Value	
Vegetables-	19X1	100.00	100.00	100.00	100.00	100.00	
	19X2	106.43	107.01	106.58	107.16	114.05	
	19X3	110.54	107.63	110.83	107.90	119.28	
Salad-	19X1	100.00	100.00	100.00	100.00	100.00	
	19X2	111.30	104.24	111.30	104.24	116.02	
	19X3	114.76	107.41	114.52	107.18	123.00	
Fruit-	19X1	100.00	100.00	100.00	100.00	100.00	
	19X2	98.55	119.24	98.55	119.24	117.51	
	19X3	97.80	116.11	98.14	116.51	113.95	
Meat-	19X1	100.00	100.00	100.00	100.00	100.00	
	19X2	101.90	100.14	101.93	100.17	102.07	
	19X3	103.44	98.62	103.27	98.45	101.84	
Fish-	19X1	100.00	100.00	100.00	100.00	100.00	
	19X2	105.67	134.48	107.66	137.01	144.78	
	19X3	121.86	171.73	120.82	170.27	207.49	
Basics-	19X1	100.00	100.00	100.00	100.00	100.00	
	19X2	107.49	106.51	107.72	106.74	114.73	
	19X3	112.34	108.20	112.95	108.79	122.21	
Overall-	19X1	100.00	100.00	100.00	100.00	100.00	
	19X2	105.59	107.60	105.92	107.94	113.97	
	19X3	109.91	111.54	110.65	112.30	123.43	

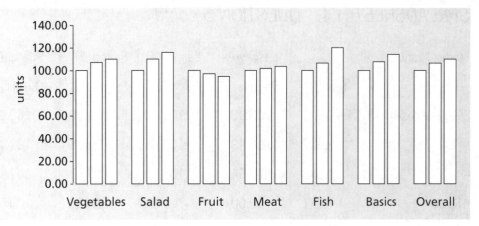

Figure H.5　Laspeyres price indices.

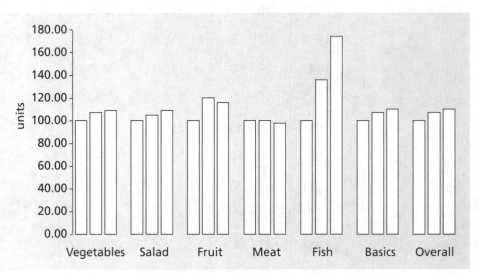

Figure H.6　Laspeyres quantity indices.

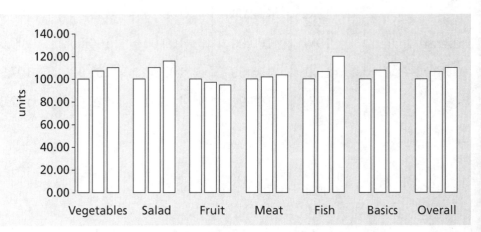

Figure H.7　Paasche price indices.

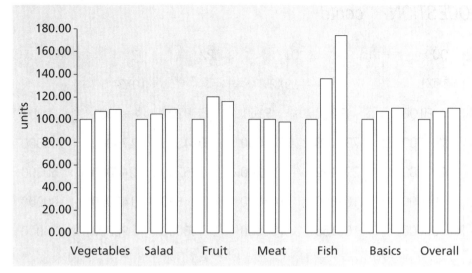

Figure H.8   Paasche quantity indices.

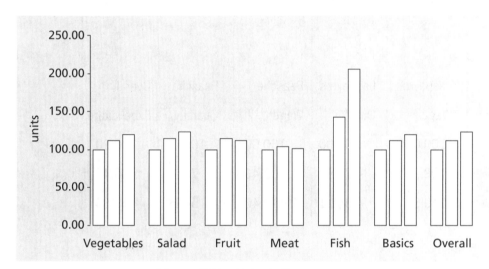

Figure H.9   Value indices.

SPREADSHEET H.5   QUESTION 6

	P0	Q0	P1	Q1	P2	Q2	
		19X1		19X2		19X3	
People	Av Wage	Number	Av Wage	Number	Av Wage	Number	
Manual	12000	135	13000	98	13260	75	2%
Supervisor	15000	18	16200	16	16524	10	2%
Middle Manager	20000	8	21000	7	21210	4	1%
Senior Manager	30000	3	35000	3	36050	1	3%

SPREADSHEET H.5   QUESTION   contd

	P0	Q0	P1	Q1	P2	Q2	
		19X1		19X2		19X3	
People	P0Q0	P1Q0	P2Q0	P1Q1	P2Q2	P0Q1	P0Q2
Manual	1620000	1755000	1790100	1274000	994500	1176000	900000
Supervisor	270000	291600	297432	259200	165240	240000	150000
Middle Manager	160000	168000	169680	147000	84840	140000	80000
Senior Manager	90000	105000	108150	105000	36050	90000	30000
TOTALS	2140000	2319600	2365362	1785200	1280630	1646000	1160000

Index Numbers		Laspeyres	Laspeyres	Paasche	Paasche	Overall	
	Year	Wage	Quantity	Wage	Quantity	Expenditure	
	19X1	100.00	100.00	100.00	100.00	100.00	
	19X2	108.39	76.92	108.46	76.96	83.42	
	19X3	110.53	54.21	110.40	54.14	59.84	

Section 3

1. The question asks for five cross-tabulations which can be quickly found using MICROSTATS. The answers are given in Tables H1 to H7, but it is quite possible to find many other cross-tabulations, and it is left to you to discover other information contained within the questionnaire data.

Table H.1

No used		Quality			
	Do not use	Very good	Good	Poor	Total
0	27	0	0	0	27
1	0	8	26	4	38
2	0	8	20	2	30
3	0	0	1	1	2
4	0	1	1	0	2
5	0	0	1	0	1
	27	17	49	7	100

(a) Whilst Table H.1 is 'correct', it is not very informative because of the small number of people who use more than 3 facilities and because of the 27 people who do not use the facilities at all. The table may be rebuilt as Table H.2.

Table H.2

No used	Quality			
	Very good	Good	Poor	Total
1	8	26	4	38
2	8	20	2	30
3 or more	1	3	1	5
	17	49	7	73

It might also be useful to show percentages rather than actual numbers of people (Table H.3). Note that percentages do not add to 100 due to rounding.

Table H.3

No used	Quality (%)		
	Very good	Good	Poor
1	11	36	5
2	11	27	3
3 or more	1	4	1

(b) Using the reduce sized table we can get Table H.4.

Table H.4

No. used	Not use if price rises	Use if price rises	Total
1	21	17	38
2	21	9	30
3 or more	2	3	5
Total	44	29	73

(c) Again, using the reduced sized table we can get Table H.5.

Table H.5

No. used	Not use if price falls	Use if price falls	Total
0	16	11	27
1	16	22	38
2	16	14	30
3 or more	2	3	5
Total	60	40	100

(d) The reduced sized table gives Table H.6.

Table H.6

Quality	Not use if price rises	Use if price rises	Total
Very good	16	1	17
Good	28	21	49
Poor	0	7	7
Total	44	29	73

(e)   The final tabulation gives Table H.7.

Table H.7

Quality	Not use if price falls	Use if price falls	Total
Do not use	16	11	27
Very good	14	3	17
Good	19	30	49
Poor	1	7	7
Total	60	40	100

2. There can be no definitive answer to this question as it will depend on how you have decided to define the 'image' and 'role' of the police force. One way of finding if your questionnaire makes sense, is to try it out on about 10 friends.

3. There is a tremendous amount of data included in this file and thus the range of possible answers is very large. The key point is that you should be able to make firm recommendations to the BPICS branch on the basis of the results obtained.

Section 4

1. To make a prediction for 19X4, the trend needs to be extended forward and seasonal adjustments made. The trend values and seasonal factors are given as follows:

    Trend: 149.5, 153.5, 157.5, 158.875, 156.125, 151.0, 147.0, 146.375

    Seasonal factors: Qtr 1   −104.75   Qtr 2   8.375
                        Qtr 3   200.1875   Qtr 4   −105.75

2. Trend: 90, 88.75, 87, 85.375, 83.25, 81, 79, 76.625

    Seasonal factors: Qtr 1   −15   Qtr 2   2
                        Qtr 3   −14.375   Qtr 4   −1.375

3. Refer to judgemental techniques.

4. Trend (5 period): 23.4, 23.8, 23.4, 23.8, 23.6, 23.8, 23.4, 23.4, 23.6, 23.8, 23.8, 24.0, 24.6, 25.0, 25.2, 25.4

Daily factors: Mon. –0.13, Tues. –3.2, Wed. 5.4, Thurs. –0.07, Fri. –2.13

5. Trend (5 period): 563.6, 570.0, 573.8, 579.0, 583.0, 586.8, 591.6, 593.2, 595.8, 598.8, 602.2

Daily factors: Mon. 98.6, Tues. 10.1, Wed. –20.5, Thurs. –37.8, Fri. –51

Linear regression gradient = 3.74 (intercept depends on values chosen for x)

Predictions: Mon. 714, Tues. 629, Wed. 602, Thurs. 589, Fri. 579

6. You will need a spreadsheet model for this problem. Trend (12 period and centred): 148.5, 149, 150, 153.5, 157.5, 161, 163.5, 165, 169, 173, 174, 174, 174, 175, 177.5, 179.5, 180.5, 181.5, 183.5, 186, 188, 190, 192, 194

7 (b) Correlation coefficient: -0.9853
   (c) Linear regression gradient = –9.8
       The intercept depends on the values chosen for x. If you let $x = 1$ for the first value then the intercept = 138.8.
   (d) Predicted number of course presentations for 1994 is 80.

8. (b) Correlation coefficient: 0.8672
   (c) $y = 14^{55} + 1.29x$
   (d) 66.15

9. Correlation between advertising and sales is 0.9825. Correlation between enquiries and sales is 0.8408.

Section 5

1. (a) Number of tests to break even is 7500.
   (c) (i)   8750 tests
       (ii) 10 000 tests (assuming fixed costs of £6000)
   (d) You need to consider the number of tests possible each year and the likely effect of variation in demand.

2. (a) Total annual cost: £60680
   (b) EOQ = 60, total annual cost = £60 600
   (c) Saving: £80

3. (a) EOB = 15.3 (approx.), total annual cost = £1716.46

4. Total scores: A: 43, B: 42, C: 33. Choose A.

5. Total scores: product A: 7, product B: 8. Choose product B.

6.   Option 1: retains £6000, simple interest of £720 per year
     Option 2: worth £7986 after 3 years
     Option 3: worth £8366.34 after 3 years

8.

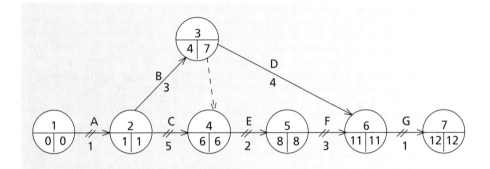

Figure H.10

9.

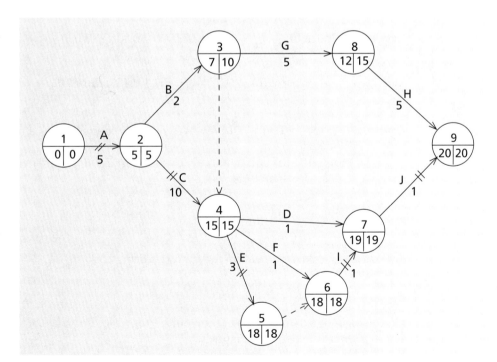

Figure H.11

Section 6

1. (a) $\dfrac{15}{64}$ (b) $\dfrac{42}{64}$ (c) $\dfrac{15}{64}$

   (d) $\dfrac{49}{64}$ (e) $\dfrac{9}{15}$ (f) $\dfrac{13}{49}$

2. (a) 0.24 (b) 0.112 (c) 0.048

3. (a) 0.21 (b) 0.308 (c) £58.55 for present system, £77.94 for proposed system

4. First option: expected value £7200
   Second option: expected value £7500
   Maximax: second option
   Maximin: first option

5. *Three options:*
   1. *Sell:* expected value £25 000

   2. *Launch without advertising:*
      Expected value $= 0.5 \times £36\,000 + 0.5 \times £10\,000$
      $= £23\,000$

   3. *Advertise in advance of launch:*
      Note: once the advertising has been evaluated you can launch or sell design (hence two more decision nodes □)

      Expected value at (a) $= 0.80 \times £70\,000 + 0.20 \times £15\,000$
      $= £59\,000$

      Expected value at point (b) $= 0.55 \times £36\,000 + 0.45 \times £10\,000$
      $= 24\,300$

      At decision node (c) you would always choose to launch (expected value of £59 000).
      At decision node (d) you would always sell (as £25 000 is greater than the expected value of £24 300).

      Expected value at point (e) $= 0.9 \times £59\,000 + 0.1 \times £25\,000$
      $= £55\,600$

      Expected value (of option allowing for advertising cost) is

      $$£55\,600 - £20\,000 = £35\,600$$

      On the basis of expected value you would:
      1. Advertise in advance of launch.
      2. If advertising were effective, launch product.
         If advertising were not effective, sell design.

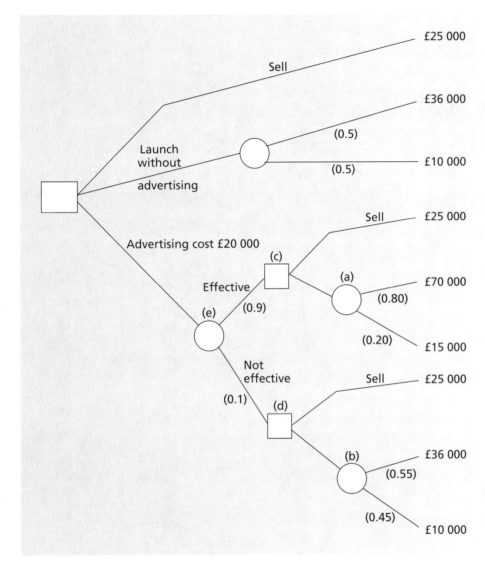

Figure H.12

Maximin: sell (avoid risk and accept £25 000)

Maximax: advertise

6. (a) 0.3859   (b) 0.0548   (c) 0.0301

7. (a) 0.02275   (b) 389 grams

8. (a) 4.01%   (b) 95.99%   (c) 0.006%

Index